LUTHER'S WORKS

American Edition

VOLUME 47

Published by Concordia Publishing House

and Fortress Press in 55 volumes.

General Editors are Jaroslav Pelikan (for vols. 1–30)

and Helmut T. Lehmann (for vols. 31–55)

LUTHER'S WORKS

VOLUME 47

The Christian in Society
IV

EDITED BY

FRANKLIN SHERMAN

GENERAL EDITOR

HELMUT T. LEHMANN

FORTRESS PRESS / PHILADELPHIA

1561D71

GENERAL EDITORS'
PREFACE

The first editions of Luther's collected works appeared in the sixteenth century, and so did the first efforts to make him "speak English." In America serious attempts in these directions were made for the first time in the nineteenth century. The Saint Louis edition of Luther was the first endeavor on American soil to publish a collected edition of his works, and the Henkel Press in Newmarket, Virginia, was the first to publish some of Luther's writings in an English translation. During the first decade of the twentieth century, J. N. Lenker produced translations of Luther's sermons and commentaries in thirteen volumes. A few years later the first of the six volumes in the Philadelphia (or Holman) edition of the *Works of Martin Luther* appeared. But a growing recognition of the need for more of Luther's works in English has resulted in this American edition of Luther's works.

The edition is intended primarily for the reader whose knowledge of late medieval Latin and sixteenth-century German is too small to permit him to work with Luther in the original languages. Those who can will continue to read Luther in his original words as these have been assembled in the monumental Weimar edition (*D. Martin Luthers Werke*. Kritische Gesamtausgabe, Weimar, 1883-   ). Its texts and helps have formed a basis for this edition, though in certain places we have felt constrained to depart from its readings and findings. We have tried throughout to translate Luther as he thought translating should be done. That is, we have striven for faithfulness on the basis of the best lexicographical materials available. But where literal accuracy and clarity have conflicted, it is clarity that we have preferred, so that sometimes paraphrase seemed more faithful than literal fidelity. We have proceeded in a similar way in the matter of Bible versions, translating Luther's translation. Where this could be done by the use of an existing

English version—King James, Douay, or Revised Standard—we have done so. Where it could not, we have supplied our own. To indicate this in each specific instance would have been pendantic; to adopt a uniform procedure would have been artificial—especially in view of Luther's own inconsistency in this regard. In each volume the translator will be responsible primarily for matters of text and language, while the responsibility of the editor will extend principally to the historical and theological matters reflected in the introductions and notes.

Although the edition as planned will include fifty-five volumes, Luther's writings are not being translated in their entirety. Nor should they be. As he was the first to insist, much of what he wrote and said was not that important. Thus the edition is a selection of works that have proved their importance for the faith, life, and history of the Christian church. The first thirty volumes contain Luther's expositions of various biblical books, while the remaining volumes include what are usually called his "Reformation writings" and other occasional pieces. The final volume of the set will be an index volume; in addition to an index of quotations, proper names, and topics, and a list of corrections and changes, it will contain a glossary of many of the technical terms that recur in Luther's works and that cannot be defined each time they appear. Obviously Luther cannot be forced into any neat set of rubrics. He can provide his reader with bits of autobiography or with political observations as he expounds a psalm, and he can speak tenderly about the meaning of the faith in the midst of polemics against his opponents. It is the hope of publishers, editors, and translators that through this edition the message of Luther's faith will speak more clearly to the modern church.

J.P.
H.T.L.

CONTENTS

CIC   — *Corpus Iuris Canonici,* edited by E. Friedberg (Graz, 1955).

C. R.   — *Corpus Reformatorum,* edited by C. G. Bretschneider and H. E. Bindseil (Halle/Salle, 1834-1860).

EA   — *D. Martin Luthers sämmtliche Werke* (Frankfurt and Erlangen, 1826-1857).

LW   — American Edition of *Luther's Works* (Philadelphia and St. Louis, 1955-   ).

PE   — *Works of Martin Luther,* Philadelphia Edition (Philadelphia, 1915-1943).

St. L.   — *D. Martin Luthers sämmtliche Schriften,* edited by Johann Georg Walch. Edited and published in modern German, 23 vols. in 25 (2nd ed., St. Louis, 1880-1910).

WA   — *D. Martin Luthers Werke.* Kritische Gesamtausgabe (Weimar, 1883-   ).

WA, Br   — *D. Martin Luthers Werke.* Briefwechsel (Weimar, 1930-   ).

WA, DB   — *D. Martin Luthers Werke.* Deutsche Bibel (Weimar, 1906-1961).

WA, TR   — *D. Martin Luthers Werke.* Tischreden (Weimar, 1912-1921).

INTRODUCTION TO VOLUME 47

This final volume in the series *Christian in Society* presents four writings dating from the last fifteen years of Luther's life. Disparate in theme, they all portray Luther in his role as polemicist, striking out with great vigor of thought and language against what he regarded as mortal threats to the gospel.

The first treatise, *Dr. Martin Luther's Warning to His Dear German People*, reflects the tumult of the period immediately following the issuance of the *Augsburg Confession* in 1530. Alarmed by the prospect that Emperor Charles V and the princes loyal to Rome might attempt to extirpate the Protestant movement by the use of military force, Luther issues this "warning" to his followers. No one who cares for the freedom of the gospel or the integrity of the church should in any way collaborate in such an enterprise, even if the emperor himself should command it. Not only passive noncooperation but armed resistance would be justified. It is this point which gives the treatise its special doctrinal and historical significance, representing as it does a departure from Luther's earlier, more passive attitude toward "the powers that be." Of interest, too, is Luther's summary in the concluding pages of the achievements of the Reformation as he saw them from the vantage point of the year 1531.

The pure teaching of the gospel, however, also faced threats from within the evangelical camp itself. Luther's treatise of 1539, *Against the Antinomians*, reflects his long-standing controversy with those who, as he believed, were grievously misinterpreting his own cardinal doctrine of justification by grace through faith, in that they took it to imply that there was no longer any need for the preaching of the law. Luther's rejection of this view, which is of great significance for Christian ethics, is grounded in his great sense of realism concerning the situation of the Christian and the church as *simul justus et peccator*. It is evident that he shared fully the desire to avoid anything like what the twentieth-century theologian Dietrich Bonhoeffer was to characterize as the preaching of "cheap grace."

The treatise *Against the Sabbatarians: Letter to a Good Friend*, although printed second in this volume in observance of chronological order, is to be grouped topically with the fourth treatise, *On the Jews and Their Lies*. The link between them is found in the fact that Luther attributed the rise of Sabbatarianism, a Christian sect which stressed the observance of the seventh day and other aspects of Old Testament law, to Jewish influence. From the law in *this* sense Christians indeed are free, Luther proclaimed. What they are called on to obey is rather the underlying *moral* law as presented in biblical teaching as well as in the natural law made known by the Creator to all men. In the final portion of the treatise, Luther deals at length with the distinction between natural-law elements and historically conditioned elements of the Decalogue, the former being still obligatory for Christians, the latter non-obligatory.

It is the treatise *On the Jews and Their Lies*, published in 1543, of which Luther's biographer Roland H. Bainton remarked: "One could wish that Luther had died before ever this tract was written."[1] Many efforts have been made to explain the treatise— whether on psychological, sociological, or theological grounds— but it cannot be explained away. The crudity of its language at many points and the inhumanity of its proposals concerning treatment of the Jews are enough to shock and sadden any reader. It is presented here for historical purposes only, in order that the record of Luther's thought and writing might be complete. An effort is made in the introduction to the treatise itself to place it in the context of late medieval cultural and theological trends, as well as Luther's own life and development. The fact that he was largely repeating the anti-Semitic commonplaces of the time and that much of his theological argumentation is borrowed from earlier Christian polemics against Judaism is a mitigating factor, though by no means an excuse for Luther's views.

[1] *Here I Stand: A Life of Martin Luther* (New York: Abingdon-Cokesbury, 1950), p. 379.

The draft translation by Martin H. Bertram was extensively revised by the undersigned and by the staff of Fortress Press, with the aid also of my colleague Wilhelm C. Linss. I am indebted to Professors Aarne Siirala and Robert H. Fischer for valuable advice based on their own research in Luther, as well as to James M. Weiss, graduate student at the University of Chicago, for his work in checking Latin texts and in compiling data for the footnotes.

F.S.

LUTHER'S WORKS

VOLUME 47

DR. MARTIN LUTHER'S WARNING TO HIS DEAR GERMAN PEOPLE

1531

Translated by Martin H. Bertram

INTRODUCTION

The context of the present treatise is the Diet of Augsburg, which commenced on June 30, 1530. Luther himself was absent from the diet, but from his refuge at Coburg Castle some hundred and fifty miles to the north he exchanged frequent communications with the evangelical representatives at Augsburg.[1] Dismayed by the efforts of Melanchthon and his colleagues to seek formulas of compromise or consensus with their Roman adversaries, Luther felt a sense of relief on learning that the negotiations had been broken off. But he felt also anger at the way the Protestants (as they now were known) had been treated at the diet, as well as alarm at the interpretation which the opposing party was putting on the outcome of the discussions. The errors of the Protestants, declared the *Recess* proclaimed by Emperor Charles V on September 23, had been "thoroughly refuted." All that remained was actually to extirpate the heresy from the several lands in which it had taken root.

The terms of the *Recess* gave the dissidents six months to accept the Catholic position as stated in the *Confutatio Pontificia,* the Romanists' reply to the *Augsburg Confession.* Proselytizing and religious publishing were to be prohibited in their domains; a common front was to be maintained against the Sacramentarians and Anabaptists; while the emperor, for his part, would use his good offices with the pope to secure the convening of a "general Christian council."[2]

Luther viewed these terms as intolerable, as did the Protestant princes and other representatives. But if submission was impossible,

---

[1] See *LW* 34, 5-7.
[2] The text of both the *Confutation* and the *Recess* is given in English translation in J. Michael Reu, *The Augsburg Confession: A Collection of Sources with an Historical Introduction* (Chicago: Wartburg Publishing House, 1930), Second Part, pp. 348-383, 390-392. For the *Confutation,* see also Henry E. Jacobs, *The Book of Concord, or the Symbolical Books of the Evangelical Lutheran Church, with Historical Introductions, Notes, Appendixes, and Indexes* (2 vols.; Philadelphia: Frederick, 1883), II, 209-241. A standard account of the Diet of Augsburg is Hans von Schubert, *Der Reichstag von Augsburg im Zuzammenhang mit der Reformationsgeschichte* ("Schriften des Vereins für Reformationsgeschichte," XLV, Part III [1930]); see also Johannes von Walter, "*Der Reichstag zu Augsburg 1530,*" in *Lutherjahrbuch,* XII (1930).

one then had to contemplate what would follow the expiration of the six-month period of grace. Luther, for one, viewed it as entirely likely that the emperor would turn to the use of force, using all the authority of his office to marshal sufficient power to bring the evangelicals to heel. It was this conviction which moved Luther to issue the *Warning to His Dear German People*. On the peril of their souls, he warned, they should in no way collaborate in such an enterprise. The emperor's authority does not extend to lordship over spiritual matters. When the gospel is at stake, one must obey God rather than men.

Luther's argument up to this point, though it amounts to advocacy of civil disobedience, does not go beyond the position he had taken already in his treatise of 1523, *Temporal Authority: To What Extent It Should Be Obeyed*, where he had counseled Christians in neighboring Ducal Saxony to disobey the edict calling for confiscation of the German New Testament.[3] For that matter, Luther himself had lived in a state of civil disobedience since the proclamation of the Edict of Worms in 1521. What distinguishes the *Warning* is that Luther goes on to sanction active, armed resistance to the emperor.

He does not find it easy to articulate this position, nor had he been quick to arrive at it. As late as March 6, 1530, he had stated in a letter to Elector John of Saxony: "According to Scripture, it is in no way proper for anyone who would be a Christian to set himself against his government, whether it acts justly or unjustly. Rather a Christian ought to suffer oppression and injustice by his government. For even if His Imperial Majesty were acting wrongly in this matter and were transgressing against his duty and his oath, neither his imperial authority nor his subjects' obligation of obedience has thereby been abolished."[4] Since the present treatise is thought to have been composed in October, 1530 (although printing difficulties delayed its publication until April, 1531),[5] there must have been a period of only six or seven months during which Luther's views on this question underwent significant alteration.

---

[3] Cf. *LW* 45, 84, n. 11.
[4] As cited in Preserved Smith and C. M. Jacobs (eds.), *Luther's Correspondence* (Philadelphia: Lutheran Publication Society, 1918), II, 519-520.
[5] For details, see *WA* 30III, 255-256.

In fact, we can see his thought still in process of development in the treatise itself. He is unwilling openly to retract what he had said before; rather he "brackets" it and almost invites his readers to disregard his former teaching. He writes "as in a dream," to use his words, or "as if there were no God"[6]—forcing himself to think in terms of the political realities that actually confront the Protestants. Even so, his final endorsement of resistance is put in cautious and negative terms. "If war breaks out—which God forbid," he writes, "I will not reprove those who defend themselves against the murderers and bloodthirsty papists, nor let anyone else rebuke them as being seditious, but I will accept their action and let it pass as self-defense."[7]

Luther's new position amounts to saying: Insurrection, to be sure, is still forbidden to the Christian; but defensive action in protection of the gospel—even if military means be used, and even if these be directed against the emperor—is not to be counted as insurrection. The use of force in such circumstances may be justified, as in the case of a "just war" according to the classic doctrine, if the end is just, the means appropriate, and if all peaceful means of settlement have failed. It is in light of such criteria that we may understand Luther's diatribes against the Romanists in the present treatise, as well as his survey, in the concluding pages, of the achievements of the Reformation. These serve to demonstrate that the Reformers' cause is just, while that of the opponents is unjust. Likewise, his emphasis on the peaceful intentions of the Protestants and their frequent efforts at accommodation serves to demonstrate that "all peaceful means of settlement have failed." Under such circumstances, the resort to force is justified.

Luther was not alone in moving toward a new position on the question of resistance during these months. The question was agitating all of the Protestant lands and cities. Of special importance for the development of Luther's views was the work of the legal advisers of Elector John, who after diligent reflection and historical research had now set forth the view that grounds could indeed be found for resistance to the emperor under certain conditions. The

---

[6] See below, p. 13.
[7] See below, p. 19.

emperor's authority, they emphasized, is not absolute, but is limited by the terms of his election. It does not extend to questions of the faith. Moreover, any authority may be resisted if it is exercised with manifest injustice. And on a technical point, they noted that it is a well-known rule of judicial procedure that execution of a sentence must be postponed if appeal has been made to a higher court; but this is just what the Protestants have done in appealing beyond both pope and emperor to a "free general council."[8]

The direct influence of these judgments of the Saxon jurists is seen in a brief but significant statement issued in late October, 1530, in the name of "Luther, Jonas, Melanchthon, Spalatin, and other theologians": "We are in receipt of a memorandum from which we learn that the doctors of law have come to an agreement on the question: In what situations may one resist the government? Since this possibility has now been established by these doctors and experts in the law, and since we certainly are in the kind of situation in which, as they show, resistance to the government is permissible, and since, further, we have always taught that one should acknowledge civil laws, submit to them, and respect their authority, inasmuch as the gospel does not militate against civil laws, we cannot invalidate from Scripture the right of men to defend themselves even against the emperor in person, or anyone acting in his name. And now that the situation everywhere has become so dangerous that events may daily make it necessary for men to take immediate measures to protect themselves, not only on the basis of civil law but on the grounds of duty and distress of conscience, it is fitting for them to arm themselves and to be prepared to defend themselves against the use of force; and such may easily occur, to judge by the present pattern and course of events. For in previously teaching that resistance to governmental authorities is altogether forbidden, we were unaware that this right has been granted by the government's own laws, which we have diligently taught are to be obeyed at all times."[9]

<hr>

[8] See the text of the jurists' statement in EA 64, 266-269 and St. L. 10, 558-561.
[9] Translated by the present editor from the text as given in EA 64, 269-270; see also St. L. 10, 562-563. This memorandum, although not printed in the Weimar edition (since its author is thought to be Melanchthon rather than Luther), is referred to in the Introduction to Warning (WA 30[III], 257), where

Luther's *Warning* thus is to be understood in the context of widespread ferment on the subject of resistance to the emperor. The pertinence of the treatise to the existing situation is shown by the fact that it ran through five editions in the year 1531. Meanwhile, early in that same year, the Smalcald League had been organized, and with the accession of the South German cities as well as the North German states it soon became a formidable European power. The final outbreak of the Smalcald War in 1546, very shortly after Luther's death, once again occasioned numerous reprintings of his treatise. The same occurred in the period 1620-1636, during the Thirty Years' War. Evidently the treatise was found useful in nerving the evangelical forces on occasions of strife.

In subsequent centuries, however, the treatise was neglected, so much so that both Luther's supporters and his critics could cite his earlier writings on the subject while quite overlooking this important modification of his position. Attention has rightly been paid to Calvin's limited endorsement of the right to resist in the final chapter of the *Institutes* (IV, XX, 31), wherein he speaks of the duty of the "magistrates of the people" to withstand the "fierce licentiousness of kings." In the later history of Calvinism, this principle proved of great effect in contributing to the rise of democracy. The reader of Luther's *Warning*, written five years before the first edition of the *Institutes*, will perceive, however, that this thought was not entirely original with Calvin. Luther's conception was similar, although it was phrased not in terms of the constitution of individual states, but in terms of the relationship between the many sovereigns of the German principalities and the superstructure of the Holy Roman Empire. In this difference lies, perhaps, one of the keys to the fact that this doctrine of the "right to resist" subsequently proved less effective in checking the rise of absolutism in Lutheran territories than it did in lands influenced by Calvinism.[10]

---

its date of composition is wrongly given as 1531 rather than the 1530 date that had been established by Enders (see Ernst Ludwig Enders, *Dr. Martin Luthers Briefwechsel* [Calw and Stuttgart, 1898], 8, 298–299). See also several similar statements on this question issued subsequently by the Wittenberg theologians in *EA* and *St. L., ad. loc.*

[10] Cf. Karl Holl, *The Cultural Significance of the Reformation*, trans. by Karl and Barbara Hertz and John H. Lichtblau (New York: Meridian, 1959), Ch. II.

Luther's *Warning* has not heretofore appeared in English. The following translation is based upon the German text, *Warnunge D. Martini Luther, An seine lieben Deudschen,* as given in WA 30ᴵᴵᴵ, 276-320. A modern German version, with certain revisions and omissions, appears in Kurt Aland (ed.), *Luther Deutsch,* Vol. IV (2nd rev. ed.; Stuttgart and Göttingen, 1964), pp. 232-250.

DR. MARTIN LUTHER'S WARNING TO HIS DEAR GERMAN PEOPLE

I issued an urgent and sincere admonition publicly to the clerical members of the Diet of Augsburg in which I implored them not to let the diet—on which all the world set such great hopes and toward which it looked with longing—adjourn inconclusively, but rather work toward the establishment of peace, the cessation of some of their abominations, and freedom for the gospel.[1] I also strove and sighed for these things with all my might in my prayers before God, as did all good Christians. However, since neither our diligent prayer to God nor our sincere warning to them availed, one can readily infer what this means: namely, that God considers them to be hardened and blinded; they are guilty of so much innocent blood, blasphemy, and shameful, impenitent living, that he does not consider that they are worthy to receive a single good thought or emotion or that they will pay any attention to a word of wholesome and peaceful admonition. Their condition is like that of the Jews at the time of Jeremiah, when God said to him (Jeremiah 15 [:1]): "Though Moses and Samuel stood before me, yet my heart would not turn to this people. Send them out of my sight, and let them go!" And in Jeremiah 7 [:16] he said, "As for you, do not pray for this people, or lift up cry or prayer for them, and do not intercede with me, for I do not hear you."

My colleagues and I must now issue this same answer and apply it to ourselves. We have prayed in vain for the clergy. With his actions, God is demonstrating mightily that he does not want to hear our intercession in their behalf, but he is letting them go and sin against the Holy Spirit, as Pharaoh did, until they are beyond hope of repentance and reform. If anything could have been attained through prayer before God and anything achieved with the clergy through admonition, pleas, humility, patience, friendly advances, truth, justice, a good cause, etc., it surely would have been

[1] Cf. Luther's *Exhortation to All Clergy Assembled at Augsburg. LW* 34, 3–61.

accomplished now at the diet. For I know how earnestly the Christians prayed, what great humility, patience, and fervor was demonstrated there, and what a good and just cause they championed.

But now that they not only have let the diet disband without bearing any fruit and without peace, but have even confirmed the discord and concluded with defiant threats,[2] my followers and I will also withdraw our prayers in compliance with God's command and, as St. John teaches [I John 5:16], not pray for the sin unto death. Rather we shall see how God will baptize the hardened Pharaoh in the Red Sea. Our prayers and supplications for peace, even though lost on the impenitent, will help us all the more. In fact, they have already performed great miracles at Augsburg. And by the grace of God they will also succeed in the end. For we were heard and must be heard. Our prayers have not failed us in the past, nor will they fail us now—that I know for a certainty. Amen! It will happen as Jesus said, that whenever the apostles' greetings or peace found no reception or no children of peace in a house, their peace returned again to them [Matt. 10:13; Luke 10:6]. So too in this case, since the clergy heed neither prayer nor peace, both prayer and peace will not be lost on that account but will revert to us.[3] And in place of prayers, nothing but curses, in place of peace nothing but discord, and both in abundance, will be the clergy's lot. Amen.

Therefore, because their plans are built exclusively on force and their cause relies on the power of the fist, over against the manifest and known truth of God, no one need fear them. Let everyone be of good cheer and unafraid before such raging foes of God; for they do not cry or pray to God, nor are they able to pray in view of their bad conscience and cause. Out of pride and spite they attack flesh and blood; to do this they need no God, nor do

[2] Luther discusses some of these threats in this treatise: e.g., that of John Eck (see below, pp. 23-24) and that of Elector Joachim of Brandenburg (in a speech delivered on August 7, 1530; see below, p. 33).
[3] In his *Exhortation to All Clergy* Luther had written that he and his followers were praying for the success of the diet and for the enlightenment of the opposition. But he also warned: ". . . may God grant that you do not set yourselves stubbornly against it, so that our prayer must again return into our bosom, as lost and scorned by you [Matt. 10:13]." *LW* 34, 11.

they dare to ask him whether he desires what they are thinking. God surely loves this and takes great delight in it; such defiance and contempt of his grace are most pleasing to him. He makes a practice of rewarding such defiance and arrogance with good fortune and victory—so that both horse and rider lie drowned in the Red Sea and everything is overturned and no one survives. We, however, are quite convinced that their mad undertaking does not rest in their might, but in the hand of God, and that their aims will not so soon be accomplished. He will want to be a Lord over them too, as has always been the case in the past. This they shall indeed experience. But for the present I will assume that there is no God, I will just imagine as in a dream that their plans and plots will proceed and prosper mightily.

If worst comes to worst, then one of two things will happen: either a war or a rebellion will occur, perhaps both at the same time. For there is indeed danger—we are now speaking as in a dream, as if there were no God—that if they initiate a war, an armed troop will organize and a mob band together, perhaps even among their own people, so that both they and we will perish. For in such an event they cannot rely on our teaching and take it for granted that no one will attack them, just because we wrote and taught so emphatically not to resort to rebellion, but to suffer the madness even of tyrants, and not to defend oneself.[4] This is what I teach, but I cannot create the doers of this teaching, since they esteem so little all the other articles of our teaching. If now the masses should reject our teaching against rebellion, especially if they were provoked by such a godless outrage and wanton war, then the devil would make real fools of them and expose them very nicely and neatly. I am still speaking in a dream. But let them see to it that the dream does not come true. The dream does not harm me, but if it hits them, so be it.

All right, if a war or a rebellion should break out as I fear (for God's wrath will have to take its course), I wish to testify before God and all the world here in this writing that we, who are derisively called "Lutherans," neither counseled it or consented to it, nor, indeed, gave any cause for it; rather we constantly and

---

[4] Cf. above, p. 6.

13

ceaselessly pleaded and called for peace. The papists themselves know and have to admit that we have preached peace up till now and have also kept the peace, and that peace was also our ardent desire now at the diet. Consequently, if a war or a rebellion should break out, it can under no circumstances be said, "See, that is the fruit of Lutheran teaching." It will rather have to be said, "See, that is the papists' teaching and its fruit; they want peace neither for themselves nor for others." Until now we have taught and lived quietly. We drew no sword and did not burn, murder, or rob anyone, as they have done in the past and still do; rather we endured their murder and pillage, their raving and raging with the greatest patience.

Furthermore, when our people were threatened and challenged, defied, jeered, and mocked at the diet by the papists, they humbled themselves most abjectly and let themselves simply be trampled underfoot. Despite all, they asked and pleaded for peace, and they offered to do all that God might want. That would have been more than enough, even if our party were mere beggars, to say nothing of the fact that they are great princes, lords, and godly and honorable people. Therefore, I believe that there have been but few instances of such a confession and of such humility and of such patience as long as Christendom has existed, and I trust this will not be exceeded before the Last Day. Yet all of this was of no avail. Münzer[5] and the insurrectionists did not act thus; they did what the papists are doing now. They, too, neither wanted to have peace nor would they grant it to others. They resorted to violence; they listened to no mediation and no overtures, but insisted on having their own way. Moreover, they refused to submit their teaching to a hearing as our people now have done at Augsburg, but without further ado they condemned all other teaching and exalted their own by every means. In the same way the papists now refuse to make their document public, and yet they condemn our teaching.[6] We shall hear more of that later. In brief, we cannot

[5] Thomas Münzer (ca. 1488–1525), radical reformer and a leader in the Peasants' Revolt of 1525. For Luther's view of him, see *Letter to the Princes of Saxony Concerning the Rebellious Spirit* (1524). *LW* 40, 45-59. For a recent study of Münzer, see Eric W. Gritsch, *Reformer Without a Church* (Philadelphia: Fortress Press, 1967).
[6] On August 3, 1530, the Roman Catholic *Confutation* (*Confutatio Pontificia*) was publicly read. The evangelical representatives were not given a copy of

be blamed or accused either before God or before the world of fomenting war or insurrection.

Since our conscience is clear and pure and assured in this matter, and that of the papists must be guilty and impure and filled with misgiving, let come what may, even the worst, be it war or rebellion—whatever God's wrath decrees. If an uprising should result, my God and Lord Jesus Christ is well able to save me and mine, as he rescued dear Lot in Sodom, and as he saved me in the recent uprising when I was in danger of life and limb more than once.[7] And yet this is the thanks I earned by my efforts from those incorrigible scoundrels; I mean the papists. If God does not see fit to rescue me, I will nonetheless praise and thank him. I have lived long enough, I have certainly earned death, and I have begun to avenge my Lord Jesus properly on the papacy. Only after my death will they begin really to take Luther seriously.[8] Even now, if I were to be murdered in such a papist and clerical uprising, I would take a throng of bishops, priests, and monks with me, so that people would say that Doctor Martin had been escorted to his grave in a grand procession. For he was a great doctor over all bishops, priests, and monks; therefore it is fitting that they go to the grave with him, lying on their backs. People will sing and talk about it. Thus in the end we will undertake a little pilgrimage together—they, the papists, into the abyss of hell to their god of lies and murder, whom they served with lies and murder; I to my Lord Jesus Christ, whom I served in truth and peace.

For it is easy to figure out that whoever kills Doctor Luther in an uprising will not spare many of the priests either. Thus we shall go to our death together, they to hell in the name of all devils, I to heaven in the name of God. No one can harm me, that I know; nor do I desire to do harm to anyone else. But whatever evil they

---

this document beforehand; afterward they were to receive a copy of it only if they promised to accept its conclusions and not to hand it around. This the evangelicals refused to do. Melanchthon therefore had to present his reply to the *Confutation* (the *Apology of the Augsburg Confession*) without access to its text.

[7] Luther is referring to his experiences in May, 1525, during the Peasants' Revolt, when he traveled through some of the possessions of the count of Mansfeld and through Thuringia.

[8] A variation of a saying with which Luther taunted the papacy; he quoted it in either German or Latin. It is translated in *LW* 34, 49, as: "If I live I shall be your plague. If I die, I shall be your death." Cf. also *LW* 54, 227.

inflict on me, I will outdo them. No matter how hard their heads may be, they will find mine still harder. Even if they had not only Emperor Charles on their side but also the emperor of the Turks, they would not intimidate or frighten me; rather I will intimidate and frighten them. In the future they will yield to me; I will not yield to them. I will survive, they will perish. They have miscalculated grievously, for my life will be their hangman, my death will be their devil.[9] This is what they will discover, nothing else; just let them laugh impudently about it now.

On the other hand, if this ends in a war, I will again have to resign myself to it, together with my followers, and await what our God will advise and decree in this matter. He has always faithfully assisted and never forsaken us. Here again we enjoy a great advantage. In the first place, it will not harm us if we die or come to grief, for it is written, "Blessed are those who are persecuted for righteousness' sake" [Matt. 5:10]. We are convinced that he who says that does not lie. The papists themselves know and confess—and may the devil thank them if they should say otherwise—that our teaching is contrary neither to any article of the Creed nor to the Holy Scriptures;[10] rather it is contrary to the customs of their church and the laws of the popes. Therefore they cannot revile us as heretics without giving their own heart and mouth the lie, since no one may be dubbed a heretic who does not teach contrary to Holy Scripture or the articles of faith. Much less may they punish us or wage war against us as heretics. As liars against themselves, as assassins and traitors, they have hitherto defamed Leonard Keiser[11] and his like as heretics, burned them at the stake, murdered and persecuted them. And they have not yet shown any contrition or repentance for this, but remain hardened in such blood and lies. Who should be afraid of such warriors?

---

[9] Cf. above, n. 8.

[10] Justus Jonas had written Luther (June 30 [?], 1530) that after the reading of the *Augsburg Confession* the bishop of Augsburg, Christoph von Stadion, had shouted out, "This is pure truth; we cannot deny it!" Cf. WA 30II, 400, n. 2.

[11] Leonard Keiser, who had studied at the university in Wittenberg for a year and a half, was burned as a heretic, because of his Lutheran views, on August 16, 1527, in Schärding, Bavaria. Cf. Luther's treatise, *Concerning Leonard Keiser of Bavaria, Burned for the Sake of the Gospel*, 1527 (*Von Lenhard Keiser in Baiern, um des Euangelii willen verbrannt*), WA 30II, 452–476.

In the second place, we know that they are unable to begin such a war in the name of God, nor are they able to pray for it and invoke God's help. And I challenge them all, collectively and individually, to say to God with a sincere heart: "Help us, God, to fight in defense of this cause!" For their conscience is too burdened, not only with lying, blaspheming, blood, murder, and all other abominations but, over and above all this, with hardened and impenitent hearts and sins against the Holy Spirit. Consequently, since they wage war with a bad conscience for a blasphemous cause, good fortune and success cannot attend them. Therefore we will speak a blessing over them, which will read as follows: "May God give you success and victory in proportion to your uprightness before God and the goodness of your cause! Amen!" You will fare as we Germans did when we ventured to break the peace with St. John Huss and fought against the Bohemians.[12] On that occasion the pope also handed us over to the slaughter, so that we had to satisfy his pleasure with our blood and heads, and we fought against truth and justice. Now you are doing the same thing, and so the pope, this most holy father and kind shepherd of our souls, will again have occasion to laugh up his sleeve if he can stir up such a welcome bloodbath among us. However, God can easily raise up a Judas Maccabeus[13] (even if my followers and I sit by quietly and suffer) who will smash Antiochus with his army and teach him real warfare, as he taught us how to wage war and how to keep the peace through the Bohemians.

Nor will my followers and I leave off praying and imploring God to give them a despondent, timid, and craven heart when on the battlefield, to prick the conscience of one and then another and prompt them to say: "Alas! Alas! I am engaged in a perilous war. We are espousing an evil cause and fighting against God and his word. What will be our fate? Where are we going?" And when they see a Maccabean warrior coming at them, they will disperse and scatter like chaff before the wind. Do you not believe that God is

---

[12] Luther is referring to the unsuccessful attempts which were made to root out the Hussites after Huss was burned as a heretic by the Council of Constance in 1415. Cf. below, n. 14.

[13] The reference is to the heroic Jewish figure who led the Jews in 166–160 B.C. during their struggle aganst the Syrian king Antiochus Epiphanes and his successors.

still able to do this? He says to his people, "I will send faintness into your hearts, so that when you go out one way against your enemies, you shall flee seven ways before them; the sound of a driven leaf shall put you to flight" [Lev. 26:36; Deut. 28:25]. Truly, that is what he also did to the obdurate Egyptians in the Red Sea. They were probably as obstinate and secure as the papists are. Yet when the hour came that their conscience smote them, they cried, "Alas, let us flee, for the Lord is fighting against us" [Exod. 14:25]. Let him who does not know what it means to wage war with a bad conscience and a despondent heart try it now. If the papists wage war, he will experience it, just as our ancestors did in a similar situation against the Bohemians and Zizka.[14] And we will not suppress our prayer but will offer it publicly; it will be the seventh psalm, which in its first combat slew all of Israel, so that twenty thousand men, together with Absalom, lay dead on the battlefield, slain by a small number.[15] For it has a sufficient stock of guns, powder, and armor—that I know for a certainty.

In the third place, it is not fitting for me, a preacher, vested with the spiritual office, to wage war or to counsel war or incite it, but rather to dissuade from war and to direct to peace, as I have done until now with all diligence. All the world must bear witness to this. However, our enemies do not want to have peace, but war. If war should come now, I will surely hold my pen in check and keep silent and not intervene as I did in the last uprising.[16] I will let matters take their course, even though not a bishop, priest, or monk survives and I myself also perish. For their defiance and boasting are intolerable to God; their impenitent heart is carrying things too far. They were begged, they were admonished, they were implored for peace beyond all reasonable measure. They

---

[14] John Zizka (1376–1424) was the great military leader of the Hussites; he successfully defied Sigismund, king of the Germans and king of Hungary, and others who led crusades against the followers of John Huss after the death of Huss in 1415. Cf. F. G. Heymann, *John Zizka and the Hussite Revolution* (Princeton: Princeton University Press, 1955).
[15] Cf. II Sam. 18:7.
[16] I.e., the Peasants' Revolt of 1525. Cf. Luther's writings on the subject in *LW* 46, 17–85: *Admonition to Peace, A Reply to the Twelve Articles of the Peasants in Swabia*, 1525; *Against the Robbing and Murdering Hordes of Peasants*, 1525; and *An Open Letter on the Harsh Book Against the Peasants*, 1525.

insist on forcing the issue with flesh and blood; so I, too, will force the issue with them through the Spirit and through God and henceforth set not one or two papists but the entire papacy against me, until the Judge in heaven intervenes with signs. I will not and cannot be afraid of such miserable enemies of God. I disdain their defiance, and I laugh at their wrath. They can do no more than deprive me of a sack of ailing flesh. But they shall soon discover of what I am able to deprive them.

Furthermore, if war breaks out—which God forbid—I will not reprove those who defend themselves against the murderous and bloodthirsty papists, nor let anyone else rebuke them as being seditious, but I will accept their action and let it pass as self-defense. I will direct them in this matter to the law and to the jurists. For in such an instance, when the murderers and bloodhounds wish to wage war and to murder, it is in truth no insurrection to rise against them and defend oneself. Not that I wish to incite or spur anyone on to such self-defense, or to justify it, for that is not my office; much less does it devolve on me to pass judgment or sentence on him. A Christian knows very will what he is to do—namely, to render to God the things that are God's and to Caesar the things that are Caesar's [Matt. 22:21], but not to render to the bloodhounds the things that are not theirs. I want to make a distinction between sedition and other acts and to deprive the bloodhounds of the pretext of boasting that they are warring against rebellious people and that they were justified according to both human and divine law; for so the little kitten is fond of grooming and adorning itself. Likewise, I do not want to leave the conscience of the people burdened by the concern and worry that their self-defense might be rebellious. For such a term would be too evil and too harsh in such a case. It should be given a different name, which I am sure the jurists can find for it.

We must not let everything be considered rebellious which the bloodhounds designate as such. For in that way they want to silence the lips and tie the hands of the entire world, so that no one may either reprove them with preaching or defend himself with his fist, while they keep their mouth open and their hands free. Thus they want to frighten and ensnare all the world with the name

19

"insurrection," and at the same time comfort and reassure themselves. No, dear fellow, we must submit to you a different interpretation and definition of that term. To act contrary to law is not rebellion; otherwise every violation of the law would be rebellion. No, he is an insurrectionist who refuses to submit to government and law, who attacks and fights against them, and attempts to overthrow them with a view to making himself ruler and establishing the law, as Münzer did; that is the true definition of a rebel. *Aliud est invasor, aliud transgressor.*[17] In accordance with this definition, self-defense against the bloodhounds cannot be rebellious. For the papists are deliberately starting the war; they refuse to keep the peace, they do not let others rest who would like to live in peace. Thus the papists are much closer to the name and the quality which is termed rebellion.

For they have no law, either divine or human, on their side; rather they act out of malice, like murderers and villains, in violation of all divine and human law. That can easily be proved; for they themselves know that our doctrine is correct, and yet they want to exterminate it. Thus a great Nicholas bishop[18] declared in Augsburg that he could tolerate it if everyone believed as they do in Wittenberg; but what he could not tolerate was that such a doctrine should originate in and emanate from such a remote nook and corner. What do you think? Are those not fine episcopal words? The papal legate, Cardinal Campeggio,[19] confessed similarly that he could easily accept such a teaching. However, this would establish a bad precedent, and one would then have to accord other nations and kingdoms the same privilege, which would be out of the question. Another important bishop declared of their scholars: "Our scholars do a fine job of defending us. They themselves concede that our cause is not based on Scripture."[20] Thus they are well

---

[17] "An invader is one thing, a transgressor is another."
[18] Luther sometimes referred to the Roman Catholic bishops as "Nicholas bishops" when he wanted to stress the dubiousness of their calling. A "Nicholas" was a comic figure in children's games and also a term of contempt for a peasant. Cf. *LW* 39, 252, n. 8. Melanchthon and Jonas attributed a statement of this nature to Matthew Lang, the archbishop of Salzburg, and it is he to whom Luther is referring. Cf. *WA* 30III, 261–262, and 283, n. 2, as well as *LW* 34, 102.
[19] Cardinal Lorenzo Campeggio, papal legate at the diet in Augsburg.
[20] Conrad Cordatus, one of the Lutheran theologians at the diet, attributed such statements to Albert, archbishop of Mainz, and to John Eck. Cf. *WA* 30III, 284, n. 1.

aware that our doctrine is not wrong, but that it is founded on the Scriptures. Yet they condemn us arbitrarily and try to exterminate this doctrine in contravention of divine law and truth.

It is also obvious that they are acting contrary to imperial and to natural law; for in the first place, they hardly gave our side a hearing, and then, when they delivered their tardy, flimsy confutation orally, they simply refused to hand us a copy of it, nor did they give us an opportunity to make reply.[21] To the present day they shun the light like bats. It is, of course, in accord with divine, imperial, and natural law, as the heathen Porcius Festus also held in the controversy between the Jews and St. Paul [Acts 25:16], not to condemn a man without a hearing. Even God did not condemn Adam until he first gave him a chance to reply. We appeared voluntarily at Augsburg and offered humbly and eagerly to render an account. This, however, was maliciously and arbitrarily denied us. Nor did they give us their confutation, no matter how often and how much we pleaded for it. Yet we were condemned by the holy fathers in God and by the Christian princes. O excellent teachers! O fine judges, who force all the world to believe and still dare not to publish what is to be believed! I am expected to believe without knowing what to believe. I am told that I am in error, but I am not shown in what I err!

O all you unfortunate people who sided with the pope at Augsburg! All your descendants will forever have to be ashamed of you. They will be unhappy to hear that they had such miserable ancestors. If we had shunned the light and refused to give answer, you would have compelled us to do so. Now we come along, not only willing and glad to give an account, but we plead, implore, and clamor for a chance to do this. We go to great expense to do so, neglect many things, and suffer every indignity, mockery, contempt, and danger, and you shamefully and maliciously refuse our request. If we had not asked for or desired to have your bat or night owl, that is, your confutation, you would have transmitted it to us against our wishes. Now that we ask for it, complain, and persist in demanding it, you deny us your confutation and refuse to receive our reply.

Shame on this diet for its disgraceful action! The like of it

---

[21] See above, pp. 13-14, n. 6.

was never held or heard of before and never will be held or heard of again. It must be an eternal blemish on all princes and the whole empire, and makes all of us Germans blush with shame before God and all the world. What will the Turk and his whole realm say when they hear of such an unparalleled action of our empire? What will the Tartars and the Muscovites say to this? Who under heaven will henceforth fear us Germans or regard us as honorable when they hear that we permit the accursed pope and his masks to hoax and dupe us, to treat us as children, yes, as dolts and clods, that we, for the sake of their blasphemous, sodomitic, shameful teaching and life, act so disgracefully, so very, very shamefully and contrary to law and truth in a public diet? Every German should on this account rue having been born a German and being called a German.

However, I am very willing to believe that a special portion of shrewdness prompts them to hold back their confutation and their fine little booklet. Their conscience must sense instinctively that it is a flimsy, empty, and meaningless thing of which they would have to be ashamed if it were made public and examined in the light of day, or if it were to be answered. For I know those highly learned doctors very well who no doubt brewed and stewed over it for six weeks. Perhaps with their babbling they can impress those unfamiliar with the subject; but when it is put on paper, it has neither hands nor feet, and lies there confounded and confused, as though a drunkard had spewed it forth. This is especially apparent in the writings of Dr. Schmid[22] and Dr. Eck.[23] There is neither head nor tail to it when they commit things to writing. For that reason they apply themselves so much the more to shouting and chattering.

I also heard that many of our opponents were astonished when our confession was read and admitted that it was the simple truth and could not be refuted with Scripture. On the other hand, when

[22] Schmid ("Smith") was Luther's name for John Faber, or Fabri (1478–1541), the archbishop of Vienna and one of the principal authors of the Roman Catholic confutation. Faber was the son of a blacksmith.
[23] John Eck (1486–1543), the Roman Catholic theologian who was Luther's opponent in the Leipzig Debate (1519) and a leading Roman Catholic participant at Augsburg.

their confutation was read, they hung their heads and admitted by their expressions that it was a flimsy and empty thing compared with our confession. Our people and many godly hearts rejoiced greatly and were wonderfully strengthened when they heard that the opponents with the utmost might and skill they could muster at the time could produce no more than this empty confutation, which—God be praised—a woman, a child, a layman, a peasant is now able to refute, buttressed with good arguments from the Scriptures and from truth. That is the true and real reason why they declined to hand us their confutation. Those fugitive, bad consciences shudder at themselves and are not prepared for truth's reply.

It is easy to see that they were very confident when they arranged for this diet and were convinced that our side would lack the courage to appear. They thought that when they brought the emperor in person to Germany, all would be frightened and say, "Gracious lords, what is your wish?" When they proved mistaken in this and the elector of Saxony was the very first to make his appearance, my heavens, how they soiled their breeches in their trepidation! How all their confidence vanished! How they put their heads together, took secret counsel with one another and whispered! No one—not Christ himself, or even I—was permitted to know what it was all about, just as little as we knew about the princes' plotting prior to this year.[24] In the final analysis they were trying to find ways and means to avoid giving our people an opportunity to be heard, for our people were the first to arrive, and they appeared to be very bold and cheerful. As this was impossible, they nevertheless did themselves the honor in the end of refusing to hand us their vapid confutation and to give us an opportunity to make reply.

Their insolent mouthpiece and bloodthirsty sophist, Dr. Eck, one of their foremost advisers, declared openly within the hearing

---

[24] In the spring of 1528 Otto von Pack, an official of Duke George of Saxony, reported to Philip of Hesse the existence of a league of Roman Catholic princes and bishops which proposed to attack and destroy the supporters of the Reformation. It was soon ascertained that Pack's story was a hoax and that his documents were forgeries. Luther, however, continued to believe Pack's account. Cf. Smith and Jacobs, *Luther's Correspondence*, II, 435.

of our people that if the emperor had followed the resolution arrived at in Bologna[25] and attacked the Lutherans promptly and swiftly with the sword upon his entry into Germany, beheading one after the other, then the problem would have been solved; but all that had come to nought when he permitted the elector of Saxony to speak and defend himself through his chancellor. What do you think of such doctors and holy fathers? How imbued with love and truth they are! Thus the secret deliberations had to come to light which the papal holiness had conducted in Bologna with the emperor. What a fine spectacle would have evolved if the emperor had followed such papistic and devilish advice and initiated this event with murder! That would have resulted in such a diet that not a fingernail either of the bishops or of the princes would have remained. And all this in these perilous times when everything is so unsettled and confused and when all the world was looking forward to a benevolent diet, as the summons had intimated and asserted. However, the expectations were not fulfilled.

Someone may interpose that the emperor was willing to hand us their confutation if we had promised not to make it public. That is true; this was suggested to our side.[26] But here let everyone feel and grope, even if he cannot see and hear, to learn what kind of people they are who do not wish or dare to have their cause exposed to the light of day. If it is really such a precious thing and so well grounded in the Scriptures, as they shout and boast, why does it shun the light? What good does it do to conceal such public matters from us and from everyone? After all, they must be taught and observed by them. But if it is unfounded and without meaning, why then did they have the elector of Brandenburg proclaim and publish in writing at the time of the first recess that our confession was refuted by Scripture and sound reason?[27] If that were true and

<hr>

[25] It was in the Treaty of Barcelona, June 29, 1529, between the pope and the emperor, that Charles agreed to take forcible measures to suppress the Reformation in Germany. Cf. Ludwig Pastor, *History of the Popes* (St. Louis: B. Herder Book Co., 1923), X, 57. This matter may also have been discussed when the pope and emperor met in Bologna (November, 1529–March, 1530) to work out a peace treaty and to crown the emperor.

[26] Cf. above, pp. 13-14, n. 6.

[27] On September 22, 1530, the emperor proclaimed an imperial recess, and the elector of Brandenburg read the emperor's verdict that the "views and confession of the elector of Saxony and his associates . . . have been refuted and

if their own conscience did not give them the lie, they would not only have had such a precious and well-documented confutation read, but they would also have handed it to us in writing, saying, "There you have it. We challenge anyone to refute that." That is what we did, and still do, with our confession.

However, Christ must remain truthful when he says: "For every one who does evil hates the light, and does not come to the light, lest his deeds should be exposed. But he who does what is true comes to the light, that it may be clearly seen that his deeds have been wrought in God" [John 3:20-21]. In accord with this judgment of Christ, God permitted our people to come away from this diet decked with such eternal glory that even our adversaries have to confess that we did not avoid the light but most boldly and cheerfully sought out and expected it. They, on the other hand, were left there covered with such eternal disgrace that they avoided and shunned the light most shamefully and obviously like night owls and bats, yes, like their father of lies and murder, and were unable to expect or tolerate a rejoinder to their loose, hollow, and obscure prattle.

It is also an indication of a fine Christian attitude that they asked our people to pledge themselves to prevent the precious knowledge and well-grounded wisdom of their confutation from leaking out and becoming public. How thoroughly God has blinded and abased the papists, so that they no longer have either reason or shame! How is it possible—to leave aside the question of whether it is right—to promise to keep such a document secret, which had passed through so many hands and had already been read once before the diet? Then if it would have been made public later on by their own faction, we would have been blamed for it.

Godless reason must take recourse to such cleverness and petty artifices because it cannot bear the truth and the light; nor can it find a better excuse for remaining in the dark and refusing to publish its confutation. Well and good, let it remain in the dark where it is; moreover, it shall ever remain in the eternal hellish darkness.

rejected on the basis of the gospel and the Scriptures with sound reason." Cf. WA 30^{III}, 287, n. 4; Reu, *The Augsburg Confession,* p. 391; and Luther's *Commentary on the Alleged Imperial Edict, LW* 34, 63–104. See especially *LW* 34, 68, n. 5.

But on the day of judgment, if not before, it will come into the light only too clearly.

Yes, you will say, but even though they did not issue their confutation or allow it to be answered, they did appoint instead a committee composed of several princes and scholars from each side and ordered them to discuss the matter at issue in a friendly manner. Little kitten, clean and groom yourself, we are going to have company![28] How stupid and foolish is that poor man Christ, not to notice such cunning. The committee did convene, that is true; but what was discussed? Nothing at all about their confutation or refutation; that remained in the dark. The committee had to help in preserving appearances, so as to provide some pretense for keeping the inane confutation under cover and not making it public. For it was not their confutation that was submitted in the committee meeting, but our confession. Their deliberations with our people revolved about such questions as how much of our confession we were willing to drop and withdraw, or how they interpreted it, or how we could make it harmonize with their views. Their one aim and objective was to enable them to make a fine pretense and to raise the hue and cry: "You see, dear people, listen, all the world, and hear how stubborn and stiff-necked the Lutherans are! In the first place, their confession was disproven with Scripture and with well-founded reasons, and then we engaged in friendly discussions with them. What more can we do? They refuse to yield, whether they are overcome or whether instructed in a friendly manner."

All right, we must put up with their clamor and their lies; however, I know that this will not help them. God, too, has already given them and their boasting the lie. For when this recess was announced by the elector of Brandenburg and it was proclaimed that our confession had been refuted with the Scriptures and with valid reason, our people did not accept it, nor did they keep silent, but boldly and publicly contradicted it before the emperor and the empire and affirmed that our confession had not been refuted, but that it was ordered and founded in such a way that even the

---

[28] When a cat washed itself it was supposed to mean that guests were coming. Luther uses this proverb in the sense of putting on a false front.

gates of hell could not prevail against it. They had to swallow this discomfiture again. For, bluntly stated, what the elector of Brandenburg read out in proclaiming the recess is not true; it is a lie. That is correct, for their well-grounded confutation has not yet been brought to light. It is perhaps still slumbering with old Tannhäuser in the Venusberg.[29]

Since it is evident that they are keeping their confutation secret and have not yet brought it to light on their own, their allegation that our confession had been refuted with the Scriptures and with sound reason is not only a manifest and impudent lie, but it represents the devil's own lie when they boast in the bargain and put up a good front and dare to cry that we are defeated but will not retract. This they do though their conscience mightily convicts them of such lies. So it is obvious that they had to resort to this pretense, as do all those who have a bad cause. They cover up miserably and hatch all sorts of dodges to keep their bad cause from coming to light. In brief, it is plain that they, despairing of their cause, expected nothing less than that our people would appear on the scene. They relied entirely on sheer force and were not at all prepared for truth and light.

The friendly intentions which they had regarding the committee are also very evident from the one point which they dared, among other articles, to propose to our people, namely, that we should teach that in addition to taking the sacrament in two kinds, it was not wrong but right to administer and take it also in only one kind.[30] If we consented to that, they would also make a concession and permit us to teach that the sacrament might be taken and given in both kinds. Does that not betoken a great friendship? Who might have looked for such love from these people? Until now they persecuted as heretics all who took the sacrament

---

[29] The Tannhäuser legend combined elements from the life of a thirteenth-century German minnesinger with those of a legendary knight who, after many wanderings, gave himself up to a life of sensual passion with Lady Venus on the Venusberg, a mountain near Eisenach.

[30] This proposal was made on August 19, 1530, and the answer from the Lutherans was given on the next day. Luther had discussed "both kinds in the sacrament" in his *Exhortation to All Clergy Assembled at Augsburg*, LW 34, 38–40. He also dealt with the matter in his letter of August 26 to Elector John of Saxony, WA, Br 5, 572–574; translated in Reu, *op. cit.*, Second Part, pp. 383 ff.

in both kinds and tormented them in every way. And now they are ready to adjudge this as correct and Christian and let it pass as such, if we but admit that they in turn also do the correct and Christian thing when they take the sacrament in one kind. That is, in plain words, speaking out of both sides of your mouth.[31] It is wrong, and yet it is accounted right, depending upon their whims and will. Yet this dare not be called a lie.

If our side had agreed to this and accepted their proposal, then they really would have boasted and shouted throughout the whole world: "See, dear people, the Lutherans are recanting their doctrine. Formerly they taught that it was wrong to take the sacrament in one kind, and now they teach that it is right. Now you note that we taught correctly, and they are found to be in error in their own confession." In that way they tried to confirm all their abominations and devil's tomfoolery in the eyes of the faithful, simple folk and to arraign us as recanters of all our teaching. Furthermore, they would thus have established their pernicious doctrine in our churches by our own lips and at the same time suppressed our doctrine with might in their churches. They would not at all have taught our doctrine among themselves. In that way they wanted to penetrate and entrench themselves in our churches by means of our own lips and, simultaneously, exclude us from their churches. Are these not fine, friendly, fitting means, well suited to friendly dealings?

As the confutation is, so is the committee. The confutation is a dark night owl, reluctant to face the light; the committee is sheer cunning and deception. The boast that they tried friendly measures with us is just as truthful and sincere as their boast that they refuted our confession with Holy Scripture and sound reason—both are sheer lying and deceit. To be sure, they would not like to be treated that way by us. However, at present I do not propose to write about the actions of this diet, nor to attack their confutation (though both shall yet be attended to if God wills),[32] but at present

---

[31] Proverbial expression which literally says, "to blow hot and cold at the same time." Cf. Ernst Thiele, *Luthers Sprichwörtersammlung* (Weimar, 1900), No. 136.

[32] Luther's *Commentary on the Alleged Imperial Edict* (LW 34, 63–104) appears to be the fulfillment of this intention. Written some months after his *Warning*, it was published almost simultaneously with it due to the delay of the latter in the press.

I merely wish to show that the papists do not want to have peace, truth, or tranquillity, but insist on enforcing their will and thus are bringing about either a war or an insurrection, whether we like it or not. Nothing will restrain them. We, however, will have to take the risk and await the outcome, since our offers, pleas, and cries for peace are unheeded and our humility and patience go for nought. Let come what cannot be prevented!

But since I am the "prophet of the Germans"[33]—for this haughty title I will henceforth have to assign to myself, to please and oblige my papists and asses—it is fitting that I, as a faithful teacher, warn my dear Germans against the harm and danger threatening them and impart Christian instruction to them regarding their conduct in the event that the emperor, at the instigation of his devils, the papists, issues a call to arms against the princes and cities on our side. It is not that I worry that His Imperial Majesty will listen to such spiteful people and initiate such an unjust war, but I do not want to neglect my duty. I want to keep my conscience clean and unsullied at all events. I would much rather compose a superfluous and unnecessary admonition and warning and impart needless instruction than to neglect my duty and then find, if things go contrary to my expectations, that I am too late and have no other consolation than the words *non putassem,* I did not intend this. The sages suggest making provision for things even if everything is secure. How much less may we trust any wind and weather, no matter how pleasant it may appear, in these difficult times when the papists' raging provokes God's wrath so terribly! Moreover, in Romans 12 Paul commands those who preside over others to look out for them.

Any German who wants to follow my sincere counsel may do so; and whoever does not want to may disregard it. I am not seeking my own benefit in this, but the welfare and salvation of you Germans. Nothing better could happen to my person than that the papists devour me, tear me, or bite me to pieces, or help me out of this sinful, mortal bag of maggots in any other way. No matter how

---

[33] Justus Jonas had referred to Luther in such terms in correspondence with him during his sojourn at Coburg, complimenting him on his steadfastness in the face of controversy, and Melanchthon was to use similar phraseology in his oration at Luther's funeral. Cf. Julius Köstlin, *Martin Luther: Sein Leben und seine Schriften* (2 vols.; Berlin, 1903),II, 215, 625–626.

angry they are, I will say to them: "Dear Sirs, if you are angry, step away from the wall, do it in your underwear, and hang it around your neck!"[34] In brief, I will not have them boast to me and defy me. For I know—God be praised—what my position is and where I shall stay. If they do not want to accept my service for their own good, then may the vile devil thank them if they show me a driblet of love or grace. If they do not need my doctrine, I need their grace still less, and I will let them rage and rant in the name of all devils, while I laugh in the name of God.

This is my sincere advice: If the emperor should issue a call to arms against us on behalf of the pope or because of our teaching, as the papists at present horribly gloat and boast—though I do not yet expect this of the emperor—no one should lend himself to it or obey the emperor in this event. All may rest assured that God has strictly forbidden compliance with such a command of the emperor. Whoever does obey him can be certain that he is disobedient to God and will lose both body and soul eternally in the war. For in this case the emperor would not only act in contravention of God and divine law but also in violation of his own imperial law, vow, duty, seal, and edicts. And lest you imagine that this is just my own idea or that such advice is dictated by my fancy, I shall submit clear and strong reasons and arguments to convince you that this is not my own counsel, but God's earnest, manifold, and stringent command. Before his anger you surely ought to be terrified and, in the end, must be terrified.

In the first place, I must say a word in defense of dear Emperor Charles' person. For he has to date, also at the diet, conducted himself in such a way that he has gained the favor and affection of all the world and is worthy of being spared all grief. Our people, too, have nothing but praise for his imperial virtues.[35] Let me cite just a few examples to demonstrate this. It demonstrates a wonderful and rare gentleness of character that His Imperial Majesty refused to condemn our doctrine even though he was vehemently incited and urged on by both the spiritual and secular princes, with un-

---

[34] A proverbial expression; cf. Thiele, *Luthers Sprichwörtersammlung*, No. 90.
[35] Cf., for example, Melanchthon's letter of June 19, 1530, to Luther: "Nor is anyone in the whole hall milder than the emperor himself." WA 30III, 291, n. 4.

relenting insistence, even before he left Spain. However, His Majesty stood his ground as firmly as a rock. He hurried to the diet and issued a gracious invitation, wanting to discuss matters in a kind and friendly spirit. He is also reported to have declared: "This cannot be such an utterly evil doctrine, since so many great, exalted, learned, and honest people accept it."

And this was borne out at Augsburg. When our confession was read before His Imperial Majesty, the opposition itself discovered that this teaching was not as evil as it had been pictured by their venomous preachers and sycophants and hateful princes. Indeed, they had not expected that it was such sound doctrine. Many of them confessed that it was pure Scripture, that it could not be refuted by Holy Scripture, and that previously they had been entirely misinformed. That is also the reason why permission to read the confession was granted so reluctantly; for the envious princes and the virulent liars were indeed worried that their vile lies would be put to shame if it was read. It was their wish that His Imperial Majesty should condemn everything at once, unread and unheard. But since His Imperial Majesty could not have it read publicly in the presence of all, he at least had it read and heard before the imperial estates, no matter how the other princes and bishops and sophists opposed this and were bitterly vexed by it.

And although the diet involved a great expenditure of money and it seems that nothing was accomplished there, I nevertheless will say for myself that even if it had consumed twice as much money, all is richly compensated for and enough has been achieved, for Sir Envy and Master Liar were disgraced in their envying and lying. They had to see and hear that our doctrine was not found to be contrary to the Scriptures or the articles of faith. For prior to this, their lies and envy portrayed our doctrine everywhere, through their writings, their sermons, and their slander, as more horrible than any other that has ever seen the light of day. This envy, I say, was put to shame at the diet, and these lies were disclosed. Therefore we must be kindly disposed toward our dear Emperor Charles and thank him for this benefit, that God through him initially adorned our doctrine and delivered it from the false and ridiculous labels of heresy and of other shameful names, and that he thus administered a sound slap on the mouth of these lying and envious people. Of course, they are brazen-faced and unashamed. But this does not matter; the beginning is good enough for us, and, I suppose, things will also improve.

Furthermore, His Imperial Majesty is reported to have said that if the priests were godly, they would not need a Luther. What else does that mean other than what Solomon said: "Inspired decisions are on the lips of a king" [Prov. 16:10]. His Majesty wishes to indicate that Luther is the priests' scourge, that they are well deserving of this, and that their conduct is reprehensible. They themselves have admitted that often enough. For the bishop of Salzburg remarked to Master Philip:[36] "Alas, why do you propose to reform us priests? We priests never have been any good." See and hear those godly people! They know and they confess that they are evil and that they are in error; moreover, they want to stay that way, remain unreformed, and not yield to the acknowledged truth. Yet they clamor and call upon the emperor and all princes to go to war for them and to protect them. What else does that mean than this: Dear Emperor, dear Germans, wage war, shed your blood, stake all your property, your life, your wife and child on protecting us in our shameful, devilish life against the truth. Certainly we know the truth but we cannot stomach it; nor do we want to mend our ways. What do you think? If you go to war and shed your blood for such people are you not a fine martyr, and do you not invest your blood and your property very wisely?

Furthermore, when our people wanted to hand His Imperial Majesty their answer to the sophists' confutation—as much of it as had been retained after the reading—and His Imperial Majesty extended his hand to receive it, King Ferdinand pulled the hand of His Imperial Majesty back, restraining him from accepting it.[37] This again reveals the identity of the people who vent their hatred and their envy under the name of His Imperial Majesty; for the latter was minded and inclined otherwise.

---

[36] Philip Melanchthon.

[37] The answer that Luther is referring to here is the *Apology of the Augsburg Confession*, which the elector of Saxony's chancellor, Gregory Brück, tried to hand to the emperor after the recess of the diet had been announced. King Ferdinand, who kept the emperor from accepting the *Apology*, was the archduke of Austria; in 1556 he succeeded Charles as emperor and reigned until 1564.

Furthermore, when the elector of Brandenburg in the recess argued with fine and high-sounding and haughty words that His Imperial Majesty, the princes, and the estates of the empire had leagued together and were staking land and people, life and property and blood on this, he wanted to intimidate our people with these words. But he failed to add "if God wills," so his words remained mere words and died as soon as they were spoken. When the sound had faded away, no one was afraid. Here His Imperial Majesty again interposed a word. To be sure, he did not say that the speaker was lying, but that he had made an overstatement. Many other great princes and lords were nonplussed and were at a loss to know how to interpret these words. Several suggested that they meant that if our side would attack any of their members by force, then they would ally themselves and come to the defense with life and goods, with blood, land, and people. However, our people never thought of doing that, but always asked and pleaded for peace, as all know very well. Several declared openly before the emperor that they did not concur in this speech of the margrave and that it did not at all reflect their opinion.

It is easy to talk about land and people; but it is another question if anyone has such power over them that he can wager blood, life, and property needlessly and against God and his law. Experience should be able to answer this question. It seems to me that the people will, at least, first have to be consulted, and that one cannot embark on such a venture without announcing it. It should also be remembered that God must not always grant and do what we may venture to think and say. I am sure that the mouths of greater lords have been found to lie miserably and that their schemes thoroughly put them to shame. But the best part of this is that they fail to invoke God in this and that they fail to bear him in mind when they brag so defiantly. However, one can sense the emperor's sentiments in this matter. He is not such a mad bloodhound, and these defiant words do not please him.

But the dear emperor must share the experience of all godly princes and lords. For whenever a prince is not half a devil and wishes to govern with mildness, the greatest rogues and villains inevitably gain a place in the government and the offices and do as they like under the ruler's name. They need not fear because they know that the prince is gentle and is ready to give them an ear. What can this godly emperor do among so many rogues and villains, especially over against that arch-villain, Pope Clement,[38] who is full of all kinds of malice, which he has to date amply demonstrated to the emperor? I, Dr. Luther, am better versed in Scripture than the emperor, and also more experienced in practical daily life, but still I fear that if I were to dwell among so many rogues and constantly heard their venomous tongues, without any information to the contrary, I would also be too gentle for them and they would overwhelm me in some matters. In fact, this has often happened to me at the hands of certain spirits and wiseacres.

Therefore no one need be astonished or alarmed if prohibitions or edicts are issued under the emperor's name which are contrary to God and justice. He cannot prevent this. Rather he may be assured that all of this is a scheme of the supreme rogue in the world, the pope, who instigates this through his tonsured goats and hypocrites in an attempt to initiate a bloodbath among us Germans so that we may perish. And I for one believe that if he fails to accomplish his end through this emperor, he will join with the Turkish emperor and set him upon us. That is where we will then find the money which we have poured into the pope's treasury these many years for his indulgences and business deals to finance the war against the Turks.

Let this suffice for the time being as an apology for the emperor. Now we want to issue a warning, giving reasons why everyone should rightly beware and fear to obey the emperor in such an instance and to wage war against our side. I repeat what I said earlier, that I do not wish to advise or incite anyone to engage in war. My ardent wish and plea is that peace be preserved and that neither side start a war or give cause for it. For I do not want my conscience burdened, nor do I want to be known before God or the world as having counseled or desired anyone to wage war or to offer resistance except those who are enjoined and authorized to do so (Romans 13). But wherever the devil has so completely possessed the papists that they cannot and will not keep or tolerate peace, or where they absolutely want to wage war or

---

[38] Clement VII (Giulio de' Medici), cousin of Leo X (Giovanni de' Medici), reigned as pope from 1523 to 1534.

provoke it, that will rest upon their conscience. There is nothing I can do about it, since my remonstrances are ignored and futile.

The first reason why you must not obey the emperor and make war in such an instance as this is that you, as well as the emperor, vowed in baptism to preserve the gospel of Christ and not to persecute it or oppose it. Now you are, of course, aware that in this case the emperor is being incited and duped by the pope to fight against the gospel of Christ, because our doctrine was publicly proved at Augsburg to be the true gospel and Holy Scripture. Therefore, this must be your reply to the emperor's or your prince's summons to arms: "Indeed, dear Emperor, dear prince, if you keep your oath and pledge made in baptism, you will be my dear lord, and I will obey you and go to war at your command. But if you will not keep your baptismal pledge and Christian covenant made with Christ, but rather deny them, then may a rascal obey you in my place. I refuse to blaspheme my God and deny his word for your sake; nor will I impudently rush to spring into the abyss of hell with you."

This first reason has awesome, far-reaching implications. For he who fights and contends against the gospel necessarily fights simultaneously against God, against Jesus Christ, against the Holy Spirit, against the precious blood of Christ, against his death, against God's word, against all the articles of faith, against all the sacraments, against all the doctrines which are given, confirmed, and preserved by the gospel, for example, the doctrine regarding government, regarding worldly peace, worldly estates, in brief, against all angels and saints, against heaven and earth and all creatures. For he who fights against God must fight against all that is of God or that has to do with God. But you would soon discover what kind of end that would lead to! What is even worse, such fighting would be done consciously; for these people know and admit that this teaching is the gospel. The Turks and the Tartars, of course, do not know that it is God's word. Therefore no Turk can be as vile as you, and you must be damned to hell ten times more deeply than all Turks, Tartars, heathen, and Jews.

It is indeed terrible that things have come so far among Christians that this warning becomes necessary, just as though they themselves did not realize how abominable and horrible it is knowingly to contend against God and his word. This indicates that among Christians there are few real Christians and that there must be far worse Turks in their number than are found in Turkey, or even in hell. The true Christians, however few they are, know this very well themselves and do not need such a warning; but the papists do need it. Though they bear the name and the outward appearance of Christians, they disgrace them and are ten times worse than the Turks. They must be warned. If it helps, good and well; if it does not help, we, at least, are blameless, and their punishment will be so much more severe. The Turk is not so mad as to fight and to rage against his Muhammad or against his Koran, as our devils, the papists, do when they rave and rage against their own gospel, which they acknowledge to be true. Such an action makes the Turk, by comparison, a pure saint, and they thereby make themselves true devils.

The second reason is this: Even if our doctrine were false—although everyone knows it is not—you should still be deterred from fighting solely by the knowledge that by such fighting you are taking upon yourself a part of the guilt before God of all the abominations which have been committed and will yet be committed by the whole papacy. This reason encompasses innumerable loathsome deeds and every vice, sin, and harm. In brief, the bottomless hell itself is found here, with every sin, all of which you share in if you obey the emperor in this instance. We shall enumerate a few of these and bring them into view, lest they be too easily forgotten.[39] For the papists would like to cover themselves and hide such abominations, unrepented and unreformed, until such a time as they can bring them into the open again and restore them.

Here you will first have to take upon yourself the whole of the shameful life which they have led and still lead. They do not intend

---

[39] Luther gives in the following pages a "catalog of vices" of the papacy and the Roman church which in the severity of its indictment and the exuberance of its language is equaled by few other passages in Luther's writings. Cf. the comments to this effect by Kurt Aland, *Luther Deutsch,* IV, 370-371, 373 (note to p. 246).

to mend this; however, you are to shed your blood and risk your life for the protection and preservation of their accursed, shameless life. Then all the whoring, adultery, and fornication rampant in the cathedrals and convents will be on your neck and on your conscience. Your heart will have the honor and glory of having fought for the greatest and most numerous whoremongers and knaves to be found on the earth and for endorsing their life of whoring and knavery. You will make yourself a partaker of all of that. Oh, that will be a great honor and a fine reason for risking your life and for serving God. For they will not reform such a life, nor can they reform it, since it is impossible that so many thousands of people should live a chaste life in the way that they try to do it.

Over and above that, you must also burden yourself with the chastity of popes and cardinals. This is a special kind of chastity, transcending the common, spiritual type. In Italian it is termed *buseron*, which is the chastity of Sodom and Gomorrah. For God was constrained to blind and to plague his enemy and adversary, the pope and the cardinals, above others, so that they did not remain worthy of sinning with wenches in a natural way, but, in accord with their merited reward, they had to dishonor their own body and person through themselves and to sink into such perversion and impenitence that they no longer considered this to be sin, but jested about it as though it were a game of cards about which they might laugh and joke with impunity. Oh, this beer is good and strong,[40] and so it is foaming and casting up all their shame and vice, as Jude says [Jude 13]. Now go and risk your life and fight for these impenitent, shameless Sodomites who even laugh and jest about such blasphemous sins.

I am not lying to you. Whoever has been in Rome knows that conditions are unfortunately worse there than anyone can say or believe. When the last Lateran council was to be concluded in Rome under Pope Leo, among other articles it was decreed that

---

[40] Luther uses a German proverb, *O dem bier ist recht gegeben*. Literally it says that the beer has been generously malted. Thiele, *Luthers Sprichwörtersammlung*, No. 64, says that this proverb is used when a know-it-all has been rebuffed or put in his place.

one must believe the soul to be immortal.[41] From this one may gather that they make eternal life an object of sheer mockery and contempt. In this way they confess that it is a common belief among them that there is no eternal life, but that they now wish to proclaim this by means of a bull. More remarkable yet, in the same bull they decided that a cardinal should not keep as many boys in the future. However, Pope Leo commanded that this be deleted; otherwise it would have been spread throughout the whole world how openly and shamelessly the pope and the cardinals in Rome practice sodomy. I do not wish to mention the pope, but since the knaves will not repent, but condemn the gospel, blaspheme and revile God's word, and excuse their vices, they, in turn, will have to take a whiff of their own terrible filth. This vice is so prevalent among them that recently a pope caused his own death by means of this sin and vice.[42] In fact, he died on the spot. All right now, you popes, cardinals, papists, spiritual lords, keep on persecuting God's word and defending your doctrine and your churches!

No pope, cardinal, bishop, doctor, priest, monk, or nun will condemn such an obviously disgraceful life; rather they laugh about it, excuse it, and gloss over it. They incite kings, princes, country, and people to defend such knaves with life and property, with land and people, and faithfully to protect them so that such vices might not be repented of and reformed, but rather strengthened, sanctioned, and approved. Now you are to hazard blood, body, and life just for the sake of saddling your neck and conscience with this. I could easily mention more examples of such abominations, but it is too shameful; I fear that our German soil would have to tremble before it. But if an impudent popish ass should come along and dispute this, he will find me ready to do him battle, and it will be quite a battle! If admonition and warning

---

[41] The Fifth Lateran Council held sessions in Rome at various intervals from 1512 to 1517 under popes Julius II (1503–1513) and Leo X (1513–1521). At the eighth session, on December 19, 1513, *Apostolici Regiminis* reaffirmed the doctrine of the immortality of the soul over against the teaching of some Averroists or neo-Aristotelians who taught that the human soul was mortal. Cf. Denzinger-Schönmetzer, *Enchiridion Symbolorum* (Barcelona, 1967), Nos. 1440–1441 (738).

[42] It is not clear to whom Luther is referring, or what basis in fact or rumor there may have been for his assertion.

will bring about repentance, these have been and still are being sufficiently administered. However, this will not help. Today it has become a commendable and common practice, almost equal to a great virtue, completely to disregard repentance. In fact, the emperor and you are to protect and preserve them in this, so that their example may be emulated and spread also to other countries, as, alas, has already too obviously happened.

Furthermore, you will have to encumber yourself with all the greed, robbery, and thievery of the entire papacy, the countless sums they have acquired falsely and fraudulently by means of indulgences.[43] Is it not sheer shameful robbery and thievery throughout all Christendom? Is not the incalculable wealth which they raked in through their false and fabricated purgatory sheer shameful robbery and thievery throughout the whole world? The incalculable wealth they have accumulated with their usurious masses and sacrificial masses, is it not sheer shameful robbery and thievery throughout the whole world? The incalculable wealth they procured through licenses to eat butter during Lent, through pilgrimages, the worship of the saints, and innumerable other deceptions, is it not sheer shameful robbery and thievery throughout the whole world? Where did the pope, cardinals, and bishops acquire kingdoms and principalities? How did they become the secular lords of all the world? Is it not entirely through their infinitely shameful robbery and thievery? What else are they than the greatest robbers and thieves on the face of the earth? And yet you find here no thought of repentance or restitution. Indeed, there is not enough good blood in their veins to enable them to administer their office a little, to give their possession of such property at least a slight semblance of honor. Instead, they condemn, revile, and persecute God's name, his word and work. And now they come and demand that you defend such thieves and robbers with your blood, so that they may not only go uncorrected but may also be encouraged to practice this kind of thing all the more. Consider what a great, mighty thief and rogue, robber and traitor you become and

---

[43] Luther's position on indulgences was spelled out early in his career. See *Ninety-five Theses* (1517), LW 31, 17–33; and *Explanation of the Ninety-five Theses* (1518), LW 31, 77–252.

are if you assist and protect such robbers and thieves with your blood and life; for you will burden yourself with all of this and share in their guilt.

Then you must also burden yourself with all the blood the pope has shed, with all the murders and all the wars he has instigated, all the misery and grief he has caused throughout the world. Who can relate all the blood, murders, and wretchedness which the pope and his followers have occasioned? Some have computed that for the pope's sake alone eleven hundred thousand men have been slain since the papacy elevated itself above the empire. Some set the figure higher.[44] How will you bear so many murders and so much blood on your conscience, since one single murder is unbearable, and since Christ condemns even anger in one's heart to hellfire, Matthew 5 [:22]? What then are you doing if you risk your life for such murderers? You share in the guilt of all of this and accord the pope your aid and approval, enabling him to do such things forever with security. For there is no sign of repentance among them; indeed, they regard this as honorable and virtuous, so that we cannot possibly hope for reform. Nor do they desire improvement. But they want you to help protect them, to enable them to murder, to shed blood, and to fill the world with misery, as they have done to date and still do without interruption, restraint, or fear. You see, these are the most holy fathers, the holy cardinals, bishops, and priests who presume to be judges over the gospel and who teach and rule the world.

I will say nothing here about the other vices, how they administer poison and engage in treason and in all that pertains to hatred and envy. Who can tell completely the shameful life in the papacy? The aforementioned items and the everyday examples demonstrate sufficiently what their life is like. For it [the papacy] is to be the Antichrist and to be against Christ in all things. Therefore it must follow that as Christ led and taught a beautiful, splendid, chaste, decent, holy, heavenly, and godly life, the Antichrist must lead and teach a correspondingly shameful, blasphe-

---

[44] Heinrich von Kettenbach, for example, in a comparison of Christ and the pope (1523), wrote: "It has been calculated that because of the pope's arrogance and wantonness over one million two hundred thousand Christians have been put to death in eight hundred years." Cf. WA 30III, 307, n. 2.

mous, unchaste, accursed, hellish, and devilish life. How else could he be Christ's foe or the Antichrist? All of this might be tolerated if they did not presume to defend it and insist with force on being in the right. But all that we have thus far mentioned is, so to speak, sport and jest. We now want to point out the true dregs and the chief abominations with all of which he must burden himself who protects the pope or who helps to preserve and strengthen him in his impenitent, hardened, anti-Christian status and conduct.

One might tolerate an evil life; but one can and must not tolerate, much less help to defend, a person who condemns doctrine and God's word and who elevates himself over God. They have disseminated so many doctrinal abominations within Christendom that these cannot be numbered. They repent of none of them, nor do they want to change them, but they openly defend them all and rigorously insist on being in the right. All of that would rest on your neck and conscience. You would make yourself a partner of all such abominations and you would be guilty if you helped to defend them. Let us mention just a few. How can your conscience bear the shameful, lying fraud of indulgences, with which they scandalously misled so many thousands of souls, yes, all of Christendom and all the world, deceiving them and defrauding them of their money and property? Yet they do not repent of this, nor do they intend to abrogate[45] this practice, although they are well aware of the great villainy they have committed thereby. They taught the people to place their trust in indulgences, and to die in that belief. This in itself is so atrocious and terrible that if they were otherwise as holy and pure as St. John the Baptist, they should properly be condemned to the depths of hell just for this; they should not be worthy that the earth bear them or the sun shine down on them, much less that we fight for them or defend them.

Think for yourself what a supreme villainy indulgences are. Whoever has comforted himself with and relied on indulgences and has died or lived thus, thereby has forfeited the Savior Jesus Christ; he has denied and forgotten him and he renounces all comfort from him. For whoever places his consolation in anything other than in Jesus Christ can have no consolation in Christ. Of course,

[45] *Ablassen*, a play on the word *Ablass* ("indulgence").

41

we all know, and their books also prove this incontrovertibly, that they taught us to place our reliance on indulgences. Otherwise who would have paid them any heed or bought them? Furthermore, like the devil's messengers and rogues they kept shamefully silent about faith in Christ, yes, even suppressed and exterminated it. For whoever knows that his comfort and his reliance are based on Christ cannot tolerate indulgences or any other object of trust. When will they make amends or restitution for such endless harm? Make amends indeed! Hardened in such malice, they even want to force you to defend them with life and blood and burden yourself with it all. If they were not entirely possessed and mad they would be at least a little ashamed to ask for such defense in view of all their unrepentant, shameless, blasphemous wickedness. That really does go to show that "priests are no good."[46]

Furthermore, how will your conscience bear the blasphemous fraud of purgatory, with which they also treacherously duped and falsely frightened all the world and appropriated almost all its property and splendor by lying and thievery?[47] For with this they also completely extinguished that one and only comfort and trust in Christ and taught Christians to place their attention and expectation and reliance in the bequests which they trust will follow them.[48] Whoever looks to and hopes in the bequests or works that follow him at death—as they taught and as they all did—must dismiss Christ from his mind and forget him. Therefore, if God had not especially preserved his own, in death they would have plunged unawares into hell's abyss, together with the Jews and heathen. It is the same as when a person falls headlong from a high mountain; he thinks that he is treading on a solid pathway and then steps aside into the air and plunges down into the valley or the sea. Oh, what murderers of souls they are! Before the day of judgment no human heart will know what great murder they have committed on souls with their purgatory. Much less can the damage and the

---

[46] Cf. above, p. 32.
[47] Purgatory was a very current concern for Luther. He had been distressed that the *Augsburg Confession* had failed to take a clear stand on this question, so in the summer of 1530 he had filled in this gap with his own *Disavowal of Purgatory (Widerruf vom Fegefeuer)*. WA 30III, 367–390.
[48] Cf. Rev. 14:13.

abominable blasphemy be estimated which they thereby have inflicted on faith and confidence in Christ. Yet there is no repentance for this or any end to it. Instead, they demand that you protect them and help defend them in it.

Furthermore, you have to load yourself down with all the abominations and blasphemies they committed, and still daily commit, throughout the entire papacy with the dear mass, with buying and selling, and with innumerable other desecrations of the holy sacrament, in which they sacrifice God's Son to him continually as though they were better and holier than God's Son. They do not let the sacrament be a gift of God, to be received through faith, but convert it into a sacrifice and a work with which they atone for themselves and for other people and acquire all sorts of grace and aid. Thus they appoint a separate mass for each saint, indeed, for each cause or need. In all their books and teachings you will not find as much as a letter alluding to faith. Everything says and sings that the mass is a sacrifice and a work. Yet nowhere else should faith be taught and practiced as firmly and diligently as in the mass or the sacrament, since Christ instituted it in remembrance of himself. It should be an occasion for proclaiming him, remembering him, and believing in him. However, instead of this, they preach their sacrifice and their work; moreover, they sell them most shamefully. There is no repentance there, but only hardened and dreadful wickedness and the attempt to defend themselves and to protect themselves with your life and limb.

The crude, outward misuse [of the sacrament] was atrocious enough in itself. This was seen in the priests' flippant treatment of the sacrament at masses for the dead, the dedication of churches, or festivals of patron saints. They dealt with it as though it were buffoonery. In a vulgar and impudent way they flocked together for the purpose of gorging and swilling and for the sake of money. Then they became intoxicated, vomited, gamed, and brawled. All the villages were full of this shameful abuse. Of this they never repented, nor has it ever been reformed, nor is it acknowledged to be sin by these incorrigible popish asses. However, this is as nothing in comparison with the fine abuse by which they perverted and transformed the sacrament from the common sacrament of the common faith into a private work and sacrifice of certain persons, namely, the priests. That is so terrible that I do not like to reflect on it; such thoughts might well kill a person. But even this abomination is surpassed in their concealment and suppression of the words of the sacrament and faith, so that, as already said, not a letter, not an iota, of it remained in the entire papacy in all the masses and books. This vice beggars description by word and thought. To eternity, no one will be able to rebuke and reprove this sufficiently. Any other vice has its own devil or band of devils to promote it; but I believe that the sacrificial mass is the common work of all the devils, in which they pool all hands, all counsel, all ideas, all wickedness and roguery and in that way have instituted and preserved this abomination. This is evident from the fact that wherever poltergeists have appeared as dead souls throughout the world, they have all asked for the mass.[49] No soul ever asked for or desired Christ; all asked for the mass. So this is a strong indication that the devils have their being nowhere else as markedly as in their servants of the mass, where they dwell shamefully with all lewdness, greed, blasphemy, and every vice. This will surely rank as God's greatest and ultimate wrath on earth prior to the day of judgment; for there can be no wrath to exceed this. There you have the true virtue of the papacy in behalf of which you are to go to war and to shed your blood for the impenitent blasphemers, soul-murderers, and malefactors.

Here someone will perhaps object that I am too free with my name calling and that I can do no more than to scold and abuse people. I should like to reply, first of all, that such scolding is nothing in comparison with the inexpressible baseness in question. For what sort of scolding is it when I call the devil a murderer, a villain, a traitor, a blasphemer, a liar? It is just as though a little breeze were striking him. But what are the popish asses other than devils incarnate who have no repentance but only hardened hearts, who knowingly defend such public blasphemy and who ask for protection in this from the emperor and you? My dear man, abuse and call a popish ass whatever you will or can—it rolls off him like

---

[49] Luther refers to such phenomena also in his treatise *The Misuse of the Mass*, LW 36, 190–198, and in *Disavowal of Purgatory*, WA 30^{II}, 385.

water off a duck's back.[50] He has overdone matters and has far, far, far outstripped your ability to abuse him adequately. Call him a papist and you have hit the mark; then you have said more than the world can comprehend. You cannot call him anything worse. Call him anything else and it is just like pricking a bear with a straw or striking a boulder with a feather.

I reply, in the second place, that the two cardinals, Campeggio and Salzburg,[51] advised and urged me to do this, in that the former said that he would rather have himself torn to pieces than to alter or abolish the mass, while the latter remarked that "priests are no good" and that they should be left unreformed.[52] These two are among the leading papists, and as they speak and believe, so the pope and all the papists surely speak and believe. Since they themselves say that they are desperate villains and want to remain villains, and that they would rather be torn to pieces than to desist from their blasphemies, I would do them an injustice before God and the world if I called them by any other name than that which they assign to themselves. If I were to address them as most reverend holy fathers in Christ, no one would recognize them, and they themselves would not know of whom I am speaking, since these names are unknown to them and since they are and remain hardened villains and blasphemers. Therefore my scolding is no scolding. It is no different from when I call a turnip a turnip; apples, apples; and pears, pears.

Furthermore, how will you endure their terrible idolatries? It was not enough that they venerated the saints and praised God in them, but they actually made them into gods. They put that noble child, the mother Mary, right into the place of Christ. They fashioned Christ into a judge and thus devised a tyrant for anguished consciences, so that all comfort and confidence was transferred from Christ to Mary, and then everyone turned from Christ to his particular saint. Can anyone deny this? Is it not true? Did we not all, alas, at one time try this and experience it? Are not books extant—especially those of the shabby Barefoot Friars and of the

---

[50] Literally, "It is as though a goose honked at him."
[51] Matthew Lang, archbishop of Salzburg. On Campeggio, cf. above, p. 20, n. 19.
[52] Cf. above, p. 32.

Preaching Friars[53]—which teem with idolatries, such as the *Marialia, Stellaria, Rosaria, Coronaria,* and they may as well be *Diabolaria* and *Satanaria.*[54] Still there is no sign of repentance or improvement, but they obstinately and impudently insist that all this must be defended, and they ask for your body and life for its protection.

Here I must call attention to an incident that occurred at the diet in Augsburg, to show what a precious reason they have for such holy idolatry. When the article regarding the invocation of the saints was being discussed in the committee, Dr. Eck cited the words found in Genesis 48 [:16], where Jacob says of Ephraim and Manasseh, "And my name shall be invoked upon those children."[55] When, after many words by Master Philip, John Brenz[56] said casually that nothing about calling on the saints could be found in Scripture, Dr. Cochlaeus,[57] to expedite matters, blurted out—profound thinker that he is—that the saints had not been invoked in the Old Testament because at the time they were not yet in heaven but in the anteroom of hell. Then my gracious lord, Duke John Frederick, duke of Saxony, etc., tightened the noose on both of them and said to Dr. Eck: "Dr. Eck, there you find the verse answered which you quoted from the Old Testament." So sure are they of themselves, so nicely do they agree with one another—these precious writers of contradictions![58] The one says that the saints were not invoked in the Old Testament, the other says that they were. They cite verses from the Old Testament, just as if we did not know that God performed all the great miracles in the Old Testament for the sake of Abraham, Isaac, and Jacob, as he

---

[53] I.e., the Franciscans and the Dominicans, respectively.

[54] *Mariale* is a medieval term for a work of Marian devotion. *Stellaria* may refer to devotions to Mary as the Star, *Coronaria* to devotions to the Crown of Mary, both being forms of the rosary (*Rosarium*).

[55] *Et invocetur nomen meum super pueros istos.*

[56] John Brenz (1499–1570) was one of the leading Lutheran theologians at the Diet of Augsburg. He was the pastor at Schwäbisch-Hall from 1522 to 1548 and later provost of the Collegiate Church at Stuttgart.

[57] John Cochlaeus (1479–1552) was, along with John Eck and John Faber, one of the authors of the Roman Catholic *Confutation* and a bitter critic of Luther whose polemical writings established the traditional Roman Catholic interpretation of the Reformer.

[58] John Faber had presented to the emperor a collection of contradictions found in Luther's writings, entitling the work *Antilogiarum, hoc est contradictionum M. Lutheri babylonica, ex eiusdem apostatae libris, per Ioh. Fabri excerpta.*

himself often declares, and that he did not perform one-half, indeed, not one-tenth, as many in the New Testament for the sake of any saint. Like fools, they spit out the first thing that comes into their mouth. Yet all this must be accounted true and be the basis of the articles of faith. All of this goes unrepented; moreover, it is defended. People are condemned and executed over it, and for this you are to war and fight, etc.

So that we may have at least one illustration in this long sermon, I shall give one—out of many thousands of such examples—which is taken from a book of devotion to Mary and which tells how the Virgin Mary must be venerated with sacrifices. There was a robber or highwayman who had not performed a single good deed in his whole life except that one day he strayed into a church by chance; it was the Candlemas of Our Lady,[59] and he noticed that people were offering pennies and candles on the altar, whereupon he did the same. Later he was arrested and hanged. Now the devils wanted to take his soul to hell, but a good angel intervened and said, "Why do you devils take him away, although you have no right to him?" They replied, "He committed many evil deeds and not a single good one." Then they all went before the judgment seat of God. Here the devils accused the robber, saying that he had performed no good work; but the good angel brought out the penny stamped with the cross[60] and the candle which he had offered on the altar. Now the Judge pronounced sentence: "The robber shall defend himself against the devils." The angel advised him to hold the penny in his left hand as a shield and the candle in his right hand as a sword or a spear, and thus fight against the devils, executing nothing but cross blows. That he did and thus repulsed the devils. His soul re-entered his body and he was taken from the gallows and lived happily ever after. That's the story.[61]

Who could think this up if it were not true? The monks and

---

[59] The feast celebrated on February 2 in commemoration of the presentation of Christ in the temple and the purification of the Virgin Mary. This feast was also the occasion for the consecration and sale of candles which were to be used throughout the year; hence the name Candlemas.

[60] The coin known as a *Creutzer* had a cross stamped on it; this is apparently the type of coin referred to here.

[61] The exact source of this legend has not been located. However, similar legends about Mary and the saints were common.

priests have scribbled so many books full of such outrageous and lying fables that they have inundated Christendom as with a flood. Never did a pope, bishop, or doctor pay this any heed or attention. But now that we preach that Christ is our Savior, they become mad and raving. However, if one preaches that a candle or coin offered to our dear Lady can save an impenitent rogue and murderer, without Christ and without faith, and can repel all the devils, and if one blasphemes and suppresses Christ's suffering and life, then all sermons are good and precious; then there are no heretics. All of this comes under the heading: "Priests never were any good."

Again: How will your conscience endure the great evil, the torment, and the violence they have done to all the world by means of their agonizing confession? They have driven so many souls to despair with this and have deprived and robbed despondent consciences of all Christian comfort; for they concealed and hushed up the power of absolution and faith treacherously and maliciously and insisted solely on the intolerable torment and impossible toil of relating one's sins and of feeling contrition for them. They promised grace and salvation in return for such contrition and recounting of sin as our own work. Thus they pointed and directed us away from Christ to ourselves. In brief, all that they do and teach is directed toward leading us away from Christ and to their own work and ours. There is no letter in their doctrine so insignificant and no work so petty that it does not deny and blaspheme Christ and defame faith in him, leading the poor heart to impossibilities and to despair. This is entirely in keeping with the true Antichrist. As implied by his name, he must live and teach in direct opposition to Christ and exalt himself over God and his word. We find this more obviously fulfilled in the papacy than we can understand. Still all of this goes unrepented. They defend this confession to the present day. Moreover, they want you to help fight for the maintenance of such torment, distress, despair, and all the plagues of this confession, and to burden yourself with the misery of all souls.

Furthermore, you have to burden yourself with the baleful misery and accursed abuse of the ban and of the office of the keys.[62]

---

[62] Cf. Luther's treatise, also written in 1530, entitled *The Keys* (*LW* 40, 321–377), as well as his comments on the ban in *Exhortation to All Clergy* (*LW* 34, 32 ff.).

This abuse in itself would be sufficient reason for us to let the papacy perish, to say nothing of fighting for it and confirming and fortifying the abuse. How furiously and madly the pope has employed this against emperors, kings, and all the world, yes, against God himself and his holy word! Whatever thoughts the devil suggested to his heart had to be accounted right and good. How many wars and how much bloodshed did he incite with this in all the world! Who can enumerate all the abominations? Whatever he wanted to see regarded as sin, that had to be sin, in name and in reality. What he wished to have accounted as holy, that had to be holy. In that way he became a terrible lord over the whole world, over body, soul, property, country, and people, over purgatory, hell, devil, heaven, angels, over God, and over all. He unlocked and locked heaven, he closed and opened hell to whomsoever he chose. He either took away or let a man retain his life, property, honor, land, empire, wife, child, house and home, money, and everything, entirely as he willed. What would the papacy amount to without the abuse of the keys?

All of this they did out of sheer caprice and without any authority, for the sake of their stomach and their dominion. And what is the worst of all, they misused God's name for this most flagrantly. For they committed all these inexpressible outrages, all this raving and raging, under the name of God, without the slightest intention of reforming matters. No, like a hard anvil, they impenitently let the blows rain down on them, meanwhile remaining adamant in their intentions. Moreover, they want to see all of this defended and strengthened with your blood and protection. It is surprising that heaven and earth do not break and tear apart in the face of such incorrigible, defiant wickedness, and that God tolerates such incessant wickedness, such defiance and unabashed resistance so long. I believe if the Turk knew himself to be in the wrong as the papists know themselves to be such incorrigible villains, he would not be so obstinate and defy God so impudently with his wickedness. For I think that the Turk would never say, "We Turks were never any good," as our papists say, "We priests were never any good." In brief, only the devil does that; he, too, knows that he is wicked and, in addition, wants to defend his wickedness. The papacy imitates his example. It recognizes its terrible wickedness, but wants to leave it unreformed; in fact, it wants you to confirm and defend it with your life and blood. If you feel any desire to fight, here you find a fine cause, for the most holy and spiritual people! But if you reflect on only the hundred-thousandth part of the wickedness of which you would make yourself a partner, your desire to engage in such a fight will surely vanish, and you will say, "Such impenitent arch-villains could endure the fire of hell's abyss before I would move a finger in their behalf, much less risk body and life for them."

Furthermore, you must burden yourself with and aid the terrible, fraudulent, shameful tomfoolery of the devil which they have promoted with relics and pilgrimages, and which they by no means intend to discontinue. O God, how it has snowed and rained in this respect. What a sheer cloudburst of lies and fraud has broken upon us! How the devil extolled dead bones, garments, and utensils as the saints' limbs and utensils! How confidently people believed all the liars! How they flocked to join pilgrimages! All of this was approved by pope, bishops, priests, and monks; or at least, they said nothing and left the people in error and took their money and goods. How much that new deception at Trier with Christ's coat alone must have netted them![63] What a great fair the devil held with this throughout the world, selling innumerable pseudo-miracles! Oh, what all might be said about this! If all foliage and grass could speak, they could not even express fully this knavery. Yet we have to witness that they do not confess and quit this villainy, but want to preserve it, confirm it, and increase it. Moreover, they want to accomplish this with your body and blood.

The very worst feature of all is that they misled the people with it and diverted them from Christ, persuading them to trust and rely on such falsehoods. For no one resorted to relics and pilgrimages without relying and depending on them. He forsook his Christ, the gospel, and faith and, in addition, despised his own vocation and thought it was worthless. The papists not only failed to fend off such seduction of souls, such denial of Christ and contempt for him and his faith, but they took delight and joy in this

---

[63] The first exhibition of the Holy Coat of Trier, alleged to be the seamless robe of Christ, took place in 1512. Cf. Luther's *Exhortation to All Clergy. LW* 34, 25, and *WA* 30II, 297, n. 2.

and embellished and strengthened it with indulgences and graces, and fattened themselves well with it, fleecing and flaying the whole world. Yet there is no sign of their repenting or reforming, but only a defiant resolution to expand and fortify all of this and to tolerate no change whatsoever. The golden year[64] is part and parcel of this, invented by those arch-liars, the popes, who have even ordered the angels to take the souls of the pilgrims to heaven.[65] But all of this is too high and too much; it beggars all description and all imagination. It is called the *abominatio in loco sancto,* "the desolating sacrilege standing in the holy place" [Matt. 24:15]. That is how Christ described the papacy with plain and yet incomprehensible words.

I truly believe that the papacy is an abomination not only by reason of such particular evils, but also because of its impenitence, because it declines reform in these matters and rather wants to see them defended. Thus the papacy not only sins in its deeds, but confirms its sin with impenitence, that is, with the sin against the Holy Spirit. This cannot be surpassed; it cannot become worse, for the devil himself can commit no higher or worse sin. You see, these are the fellows who presume to be judges of God's word. They dare to demand that we recant and repent of our doctrine and that we venerate all such abominations as God's word and work. But they insist on remaining unreformed; in brief, they will not tolerate any renewal. If that is not inciting to sedition, then what do you call inciting to sedition? If that is not provoking pestilence, famine, Turks, war, murder, and all of God's wrath and plague, what might be evil enough to provoke these? However, I must stop here with the enumeration of these abominations, though there are many more, such as the religious fraternities, the vows to the saints, and the great fair at which priests and monks sell their good works and their cowls to the whole world, vesting people with them at death

---

[64] During a jubilee year special indulgences were granted. Cf. *Exhortation to All Clergy.* LW 34, 16, n. 14.

[65] When a large number of pilgrims died in the jubilee year 1500 while making a pilgrimage to Rome, a bull was published (ostensibly by Pope Clement VI, though its authenticity is uncertain) commanding the angels to carry the souls of such pilgrims to heaven. Cf. Henry Charles Lea, *History of Auricular Confession and Indulgences in the Latin Church* (Philadelphia: Lea, 1896), III, 203, and WA 30II, 282, n. 2.

and thereby leading them to heaven.[66] If I were to continue, it might rob and bereave one of his senses. Unfortunately, one half of a single item of these is too much.

The third reason why you must refuse obedience to the emperor in such a call to arms is this: if you did otherwise you would not only burden yourself with all these abominations and help strengthen them, but you would also lend a hand in overthrowing and exterminating all the good which the dear gospel has again restored and established. For those villains are not satisfied with preserving such devilries and outrages; as the edict states, they will tolerate no changes but will eradicate and utterly destroy all that we have ever taught, lived for, and done, and still live for and do. This reason also encompasses a great deal; for our gospel has, thanks be to God, accomplished much good. Previously no one knew the real meaning of the gospel, Christ, baptism, confession, the sacrament [of the altar], faith, Spirit, flesh, good works, the Ten Commandments, the Our Father, prayer, suffering, comfort, temporal government, the state of matrimony, parents, children, masters, manservant, mistress, maidservant, devils, angels, world, life, death, sin, justice, forgiveness, God, bishop, pastor, church, a Christian, or the cross.[67] In brief, we were totally ignorant about all that it is necessary for a Christian to know. All of this was obscured and suppressed by the popish asses. They are, as you know, just that— great, coarse, ignorant asses in Christian affairs. For I too was one, and I know that I am telling the truth on this matter. All devout hearts will bear witness to this; for they would gladly have been instructed about even one of these items, but they were held captive by the pope as I was and could gain neither the opportunity nor the permission to be instructed. We did not know otherwise than that priests and monks alone were everything, and that we relied on their works and not on Christ.

But now—praise be to God—it has come to pass that man and woman, young and old, know the catechism; they know how to believe, to live, to pray, to suffer, and to die. Consciences are well

---

[66] Luther is referring to the practice of burying a layman in a monk's cowl, thereby supposedly assuring his salvation. Cf. *Exhortation to All Clergy.* LW 34, 21.

[67] Cf. the parallel list in Luther's *Exhortation to All Clergy.* LW 34, 53.

instructed about how to be Christians and how to recognize Christ. We preach the truth about faith and good works. In brief, the aforementioned items have again come to light, and pulpit, altar, and baptismal font have been restored to their proper place, so that—thank God—the form of a Christian church can again be recognized. But you will have to assist in the extermination and destruction of all of this if you fight for the papists. For they will not tolerate that any of these doctrines should be taught and established by us, but, as they say, they want to restore the *status quo ante,* the old state of things, and not permit a single change. You will have to help burn all the German books, New Testaments, psalters, prayer books, hymnals, and all the good things we wrote, and which they themselves admit to be good. You will have to help keep everyone ignorant about the Ten Commandments, the Lord's Prayer, and the Creed; for this is the way it used to be. You will have to help keep everyone from learning anything about baptism, the sacrament, faith, government, matrimony, or the gospel. You will have to help keep everyone from knowing Christian liberty. You will have to help keep people from placing their trust in Christ and deriving their comfort from him. For all of that was non-existent before; all of it is something new.

Furthermore, you will have to help to condemn and disgrace the children of our pastors and preachers, poor forsaken orphans, as the children of whores. You will have to help people to rely again on the works of monks and priests instead of on Christ, and on buying their merits and their cowls for the hour of death. You will have to help them fill Christendom again with whoring, adultery, and other unnatural, shameful vices, instead of getting married. You will have to help restore the atrocious carnival of the sacrificial mass. You will have to help in the defense of all their avarice, robbery, and thievery, by means of which they acquire their riches. But why should I enlarge on this? You will have to help in the destruction of Christ's word and his whole kingdom and in the rebuilding of the kingdom of the devil. For that is the aim of the scoundrels who are bent on restoring the *status quo ante,* the old state of things. They are of the Antichrist, or Counter-Christ; therefore they can only do what is against Christ, especially in the cardinal doctrine according to which our heart is to look to Christ alone for consolation and assurance and not to look to our own works; that is, we are to be delivered from sin and to be justified by faith alone, as is written in Romans 10 [:10], "For man believes with his heart and so is justified."

This doctrine, I say, they will not tolerate under any circumstances. We are able to forego it just as little; for if this doctrine vanishes, the church vanishes. Then no error can any longer be resisted, because the Holy Spirit will not and cannot dwell with us apart from this doctrine. For he is to glorify Christ to us [John 16:14]. The world has often gone to wrack and ruin over this doctrine by deluge, tempest, flood, war, and other plagues. On account of this doctrine Abel and all the saints were slain; on account of this, too, all Christians must die. Yet it has remained, and it must remain, and the world must continue to perish on account of it. Thus the world must also submit to it now and be overthrown on account of it. No matter how the world rages and rants, it must let this doctrine stand, and it must fall into the depths of hell on account of it! Amen. So reflect on this and examine yourself closely. If you fight against God and his word and against all that is of God, if you burden yourself with all the abominations of the papacy, with all the innocent blood that has been shed, beginning with Abel's, if you help to exterminate all the benefits which we have gained from the gospel and ultimately help to destroy Christ's kingdom and rebuild the devil's—just think what sort of victory you will gain and with what kind of conscience you will obey the emperor's summons!

If you are open to advice, this warning against obeying the emperor and your prince in such circumstances will suffice. As the apostles say, "We must obey God rather than men" [Acts 5:29]. If you accept this advice, good; if not, never mind—go ahead and fight confidently. Christ will not be afraid of you and will also (God willing) stand his ground against you. But if he does, you will have quite a battle on your hands. In the meantime we shall be watching to see who will overwhelm the other with his defiance and hold the field.

These things I wanted to say to my dear Germans by way of

warning. And as I did above,[68] I testify here again that I do not wish to incite or spur anyone to war or rebellion or even self-defense, but solely to peace. But if the papists—our devil—refuse to keep the peace and, impenitently raging against the Holy Spirit with their persistent abominations, insist on war, and thereby get their heads bloodied or even perish, I want to witness publicly here that this was not my doing, nor did I give any cause for it. It is they who want to have it that way. May their blood be on their heads! I am exonerated; I have done my duty faithfully. Henceforth I shall let Him judge who will, must, and also is able to do so. He will not tarry, nor will he fail. To him be praise and honor, thanks and glory in eternity! Amen.

---

[68] Cf. above, pp. 13-14, 18, 34.

AGAINST THE SABBATARIANS: LETTER TO A GOOD FRIEND

1538

Translated by Martin H. Bertram

INTRODUCTION

The present treatise, which takes the form of an open letter, was occasioned by Luther's receipt of a communication from his friend Graf Wolfgang Schlick zu Falkenau, reporting on Sabbatarian tendencies among the Christians of Bohemia and Moravia. We owe the identification of Count Schlick as Luther's correspondent to John Mathesius, who in his *Doctor Martin Luthers Leben,* a volume of biographical sermons first published in Nürnberg in 1566, speaks of the treatise as "addressed to Count Wolf Schlick zu Falkenau under the name of a 'Good Friend,' as I have ascertained from three fine letters to the gentleman in the Doctor's handwriting."[1] Count Schlick was a member of a prominent Moravian family sympathetic to the Reformation.

The term "Sabbatarians" has been used to refer to a number of movements, occurring in various epochs of church history, which have as their common denominator an insistence on a return by Christians to the essentials of Jewish Sabbath observance. Usually they are also characterized by an intense eschatological expectation, together with an inclination toward literalism in the interpretation of both the Old and the New Testaments. Concerning the specific movement to which Luther refers, however, relatively little is known, since no primary documents have come down to us. We do know that they were condemned by all the other parties of the sixteenth century—Romans, Lutherans, Zwinglians, and Calvinists, and even by many Anabaptists.

The two names definitely attached to the movement are those of Oswald Glait and Andreas Fischer, both of whom had written treatises sometime between 1528 and 1532 espousing the Sabbatarian position.[2] A reply to Glait's book was published by Caspar Schwenckfeld in early 1532 under the title *On the Christian Sabbath and the Difference Between the Old and New Testaments* (*Vom Christlichen Sabbath und Unterschied des Alten Testaments*

---

[1] Jubilee Editon (St. Louis: Concordia Verlag, 1883), pp. 62–63.
[2] See the articles on "Glait, Oswald" and "Sabbatarian Anabaptists" in *The Mennonite Encyclopedia* (Scottdale, Pa.: Mennonite Publishing House, 1955 ff.).

und Neuen Testaments). The true Sabbath, Schwenckfeld argues, is spiritual; moreover, anyone who undertakes to observe the Sabbath literally thereby obligates himself to obey the whole of Jewish law (a point also to be stressed by Luther).

In view of Luther's emphasis on Christian freedom, based on a clear distinction between law and gospel, it was predictable that he would vigorously oppose the Sabbatarian position. What gives special point to Luther's treatise is his assumption that Jewish agitation and efforts at proselytization lay at the root of the movement. In his first explicit reference to Sabbatarianism (a remark recorded at table in the fall of 1532), he speaks only in general terms of "the new error concerning the Sabbath"; there is no mention of direct Jewish influence.[3] In a similar vein are the remarks in his *Lectures on Genesis*, begun in 1535: "In our time there arose in Moravia a foolish kind of people, the Sabbatarians, who maintain that the Sabbath must be observed after the fashion of the Jews. Perhaps they will insist on circumcision too, for a like reason."[4] A few sentences later, he uses the phrase "the Jews and their apes, the Sabbatarians." Such phraseology, as well as the passage as a whole, suggests that the initiative may have come from Christians, moved perhaps simply by Old Testament literalism.

On the other hand, it is known that fraternal relations did exist between members of the Jewish community and various leaders of Christian reform movements, as indeed they had once existed between Luther and the Jews.[5] Direct proselytizing activities by Jews were uncommon, but not unknown. Former Jews who had been converted to Christianity—perhaps under unsavory conditions such as the pressures of the Inquisition—offered a prime target for re-conversion; and such efforts became more feasible when the monolithic power of the medieval church was broken by the Reformation.

The question of the precise origins and nature of the Sabba-

---

[3] *LW* 54, 51–52 (No. 356).
[4] *LW* 2, 361.
[5] Cf. Luther's comment below, p. 191. On the whole question of the relation between Judaism and the Reformation, see Louis Israel Newman, *Jewish Influence on Christian Reform Movements* (New York: Columbia University Press, 1925), especially pp. 435–630.

tarian movement can hardly be solved at this historical distance. What is important for our present purposes is that at the time of writing the treatise, Luther himself was convinced that the Jews were responsible for the movement. He devotes the greater part of the treatise, therefore, to direct attacks upon the Jews rather than upon the Sabbatarians as such.

Evidence of the chill that had come over Luther's attitude toward the Jews and of the role he was now attributing to them is provided by an entry in the *Table Talk* dated "Between May 27 and June 18, 1537," where we read: "A letter was delivered to Dr. Martin from a certain Jew who requested and pleaded (as he had often written to the doctor before) that permission be obtained from the elector to grant him safe entrance into and passage through the elector's principality. Dr. Martin responded, 'Why should these rascals, who injure people in body and property and who withdraw many Christians to their superstitions, be given permission? In Moravia they have circumcised many Christians and call them by the new name of Sabbatarians. . . . I'll write this Jew not to return.' "[6]

Luther's correspondent was no ordinary man. He was Rabbi Josel of Rosheim (*ca.* 1478-1554), one of the most prominent Jewish leaders of the age and a frequent spokesman for his people before the highest secular and ecclesiastical authorities. Contrary to the impression of the recorder of Luther's remark, it appears that not only Rabbi Josel's safety and freedom but that of Jewry as a whole in Saxony was in question. Edicts had recently been issued by Elector John Frederick forbidding Jews to reside in his territory or even to travel through it.[7] Luther's reply to Josel's

---

[6] LW 54, 239 (No. 3597).

[7] On the general situation of the Jews in Germany at the time of the Reformation, as well as the specific measures mentioned, see Wilhelm Maurer, "Die Zeit der Reformation," in Karl Heinrich Rengstorf and Siegfried von Kortzfleish (eds.), *Kirche und Synagoge, Handbuch zur Geschichte von Christen und Juden: Darstellung mit Quellen*, I (Stuttgart, 1968), pp. 363–375, especially p. 370. On the role of Josel of Rosheim, see Ludwig Feilchenfeld, *Rabbi Josel von Rosheim, Ein Beitrag zur Geschichte der Juden in Deutschland im Reformationszeitalter* (Strassburg, 1898), or Selma Stern, *Josel of Rosheim: Commander of Jewry in the Holy Roman Empire of the German Nation*, trans. by Gertrude Hirschler (Philadelphia: Jewish Publication Society, 1965).

request for him to intercede with the authorities, however, is negative:

My dear Josel:

I would have gladly interceded for you, both orally and in writing, before my gracious lord [the elector], just as my writings have greatly served the whole of Jewry. But because your people so shamefully misuse this service of mine and undertake things that we Christians simply shall not bear from you, they themselves have robbed me of all the influence I might otherwise have been able to exercise before princes and lords on your behalf.

For my opinion was, and still is, that one should treat the Jews in a kindly manner, that God may perhaps look graciously upon them and bring them to their Messiah—but not so that through my good will and influence they might be strengthened in their error and become still more bothersome.

I propose to write a pamphlet about this if God gives me space and time, to see if I cannot win some from your venerable tribe of the patriarchs and prophets and bring them to your promised Messiah. . . .[8]

Opinions of modern scholars differ as to whether *Against the Sabbatarians* is or is not the pamphlet promised by Luther in the last sentence quoted. Arguing for it is the fact that this treatise does deal with the general subject of the Jews and that its composition followed Luther's letter to Josel by only a few months. Arguing against it is the fact that the treatise does not seem to be directed at the apologetic and missionizing purposes indicated by Luther in the letter. Rather he expresses great pessimism concerning the prospects of converting the Jews. He is writing, he explains, chiefly to strengthen Christians to resist the Jews and to refute their arguments. There is no other writing by Luther, however, which more closely corresponds to the intention expressed in his letter to Josel.

The treatise came from the press of Nickel Schirlentz in Wittenberg in early March, 1538. To secure an international reader-

---

[8] Translated by the present editor from the letter as printed in *WA*, Br 8, 89 ff. (No. 3157).

ship, Luther's friend Justus Jonas translated it into Latin; this version was published in 1539. The following translation is based on the text, *Ein Brieff D. Mart. Luther Wider die Sabbather An einen guten Freund,* as found in *WA* 50, 312-337. The treatise appeared in a modern German version in the second Munich edition of Luther's works: H. H. Borchert and Georg Merz (eds.), *Martin Luther: Ausgewählte Werke,* Vol. III of the *Ergänzungsreihe* (Munich, 1936), pp. 29-60.

For a further discussion of Luther's attitudes toward the Jews, see below, pp. 123-126.

AGAINST THE SABBATARIANS: LETTER TO A GOOD FRIEND

Grace and peace in Christ! I received your letter and the oral request of your messenger. However, I was kept from answering as promptly as I should have liked, and as I promised to do, by many unavoidable obstacles. Please excuse me for this.

You informed me that the Jews are making inroads at various places throughout the country with their venom and their doctrine, and that they have already induced some Christians to let themselves be circumcised and to believe that the Messiah or Christ has not yet appeared, that the law of the Jews must prevail forever, that it must also be adopted by all the Gentiles, etc. Then you inquired of me how these allegations are to be refuted with Holy Scripture. For the time being and until I am at greater leisure, I will convey my advice and opinion briefly in this matter.[1]

[Part One]

In the first place, the Jewish people have become very stubborn because of their rabbis.[2] As a result they are difficult to win over.

---

[1] As indicated above in the Introduction, the present treatise in the form of an open letter was occasioned by Luther's receipt of a report from his friend Count Wolfgang Schlick zu Falkenau of Judaizing tendencies among the Christians in Moravia. Luther's aim is to provide the count and other interested readers with biblical, theological, and historical arguments against the Sabbatarian position. The further treatment of the question promised by Luther in the second paragraph found expression in three treatises published in rapid succession in the year 1543. *On the Jews and Their Lies* is published for the first time in English translation in the present volume. *On the Ineffable Name and on the Lineage of Christ (Vom Schem Hamphoras und vom Geschlecht Christi)* is not available in translation; for the original, see WA 53, 579–648. *The Last Words of David (Von den letzten Worten Davids)* appeared in English translation in Henry Cole (ed.), *Select Works of Martin Luther*, Vol. II (London, 1826), pp. 175–335.

The designation "Part One" for what follows is not in Luther's text but is implied by the "Part Two," below, p. 79.

[2] As the argument of this and the subsequent treatises makes clear, by "their rabbis" Luther means not only contemporary teachers but also the whole tradition of rabbinic theology and exegesis.

Even when one persuades them out of Scripture, they retreat from the Scripture to their rabbis and declare that they must believe them, just as you Christians (they say) believe your pope and your decretals. That is the answer they gave me at one time when I disputed with them and adduced Scripture against them. Therefore, to fortify the Christians, you must enlist the old argument which Lyra[3] and many other have employed and which the Jews have not been able to refute down to the present day, even though they have shamefully perverted many Scripture passages while trying to do so, in contradiction of their own most venerable teachers. However, time and space are lacking for a discussion of that now.

This is the argument: The Jews have been living away from Jerusalem, in exile, for fifteen hundred years, bereft of temple, divine service, priesthood, and kingdom. Thus their law has been lying in the ashes with Jerusalem and the entire Jewish kingdom all this time. They cannot deny this, for it is proven clearly and emphatically by their wretched situation and experiences and by the place itself, which is even today called Jerusalem and which lies desolate and devoid of Jewry before the eyes of all the world. However, they cannot observe Moses' law anywhere but in Jerusalem—this they themselves know and are forced to admit. Outside of Jerusalem they cannot have or hope to have their priesthood, kingdom, temple, sacrifices, and whatever Moses instituted for them by divine command. That is one point, and it is absolutely certain.

Now you must ask them the nature and name of the sin that caused God to punish them so cruelly, obliging them to live in exile so long, without priestly and princely, that is, Mosaic, office and government, without the sacrifices and the other regulations of the law, and particularly without Jerusalem. For God's promise —of which they also boast—is that the law will endure forever,

---

[3] Nicholas of Lyra (ca. 1270–1349), an eminent biblical scholar and commentator whose influence can be discerned in much of Luther's exegesis, and who in turn had been deeply influenced by the Jewish biblical exegete Rashi (Rabbi Solomon ben Isaac, 1040–1105). Lyra's commentary, the *Postillae perpetuae, sive brevia commentaria in universa Biblia,* was the first such work to be printed (5 vols.; Rome, 1471–1472) and had a wide circulation. For an extended discussion of Lyra, see Herman Hailperin, *Rashi and the Christian Scholars* (Pittsburgh: University of Pittsburgh Press, 1963), pp. 135–246.

that Jerusalem shall be God's own residence, and that both the princes of the house of David and the priests of the tribe of Levi will forever remain before God. The prophets and the Scriptures are filled with such promises, as they know and (as said) of which they boast. Yet these glorious, great, and numerous promises have failed of fulfillment all these fifteen hundred years. Of this they are woefully aware.

Since it is nonsense to accuse God of not keeping his promise and of having lied for fifteen hundred years, you must ask what is wrong, for God cannot lie or deceive. They will and must reply that this is due to their sins. As soon as these are atoned for, then God will keep his promise and send the Messiah. Here again you must be persistent and ask them to name these sins. For such a terrible, long, and gruesome punishment indicates that they must have committed gruesome and terrible sins previously unheard of on earth. For God never tormented even the heathen for that long a time, but destroyed them quickly. Why, then, should God torture his own people so long and in such a way that they foresee and can foresee no end of it?[4]

Of course, it is meaningless if they declare that this is because of their sin and yet they cannot name this sin. They might as well say that they had committed no sin—since they are not aware of any sin that they can name—and therefore that they were being punished unjustly by God. Therefore you must press them hard to name the sin. If they do not do it, you have made the point that they are employing lies and are no longer to be believed.

If they do name the sin, well and good, note it carefully. For this argument hurts them; and even if I were a Jew and had been born from the body of Abraham and taught most diligently by

---

[4] In this and the two preceding paragraphs, Luther lays out the essentials of the argument which will occupy him throughout Part One of the treatise. Its structure seems to be as follows: (a) The Jews are experiencing and for fifteen hundred years have been experiencing unprecedented suffering and exile. (b) This suffering far exceeds what could plausibly be attributed to divine wrath over a particular sin or sins, especially in view of God's forgiving nature and the firmness of his promises. Therefore (c) the Jews' suffering must be due to their rejection of the Messiah, whose coming God would not delay on account of even the most heinous sin. Luther supports the first point by appeal to history and contemporary observation; the second and third points he bases on logic and scriptural testimony.

Moses, I surely would not know how to answer this question. I should have to forsake Mosaic Jewry and become what I became.

Some of their rabbis, to comfort and to blind their poor people, answer this question by saying that this sin was their fathers' worship of the calf in the wilderness, and that they now have to atone for it until, etc.[5] Isn't that terrible blindness? And what sense does it make to those who read Scripture? If that sin were really so great, why then did God subsequently confer so many blessings on the people of Israel? Why did he ever and again perform so many miracles through prophets and kings, also through peasants and women, as the books of Moses, Joshua, Judges, Kings, etc., testify? He would not have done any of this if he had not graciously forgiven all sin, except for this one, which was duly punished at the time. Why did he not forsake his people then because of this sin as he forsakes them now, instead of taking them, despite this sin, into the Promised Land, lavishing all good things on them, and elevating and honoring them above all the Gentiles? If God is withholding his Messiah now because of this sin (which was atoned for at the time) he might also have said then, "I will not lead you into the land nor honor you so highly as I promised; for you committed this sin which I will never forgive or forget."

But if no sin prevented God at that time from keeping his promise made to Abraham—as he never has forsaken his promise because of men's sin—why should he now delay so long with his Messiah by reason of this sin, in view of his glorious promise made to him that the throne of David and the sacrifices of the priests would not end before the Messiah came? Many other sins were committed at that time under Moses—the sins with Baal Peor,[6] the

---

[5] Although Luther appears to have had some direct acquaintance with rabbinic literature, he was largely dependent for points such as this upon the contra-rabbinic treatises produced in the late medieval period. Nicholas of Lyra, for example, in addition to his great commentary (see n. 3, above), wrote a work entitled *Pulcherrimae quaestiones Iudaicam perfidam in catholicam fide improbantes (Excellent Issues Proving the Jewish Perfidy Against the Catholic Faith)*. Paul of Burgos (*ca.* 1350–1435), a converted Spanish Jew who rose to the rank of archbishop, wrote an apologetic treatise entitled *Scrutinium Scripturarum (Scrutiny of the Scriptures)*, as well as an extensive gloss on Lyra's commentary which is known as the *Additiones*. The argument attributing the Jews' misfortunes to the worship of the golden calf is explicitly mentioned by Burgos in his *Scrutinium*, Part II, Dist. 6, Ch. 2. For other literature on Jewish faith and practice known to Luther, see below, p. 130.
[6] Cf. Num. 25:1–5.

sin of tempting God so often, etc., for which, as Moses' books attest, they were severely punished. Why do they not also mention those sins here? Dear friend, to such Jews you must say that this is foolishness, as they know, or ought to know.

Furthermore, at that time the Messiah had not yet been promised to David. For this reason their sinning with the calf cannot come into consideration here. Therefore let them name some other sin because of which they are suffering such misery and exile. If they should mention one or several, I ask you most kindly to inform me at once of this in writing. Then I, old fool and miserable Christian that I am, will immediately have a stone knife made and become a Jew. And I will not only circumcise that one member but also my nose and my ears. However, I am convinced that they can name none.

The Scriptures record that the Jews committed many more and graver sins before the Babylonian captivity than they can point to in connection with this Roman captivity. Yet the Babylonian captivity did not last more than seventy years, and at that time they were also very much comforted with the presence of prophets, princes, and the promise, as I shall show later.[7] We find none of these in the Roman captivity; and yet we behold this terrible punishment. Whoever is able, let him say: Dear Jew, tell me, which sin is it, what is this sin, that prompts God to be angry with you so long and to withhold his Messiah?

In the second place, even if the Jews could name the sin—and it is quite indifferent whether they call it A or B (though they are able to do neither)—that still would not help them. They would still be caught in their lie. For in Jeremiah 31 [:31-34] we find recorded: "Behold, the days are coming, says the Lord, when I will make a new covenant with the house of Israel and the house of Judah, not like the covenant which I made with their fathers when I took them by the hand to bring them out of the land of Egypt, my covenant which they broke, though I was their husband, says the Lord. But this is the covenant which I will make with the house of Israel after those days, says the Lord: I will put my law within them, and I will write it upon their hearts; and I will be

---

[7] Cf. below, pp. 76-77.

their God, and they shall be my people. And no longer shall each man teach his neighbor and each his brother, saying, 'Know the Lord,' for they shall all know me, from the least of them to the greatest, says the Lord; for I will forgive their iniquity, and I will remember their sin no more."

This beautiful passage embraces many points, but since the Jews always flit and flutter from one subject to another when they feel themselves trapped, you must avoid all the others at this time and tenaciously stick to the issue for which this passage is now cited—namely, because the Jews claim that the promised Messiah's advent is being delayed as a result of their sin. Quite to the contrary, God here declares that he will make a new covenant or law, unlike Moses' covenant or law, and that he will not be prevented from doing this by the fact that they have sinned. Indeed, precisely because they failed to keep the first covenant, he wants to establish another, a new covenant, which they can keep. Their sin or their breaking of the previous covenant will not deter him. He will graciously forgive their sin and remember it no more.

You must base your argument on this passage and hold it before the Jews' eyes. For how do these things agree? How do they accord? The Jews say that the Messiah's advent is being impeded because they have not kept God's covenant but have sinned against it. God says, "No, I will not regard such sin. The fact that they did not keep my covenant will not hinder me. I am prompted to issue a new covenant all the more because they did not keep the old one, in order that such sin might be eternally forgiven and forgotten through the new covenant." Now it is time to pose the question: Who is lying here? God or the Jew? For they contradict one another. The Jew says "Yes," and God says "No." However, the question is quite superfluous, for it is proven that the Jews are lying and that their excuse that the Messiah is delayed because of their sin is worthless. God remains truthful when he declares that he is not stayed by any sin, but that he has held to his promise and the Messiah's coming, and that he still does so, regardless of their sin and their violation of his covenant.

Here you might well refer the Jews to the ninth chapter of Deuteronomy (the fifth book of Moses), where Moses tells them in a powerful sermon and in many words that they are not entering the land of Canaan because of their righteousness, since they are a stiff-necked, base, and disobedient people, who always have provoked God to anger. "You have been rebellious against the Lord," he says, "from the day that I knew you" [Deut. 9:24]. No, they were entering the land because God wished to punish the heathen who dwelt therein and because of his promise sworn to Abraham, Isaac, and Jacob, as anyone will discover in the same chapter who will read and note it.

Note that here Moses himself testifies that the Jews were not brought into the land of Canaan on account of their righteousness or their penitence, but by virtue of God's promise which he had sworn to the patriarchs. God was not prevented from keeping such an oath even though the Jews with their sins deserved complete destruction, if he had not recalled his oath and promise. In his prayer found in the same chapter, Moses also indicates that he allayed God's anger by the sole word that God should remember Abraham, Isaac, and Jacob, who, though long dead, were still remembered for the sake of the promise, who lived before God and who were able to do all things, etc. [Deut. 9:26-29].

If God at that time was not restrained by the people's terrible sin from keeping his promise and from bringing them into the land, although their sin was clearly and distinctly named and known, as everyone can read in the Scriptures, why should he now, because of the people's sin—which they themselves do not know, which they cannot name or recognize, which is not mentioned anywhere in Scripture, and which no one can think of—delay such glorious, mighty promises about the Messiah so long beyond the time, or not keep them at all, and thus become a liar, because of the Jews' unknown sin?

Why should it happen to good King David that the promise sworn to him by God should not be kept, either in the past or the future, because of the Jews' sin? Even his own sins which he committed and which are very clearly named in Scripture can be read of there, such as his adultery, the murder of his pious servant Uriah, his blasphemy, etc.—even these did not obstruct God's promises, which David repeats and exults in on his deathbed as part of his last words and testament.[8] He says that God made a firm and certain covenant with his house, as we can read in II Samuel 23 [:5], and he prophesies at the same time that the ungodly, unbelieving Jews will be rooted out and consumed [vv. 6-7].

Moreover, what about the arch-patriarch Abraham? Should God's promises, given him so richly long before any Jew or Israel existed—much less had sinned—not have been kept for him because of the sins of his descendants, since he, being holier than David, did not sin after he was called from Chaldaea? The same may be said about Isaac and Jacob, to whom God also gave and confirmed such a promise. Because of this, he also calls himself the God of Abraham, Isaac, and Jacob throughout the Scriptures. Manifestly, he could not cease being their God or become a liar because of their disobedient children and descendants, as Moses calls them. No, the Jews make themselves liars and blasphemers with such inane excuses.

Finally, we read at the end of the first commandment[9] that God will be angry with the disobedient children of Israel, to whom this commandment is given, to the third and fourth generation. At present the Jews have been under God's wrath for fifteen hundred years, with no end in sight. This covers far more than three or four generations. No heathen were ever afflicted as long as this, and they never had a promise from God. How could he then so shamefully forget the promises given to Abraham, Isaac, Jacob, David, and all the prophets and delay so long and, moreover, fail to indicate when this misery is to end? For Scripture insists that God will be and remain the God of Abraham, Isaac, and Jacob and of their seed, and that he will not let David's throne topple or cease. Yet we know that this has been toppled and has ceased to exist for fifteen hundred years, as they themselves must feel and grasp even if they could not see or hear it.[10]

---

[8] II Sam. 23:1–7. Subsequently Luther was to write an extended study of this passage (*The Last Words of David;* see n. 1, above).

[9] Exod. 20:5; Deut. 5:9 (counted in other traditions as the second commandment).

[10] The implication here is that since the advent of the Messiah, these promises find their fulfillment in Christ's kingship and in the church as the New Israel, rather than in the Jewish people as such. This is a fundamental tenet

Since it is clear and obvious that the Jews are unable to name a sin because of which God should delay so long with his promise and thus be a liar in this matter, and that even if they could mention one or more, God's word still stamps them as liars, since he assures them that he will never fail because of their sins in his promise to send the Messiah and to preserve the throne of David forever—it follows incontestably that one of the following two things must be true: either the Messiah must have come fifteen hundred years ago, or God must have lied (may God forgive me for speaking so irreverently!) and has not kept his promise. I repeat, either the Messiah must have come fifteen hundred years ago when the throne of David, the kingdom of Judah, the priesthood of Israel, the temple, and Jerusalem were still intact, when the law of Moses and the worship he instituted still endured, and the people were still living under their government in Jerusalem, before all of this had collapsed and been destroyed so miserably; or if not, God has lied. Those Jews who are still in possession of their reason cannot deny this. The hardened ones may wriggle and writhe, bend and twist with whatever artifices they may or can find, but their expedients and subterfuges are nothing over against such obvious truth.[11]

The Messiah has come and God's promise has been kept and fulfilled. They, however, did not accept or believe this, but constantly gave God the lie with their own unbelief, etc. Is it any wonder that God's wrath destroyed them together with Jerusalem, temple, law, kingdom, priesthood, and reduced these to ashes, that he scattered them among all the Gentiles, and that he does not

---

in Luther's view of the relationship of Christianity and Judaism and of course had long been part of the common Christian tradition, traceable to the New Testament itself.

[11] Luther was to elaborate this argument concerning the timing of the Messiah's coming in his treatise *On the Jews and Their Lies.* The key text was Gen. 49:10, to which he had already alluded in his treatise of 1523, *That Jesus Christ Was Born a Jew* (see LW 45, 213–216): "The scepter shall not depart from Judah,/nor the ruler's staff from between his feet,/until he comes to whom it belongs" (in Luther's text: "until Shiloh comes"). The end of the political kingdom of the Jews and the beginning of the spiritual or messianic kingdom had to coincide; according to Luther and other earlier Christian apologists, this in fact happened in the first century. The coming of the Messiah coincided with the destruction of Jerusalem and the final loss of Jewish independence.

cease to afflict them as long as they give the lie to the divine promise and fulfillment and blaspheme them by their unbelief and disobedience? For they should have accepted the new covenant (as promised by Jeremiah) from the Messiah and received him. He was commissioned to teach them properly concerning the throne of David, the priesthood, the law of Moses, the temple, and all things. As Moses writes in Deuteronomy 18 [:15]: "The Lord your God will raise up for you a prophet like me from among you, from your brethren—him you shall heed." For God says that he will put his words in the prophet's mouth and speak with them.

They may object here that God has indeed often withheld his help because of sin; as when he let them be afflicted so long in Egypt, and later when he prolonged the forty days in the wilderness into forty years in view of their sin, and finally also when he let them live in exile and prison in Babylon for seventy years, etc. Well, if that is the point they want to make, then they are on the right track, and you must accept such an argument to catch them again in a patent lie and empty subterfuge. Just say: God does of course punish the sinner, and he also tests his dear saints with misfortune. However, he does not let his promise become a lie or go unfulfilled, for he is Truth itself by his very nature, so that he cannot lie. His afflicting and testing of the children of Israel in Egypt was not an indication that he had renounced his promise. Quite the contrary, before the children of Israel were created or born, also before Abraham had a child, God provided so solicitously for them that he proclaimed and promised to Abraham (in the sixteenth chapter of Genesis [15:13-14]) that his seed, not yet existent, should dwell in exile for four hundred years, and that he would then lead them forth in prosperity. This promise he truly kept and he led them from the Egyptian exile after four hundred years, although there were sins aplenty. For they opposed Moses vigorously, as they themselves boast in Exodus [14:12]: "Is not this what we said to you in Egypt, 'Let us alone and let us serve the Egyptians'?"

But the Jews do not have now, nor did they ever have, such a promise regarding their present exile. Furthermore, at that time God gave to the children of Israel the patriarchs, who were great prophets, and he sent Joseph in advance of them to prepare a home for them, so that they should be properly received prior to the exile. Thus God was with them at all times and upheld his prophecy and promise, so that they were certain that they would be led out of Egypt. Joseph, too, said this on his deathbed, and for this reason commanded that his bones be taken along from Egypt.

But now in their last, Roman exile, [12] there is none of this. There is no prophet, and they have no word from Scripture telling them how long this exile will endure. They must be so pitifully afflicted for an indefinite time, wandering aimlessly about without prophets or God's word. God never did this before, and he would not do it now if his Messiah had not come and his promise had not been fulfilled. For he promised that David's throne would not fail or the priestly sacrifices be discontinued; and yet both David's throne and Moses' altar, together with Jerusalem itself, have been destroyed and have lain desolate for fifteen hundred years. Meanwhile God keeps silent, as he never did in Egypt or in the other exile. Nor will he or can he do so, lest he be untrue to his promise.

Likewise in the wilderness where they were afflicted for forty years, he did not forget his promise given to Abraham that his descendants should come into the land of Canaan and occupy it as an inheritance. Just as he had said, he brought them into the land. However, he had not defined the time or the number of days in which he would do this. If they had not sinned, they would have entered the land very promptly. But when they sinned, he promised them in his anger that they should not enter the land before forty years had passed, corresponding to the forty days which the spies had spent in spying out the land. Thus their murmuring protracted the forty days into forty years, as the text tells us [Num. 14:34]. Still God kept his promise, and despite his anger at that time they did enter the land after forty years.

Moreover, God did not desert them in the meantime, but gave evidence of his presence among them through many miraculous deeds. He had pillars of cloud and fire serve them day and night. He fed them daily with bread from heaven, he gave them water

---

[12] The condition of Jewry after the first century was characteristically called "exile"—*captivitas*—by writers of Luther's time.

from a rock, and supplied them with meat and birds. He did not permit their garments or their shoes to wear out. He constructed a tabernacle; he regulated the tribes of Israel; he was with Moses, Aaron, and other prophets. He punished Korah, Dathan, and Abiram. And he conferred many other similar favors on them, from all of which they could conclude that God was with them, that he was not abandoning them because of their sins, but was keeping his promise faithfully above and in spite of all their manifold wickedness. Their sins and their malice are referred to frequently in this passage;[13] they were by no means unknown.

But now in this last exile there is none of all of this. No sin is named to which they might point. There is no prophet; there is no time limit defined; there is no sign, no miracle, no manifest blessing which might let them sense God's grace. Nor is a definite place and location specified for their exile, as Egypt and the wilderness has been specified; but they are forever without established home and are cast about from place to place. Today they build their nests at one spot, tomorrow they are driven off and their nests destroyed. There is no prophet to tell them: Flee to this place or to that! No, even the place of their exile must remain uncertain to them, and they flutter wherever the wind carries them. All of this is without precedent. Egypt, the wilderness, and Babylon were definite places in which they suffered their exile. There they always had God's word and the prophets with them, and God's clear revelation. But here they are utterly forsaken, and it has been so long that David's throne has lain desolate and Moses' law neglected in the temple in Jerusalem, for which it was ordained.

Similarly, when they were driven into the Babylonian captivity, God did not forget his promise nor did he desert his people, but he fixed a definite time (namely, seventy years) and a definite place (namely, Babylon) and assured them that they would return to Jerusalem after those twenty years and that their kingdom and priesthood would remain. In addition, he granted them excellent prophets such as Jeremiah, Ezekiel, Daniel and his friends, through whom they meanwhile were comforted and sustained. He

---

[13]Luther apparently refers particularly to the story of Korah's rebellion, Numbers 16.

also demonstrated by great miracles and benefactions performed by Daniel that he was with them and had not forsaken them. The royal person of Jehoiachin was elevated by the king of Babylon far above all the other kings, so that the throne of David and the priesthood did not become extinct, and even the persons remained to the end of the exile. Through Isaiah he had also long before this named King Cyrus to liberate them (Isaiah 45). The same prophet also foretold many things about this captivity. He did not keep silent about the sin, but like Jeremiah, mentioned it distinctly, so that it is well known for what sin they were punished in this manner.

Therefore those three punishments or exiles—in Egypt, in the wilderness, and in Babylon—cannot be compared with this last Roman exile. For in regard to the former, the sin is known, there are prophecies and promises, there are prophets and persons, for both the throne of David and the altar of Moses; and there is a definite time specified. In brief, where God is so disposed toward his people and where he deals thus with them and diligently keeps them and reassures them, one cannot say that he has forsaken them or has forgotten his divine promise. Nor can they be called forsaken, when God provided for the children of Israel in Egypt before they were born, determining the time for Abraham before he ever had a child. Read Jeremiah 30 and 31 and you will discover how God bemoans, like a weeping mother, the exile of his people in Babylon. He did this even before they went into exile and without any regard for their sin on account of which they were to be driven into exile.

Why, then, should God forget his promise so woefully in this exile or let it fail of fulfillment or be so hostile to them, since they have no sin which they can name, and yet this promise of the Messiah is the most glorious and the mightiest promise, upon which all other prophecy, promise, and the entire law are built? For the other promises such as those pertaining to Egypt, the wilderness, and Babylon, are to be esteemed very small in comparison with this chief promise of the Messiah. If God kept his less important promises there and then and comforted the people so heartily in lesser exiles; if he specified the time; if he proved himself their faithful God by means of persons and blessings and in every way, and always provided for them—how is it possible, how is it credible, how is it consistent that he would fail to keep, in this terrible, long, and great exile, his glorious promise given to David that his throne should remain established forever, as David exults in his last words (recorded in II Samuel in the first chapter [23:5]) and as we find in many other writings of the prophets, for example, in Isaiah and Jeremiah?[14]

The Jews may say what they want about the sins for which they are suffering (for they are lying). God did not promise and pledge an eternal throne to their sin or their righteousness, but to David. Even if he were disinclined to keep this promise to the Jews because of their sin (which they cannot even name), he would not for that reason lie to David and fail him to whom he promised this. This is what David sings in Psalm 89 [:4-52]. However, since David's throne, which God declares is not to be destroyed or fall, has been destroyed now for fifteen hundred years, it is incontrovertible that either the Messiah came fifteen hundred years ago and occupied the throne of his father David, and forever occupies it, or God has become a liar in his most glorious promise because of evil men and disobedient Jews. But this God did not want and never will want. No, the Jews are slandering God and deceiving themselves when they accuse God of breaking faith and trust with David because he did not send the Messiah in the manner they would have liked and as they prescribe and imagine him to be.

I know this argument is true. Where there are still reasonable Jews, it must move them, and it must even upset the obdurate ones a little, for they cannot bring any substantial evidence against it. But if it does not move them or make them waver, we have nonetheless substantiated our own faith, so that their foul and worthless lies and idle chatter cannot harm us. And if they do not stick to the point of the argument but evade the issue by resorting to other twaddle, as they like to do, let them go their way and you go yours. It only shows you how they are given to babbling and lying.[15]

---

[14] Cf. Isa. 9:7; 55:3; Jer. 17:25; 33:17.
[15] This paragraph is in the vein of Luther's later treatises, especially *On the Jews and Their Lies.*

Part Two

You write that the Jews boast that their law will endure forever and that we Gentiles must become Jews. You must reply: In the first place, if it is true that the Messiah has come, then they themselves know that their law has ended. For Moses is to be binding only till the advent of the Messiah. In Deuteronomy 18 [:15] Moses declares that they must heed the prophet whom God will raise up after him. The following saying is current also among their own teachers: *Cum venerit Sanctus Sanctorum, cessabit unctio vestra;* that is, "When the Saint of all Saints appears, your anointment will terminate."[16] "Anointment" here refers to the priesthood and kingdom established upon them and among them by Moses. The Messiah will establish a new and better one for the people of Israel and the throne of David.

Second, how does their assertion that their law will endure forever agree with the fact that it has lain in ashes for fifteen hundred years, together with priesthood, temple, kingdom, and worship? It would seem to me that this means the end of the law; for they cannot keep Moses' anointment or law outside the land and outside Jerusalem, as they well know and cannot deny.[17] And God surely would not have allowed such laws to fall or to lie for so long if he had planned to have them observed forever and ever. So you must tell them that they themselves should take the initiative in keeping Moses' law and becoming Jews. For they are no longer Jews, since they do not observe their law. When they have done this, we shall promptly emulate them and also become Jews. However, they should have begun to do so fifteen hundred years ago when they still dwelt in the land and in Jerusalem, when they still had their temple, priesthood, and government. They should have been concerned or done their part so that it would not have fallen or ceased for these fifteen hundred years and thus have lost its

---

[16] A specific source for this saying has not been located.

[17] Luther obviously has in mind here the ceremonial laws which presuppose a temple cultus in Jerusalem, together with the civic or judicial ordinances which presuppose an independent state. Under the conditions of the "Roman exile," both these aspects of the law fall away, while the "moral" aspects—especially insofar as they agree with the natural law—retain their force. On the latter point, see Luther's argument below, pp. 88-95.

eternity. Then they themselves would not now have become such miserable non-Jews and be bereft of Moses.

But since this was neglected and did not come to pass, let them even now travel to the land and to Jerusalem, build the temple, establish priesthood, kingdom, and Moses with his law, and thus again become Jews and possess the land. After that is done they will soon find us on their heels, coming right after them, and we will also become Jews. If they will not do this, it would be extremely ridiculous for them to convert us Gentiles to their expired law, which has been in decay and has not been a law for fifteen hundred years. Should we be expected to observe that which they themselves do not and cannot observe as long as they are not in possession of Jerusalem and the land? They dream that they will observe it at the time when the Messiah appears. We wish to retain our freedom meanwhile and not believe in their dream until it comes true.[18]

From this, dear friend, you can infer what empty, meaningless folly the Jews are given to in declaring that their law of Moses will endure forever. It has been in ruins for fifteen hundred years now and did not survive, and they do not yet know for how long this situation will prevail. We Christians, however, know that it has ceased forever and that it is entirely abrogated through the Messiah, not only among us Gentiles, to whom this law of Moses was never issued and commanded and on whom it never was imposed, but also among the true Jews and posterity of David. For since God himself has let it lapse for these fifteen hundred years, it is reasonable to assume that he pays it no heed and that he is not interested in obedience or service to such a law. Otherwise he would never have let it collapse or, at least, he would have determined how long he would let it lie in decay (as he did in the abovementioned instances), and with new promises, as well as

---

[18] Jewish people had continued to live at Jerusalem and elsewhere in Palestine throughout the Middle Ages, enjoying now greater, now less freedom as control of the land alternated between Christian and Muslim rulers. On the whole, the latter proved the more tolerant. During Luther's lifetime, the hegemony of the Egyptian sultans was succeeded by that of the Ottoman Turks, who were to retain control for four hundred years. The event with whose unlikelihood Luther taunts the Jews in the present passage—the re-establishment of an independent Jewish state—finally occurred in 1948.

prophets and other persons, he would have secured and regulated it. But he did not do this. Therefore the law of Moses is finished. It does not stand as a law that endures forever; rather it has become a law that is forever abandoned.

But when the Jews bandy about the word *le-olam* to prove their point, quoting Moses' command to keep such and such laws which he gave them *le-olam*, that is "eternally," these rascals are well aware that this is empty talk designed to dupe those not versed in the Hebrew language. They would not dare to confront me or anyone else who understands a little Hebrew with this,[19] unless to make a joke or to provoke some laughter. In Exodus 21 [:5-6] Moses himself writes that when a slave, after serving his term, does not choose to leave his master but wishes to stay on with him, the master shall bore his ear through with an awl at the doorpost as a sign that he wishes to remain attached to the house eternally. And he shall remain the master's servant *le-olam*, that is, eternally. The Jews know very well that neither master, slave, nor house will abide eternally, but that these must die and pass away, and all will be changed. Yet Moses uses the word *le-olam* here, which means eternally. They themselves interpret this to mean "on and on," that is, without a definite end among the children of men. There are no doubt other examples in the Scriptures of the use of this word *le-olam*.

If I were Moses, I would give my pupils, the Jews, a good

---

[19] Luther is modest concerning the degree of his own expertise in Hebrew. In this case, however, he had the assistance of his predecessors Nicholas of Lyra and Paul of Burgos, both of whom had explored the meaning of the term *le-olam*. See especially Burgos' *Scrutinium Scripturarum*, Part I, Dist. 8, Ch. 5; his position is similar to Luther's. A modern authority, the Brown-Driver-Briggs *Hebrew and English Lexicon of the Old Testament* (Oxford: Clarendon Press, reprinted 1953), states the following as the meaning of *olam* with a preposition indicating futurity: *"for ever, always* (sometimes=*during the lifetime*)."* Hermann Sasse, in his discussion of the Hebrew background of the Greek terms *aion, aionos,* attributes the differences in meaning of *le-olam* such as those pointed to by Luther in part to historical developments in Hebrew thought and language. See his article in Gerhard Kittel, *Theological Dictionary of the New Testament,* trans. and ed. by Geoffrey W. Bromiley, Vol. I (Grand Rapids, Mich.: Eerdmans, 1964), pp. 197-209. Luther deals with the same point in his *Lectures on Genesis,* commenting on Gen. 17:9: the covenant of circumcision is to be kept by Abraham and his descendants "throughout their generations"; i.e., according to Luther, "as long as the kingdom and priesthood continue to exist" (*LW* 3, 127).

box on the ears. How often, I would say, have I used not only the word *le-olam*, but also the words *le-dorotham, benothekem, ledorothekem, moshebothekem*,[20] when I meant "as long as you live or remain in your dwellings." This cannot be understood otherwise than to mean, "It shall be kept by you forever so long as you live or remain in your dwellings." But they have now been expelled from their dwellings (that is, from the land of their dwellings) for fifteen hundred years. They did not remain the nation that Moses founded. For fifteen hundred years they have been without their own dwelling place; nor do they have a promise or a specified time indicating how long they must still be in exile outside their dwelling place, perplexed and uncertain. Moses thus protected himself nicely against misunderstanding, for he did not wish to have his institution and his law remain eternally any longer than his nation would remain and keep its dwelling place. In view of these qualifications, *le-olam* cannot mean "eternal" in the ordinary sense of the word, where it means literally eternal without any qualification, as God's promises are and as he himself is.

We Germans use the word *ewig* ["eternal" or "eternally"] in the same sense when we say: Am I to suffer or to do this eternally? —that is, as long as I live. Under the papacy many "eternal" masses for the dead were endowed, which means, to be maintained as long as possible. And fiefs are conferred "hereditarily and eternally"; that is, as long as the fiefs and the heirs exist or remain alive. But whenever God, who is truly eternal without qualification, speaks of eternal things, these are eternal indeed, for he is able to make them eternal—things such as David's throne, the Messiah, and the eternal blessing which he has brought to us lost men. For he does not change as the dwellings of the Jews or the feudal estates of the Gentiles change, which are changed as one changes a garment.

Therefore the Scriptures differentiate between the human *le-olam* or eternal and the divine *le-olam* by adding a negative to the latter, to indicate that it shall not change. For instance, Daniel 7 [6:26] declares of the Messiah: "He is the living God, enduring

---

[20] Literally, "to their generations," "your daughters," "to your generations," "your dwellings."

for ever; his kingdom shall never be destroyed." Here we find the word *ewig* ["eternally" or "for ever"], but to insure that this might not be construed as a human but as a divine "eternal," the negative phrase "shall never be destroyed" is added. Similarly, David prophesies of the eternal Priest, the Messiah, in Psalm 110 [:4], "The Lord has sworn"—this would have sufficed for the oath of such a Lord, but lest it be conceived as a temporary oath, the words are added—"and will not change his mind." That is to say that this Priest will be eternal, not in the Mosaic or human sense, but in the sense of without end and truly eternal.

And Isaiah in chapter 9 [:7], also speaking of the Messiah—as the Jews are very ready to admit—declares: "Of the increase of his government and of peace there will be no end, upon the throne of David, and over his kingdom," etc. Here the prophet does not content himself with saying that the kingdom of the Messiah (the Prince of Peace, as he calls him) will be great, but he states that there will be no end to peace, as though he were to say: It will not only be eternal, but eternal without any hindrance. And who knows—for I am not an expert in Hebrew—whether the closed Mem, which here conveys much subtlety to the Hebrews (as they claim), does not mean just this: that this Messiah's kingdom shall be thus eternally great, since it is not an open Mem, which might signify an earthly eternal, but a closed Mem, which excludes every other possibility than that of the truly eternal.[21]

But if the Jews claim here that they have indeed kept the law of Moses down to the present time, for instance with regard to circumcision, also with regard to abstinence from certain fish and meat, etc., and that the law, in view of this, has not come to an end, we say that this is empty talk. For we are speaking of the entire law of Moses which they are obliged to keep, especially the truly chief paragraphs and sections: namely, those dealing with the priesthood, the kingdom, the temple, worship, Jerusalem, and the

---

[21] The Hebrew letter Mem is customarily written in closed fashion only at the end of a word, whereas in this passage a closed Mem occurs in the middle of the word *le-marbeh*, "of the increase." Luther's speculation is typically medieval. Another opinion held that the closed Mem signified the closed womb of the Virgin from whom the Messiah was to be born. Modern scholars make the more pedestrian suggestion that it might be due to a scribal error.

whole country, all of which are basic to the law of Moses and which it has instituted. He who would keep Moses' law must keep it in its entirety, especially in the chief parts, or his keeping of the law goes for nought. It is just as though I were to ask for a pot and they would show me the shards or small fragments of a shattered vessel. Isaiah in chapter 30 [:14] uses this very simile against them, saying that they will become like a pot that is smashed into such small pieces that one cannot find a shard of it which could serve to carry fire or dip water.

So in this instance, we ask them where their entire law concerning priesthood, temple, city, country, and government is now, and they show us the battered fragments and small shards of their eating of fish and meat, etc. Was there ever a city or country destroyed of which some slag, bits, and pieces have not been found? Is a house ever so completely consumed by fire that not a vestige of lime, stones, bricks, nails, iron, or glass remains in the ashes? If I were to inquire about the house and someone showed me a brick or two or some nails in the ashes to persuade me that this was the house about which I had asked, what in the world should I think of him? Either I would think he was a mischievous fellow who was trying to make fun of my question, or if I felt he did not understand, I would say to him: Dear friend, these odds and ends indicate, to be sure, that a house once stood here; but it has disappeared and is here no longer.

Thus the Jews show us with their leftover shards and slags of eating fish and meat, etc., that they did once have the law of Moses, but that it has disappeared from the scene, since the house, the government, the land, the city, the temple, and the whole true head and body of the law have been absent and destroyed for fifteen hundred years. If they refuse to believe that their law is temporary and not eternal, then let them explain how their land, Jerusalem, the temple, Moses' ordinances and law, happen to be torn to bits and they themselves destroyed and dispersed. They may call it an eternal thing, but we perceive that it has fallen, and been at an end for fifteen hundred years, and will never be restored. For there is no prophet, no promise, which foretells its restoration, as happened in Babylon and Egypt. Therefore the Jews' hope is doomed, for it has no basis in God's word.

Nor is circumcision a law of Moses, for it was given to Abraham much earlier.[22] Thus our Lord testifies in John 5 [7:22]), "Circumcision is not from Moses, but from the fathers." This the Jews cannot deny. Furthermore, this circumcision is not eternal; it did not exist prior to Abraham and it was entirely directed to the future Messiah, Abraham's seed. Him they should have heard. And circumcision did not extend beyond Abraham and his seed. There are many examples in the Scriptures which demonstrate that God accepted great kings and nations from among the Gentiles. They were not forced to be circumcised, much less to obey the law of Moses. First there was Pharaoh and his princes and priests, and doubtless also many of the people, who had learned to know the true God through Joseph. Psalm 105 [:22] testifies that the king set Joseph "to instruct his princes at his pleasure and to teach his elders wisdom." In that way the Egyptians obtained a knowledge of God through Joseph, and yet, since they were not Abraham's seed, they were not burdened with circumcision, much less with the law of Moses, which was not yet promulgated.

Later Jonah was dispatched to Nineveh to preach repentance to them. The text declares that the king with his princes and people accepted faith in God and became believers, so that God was gracious to them and averted their punishment [Jonah 3:5-10]. These people of Nineveh, too, came to grace without circumcision and the law of Moses and were preserved by their faith and good works. This the prophet Jonah shows clearly.

Similarly, the evil king Nebuchadnezzar in Babylon was so thoroughly converted by Daniel's message and by God's punishment that he had a public pronouncement issued in his name, ordering that the God of Israel be regarded as the true God since he was in fact the true God [Dan. 4:34-36]. Notice that the king himself became a believer in God and a pious person, and indubitably many others in his kingdom with him; and yet he was not circumcised, nor was the law of Moses imposed on him. Daniel

---

[22] Cf. Gen. 17:9-13.

surely would not have omitted to indicate and impose this on him unless he knew that Moses' law was to be imposed solely on the Jews and circumcision solely on Abraham and his seed, until such a time, as the true Teacher, the Messiah, would come from his race.

Later King Darius and Cyrus in Persia became believers through the same Daniel and other Jews, who acquainted the latter with the prophecy of Isaiah recorded in Isaiah 45, to the effect that God had long before called this king Cyrus by name, speaking of him as his own king or anointed one, and had gloriously proclaimed that he should build for God his city of Jerusalem and release his people from Babylon, etc. This Cyrus did and publicly promulgated his confession throughout his land, as the God of heaven had commanded him, etc. (II Chronicles 36 [:22-23] and Ezra 1 [:2]). He was not circumcised either, nor was he subjected to the law of Moses; nor was anyone else in his kingdom of Persia. Daniel and his assistants would surely not have permitted this had they considered it necessary to impose Moses' law and circumcision on the Gentiles, who were not Abraham's seed or Moses' people. If it had indeed been necessary to observe them, then these kings would have been sufficiently instructed by Daniel, they would not have been true believers in God, and they would not have been saved; and all this would have been Daniel's fault.

Similarly, Job and his family and friends were endowed richly with knowledge of God and faith, and yet he was not circumcised or forced to obey the law of Moses. And there must have been many more such people dispersed throughout the lands, such as Hiram, the king of Tyre in the days of Solomon [I Kings 5:1-12], and others, too, who are not mentioned in the Scriptures.[23] These believed in the true God of Abraham, and in that way were saved. It is surprising to see that Moses, amid so many laws, does not at all mention circumcision after the exodus from Egpyt, when his law went into effect, while yet he urges so intensely and extravagantly many less important laws upon his people, the Jews. It is as though he wished to say, "Circumcision is not my law." In Exodus 12 [:43 ff.], where he speaks of foreigners who wished to eat the Passover with the Jews, he says merely that no uncircum-

---

[23] Very likely Luther was using a traditional list of "believing Gentiles."

cised should eat it; he does not force the foreigners to eat the Pass-over, or to be circumcised. He only insists that those who wanted to eat the Passover be circumcised. So it was something quite novel when the Jews later on made proselytes or converts to Judaism from among the Gentiles and commanded them to be circumcised. Moses does not force the Gentiles to adopt any of his laws against their will, because he was appointed a prophet solely to the people who were led out of Egypt, until the advent of the Messiah, who was to become the Prophet, Teacher, and Lord of all the world.

Since circumcision and the law of Moses were not necessary for the kings and heathen in Egypt, Assyria, Babylon, Persia, and elsewhere who nevertheless believed in the God of Abraham and were saved without circumcision and the law of Moses at the very time when these were flourishing and when the people had their government in Jerusalem and in the land, why then should we Gentiles be required to keep a circumcision and a law which has now ceased and which they themselves cannot keep because they have lost country, city, government, and all that Moses instituted, without any promise of ever retrieving them? From this, I am sure, you can gather that the Jews have been smitten with blindness. They put forth these crass lies and this foolishness about their law to us Gentiles, telling us that it is eternal and is to be imposed upon all the Gentiles, whereas it has really been abolished and com-pletely forsaken by God once and for all, without any prophecy. Even when still in force, it never extended, nor was intended by God to extend, beyond the people of Moses whom he led out of Egypt, and Abraham's seed, until the time of the Messiah.

In conclusion you should again introduce the passage in Jeremiah 31 [:31-32]: "Behold, the days are coming, says the Lord, when I will make a new covenant with the house of Israel and the house of Judah, not like the covenant which I made with their fathers when I took them by the hand to bring them out of the land of Egypt, my covenant which they broke, though I was their hus-band, says the Lord. . . ." This verse really pains the Jews; for they fret and sweat remarkably in an attempt to make their first cove-nant eternal even though the text states clearly and lucidly that it will not be eternal, but there will be another, a new covenant. Let them carry on here as they will, saying, for example, that at the time of the Messiah their law will be renewed and will be observed by all. Jeremiah does not say that the old covenant will be renewed, but that it will not be the same covenant that they received through Moses at the time of the exodus from Egypt. It will not be the same one, but a new and different covenant. Now it is well known what kind of a covenant Moses made with them at that time. Therefore it is also clear what is meant by saying that it is not to be the old covenant; for "not to be" does not mean to renew the old, but to abolish the old and to institute something different and new. You must adhere firmly to this verse and not listen to the prattle which they dream up. For this verse declares that the old, former covenant will not remain or be renewed, but that there will be a different, a new covenant, and that God no longer wants the old one.

Now let us consider whom it is more reasonable for us to believe, the faithful and truthful God or the false and lying Jews? God declares that Moses' covenant will not endure forever, but that it will terminate at the time of the Messiah.[24] The Jews assert that it will endure eternally and will never terminate. Thus to the Jews God must ever be a liar. And yet they wonder why they suffer such miserable exile. They insist that they are in the right and that God is in the wrong.

If at this point they try to escape and blaspheme, saying, "Your Jesus himself stated that he had not come to abolish the law, not a dot, not a letter of it," etc., you must answer that they should stick to the passage in Jeremiah and give a correct and thorough answer. Since they do not believe our Jesus at all, they cannot appeal to him. They must either refute Jeremiah or defend themselves against him with plausible reasons and valid statements. In any event, they are lying when they claim that our Jesus was referring to the law of Moses when he said that the law will not pass away; for, as everyone may read, our Lord Christ is here not at all speaking of circumcision or of the law or ordinance of Moses, but rather is speaking of the Ten Commandments.[25] But why should they

---

[24] An interpretation which, if based on Jer. 31:31-32, presupposes the equation of "the time of the new covenant" with "the time of the Messiah."
[25] Luther invokes again the distinction between the ceremonial, judicial, and

leave our books and writings uncorrupted and inviolate when all their studies are nothing but a corruption even of their own prophets and sacred writings with lies and falsehoods? We have neither time nor space to discuss what our Lord Christ says here about fulfilling the law. Moreover, the Jews cannot understand this, and we would only be diverted from our subject. Christians must deal with such words of Christ, for they understand them and—God be praised!—know their meaning well.

Finally, we also want to discuss the Ten Commandments. For perhaps the Jews will also call the Ten Commandments the law of Moses, since they were given on Mount Sinai in the presence of none but Jews or children of Abraham, etc. You must reply: If the Ten Commandments are to be regarded as Moses' law, then Moses came far too late, and he also addressed himself to far too few people, because the Ten Commandments had spread over the whole world not only before Moses but even before Abraham and all the patriarchs. For even if a Moses had never appeared and Abraham had never been born, the Ten Commandments would have had to rule in all men from the very beginning, as they indeed did and still do.[26]

For all creatures rightly regard God as God and honor his name, as do also the angels in heaven. Thus we and all human beings are obligated to hear his word, to honor father and mother,

---

moral aspects of the Mosaic law which underlies his whole argument in Part Two.

[26] The concept of natural law is deep-rooted in Luther's thought. His essay of 1525, How Christians Should Regard Moses (LW 35, 155-174), had already employed the distinction made here between the natural-law elements and the historically conditioned elements in the Mosaic code. "We will regard Moses as a teacher," Luther affirmed, "but we will not regard him as our lawgiver—unless he agrees with both the New Testament and the natural law" (LW 35, 165). He took the same tack in his pamphlet Against the Heavenly Prophets, published in the same year: "Where then the Mosaic law and the natural law are one, there the law remains . . ." (LW 40, 97). For the rest, the Mosaic code is merely the Sachsenspiegel of the Jews—their ancient equivalent of the social and economic laws obtaining in Luther's own sixteenth-century Saxony. See also the references to natural law in Luther's treatises Warning to His Dear German People and Against the Antinomians in the present volume. For brief studies from among the voluminous modern literature on the question, see John T. McNeill, "Natural Law in the Thought of Luther," Church History, X (1941), 211-227, and Heinrich Bornkamm, Luther's Doctrine of the Two Kingdoms, trans. Karl H. Hertz ("Facet Books, Social Ethics Series," No. 14; Philadelphia: Fortress, 1966).

to refrain from killing, from adultery, from stealing, from bearing false witness, from coveting one's neighbor's house or anything else that is his. All the heathen bear witness to this in their writings, laws, and governments, as can be clearly seen; but nothing is said therein of circumcision or of the laws Moses gave to the Jews for the land of Canaan.

Moses did precede all other legislators, however, in revealing in his history the genesis of all creatures and the coming of death into the whole world through Adam's fall or sin. And later when he wants to set up a special law and nation apart from all others, as he has been commanded to do, he first introduces God himself; he is the universal God of all the nations, who gives the universal Ten Commandments—which prior to this had been implanted at creation in the hearts of all men—to this particular people orally as well. In his day Moses fitted them nicely into his laws in a more orderly and excellent manner than could have been done by anyone else. Circumcision and the law of Moses, however, were not implanted in men's hearts; they were first imposed by Abraham and Moses on their people.

We and all Gentiles are just as duty-bound as the Jews to keep the first commandment, so that we have no other gods than the only God. But we Gentiles have no use and can have no use for the phrase with which he modifies this commandment and which applies solely to the Jews, namely, "who brought you out of the land of Egypt, out of the house of bondage." For if I were to approach God and say, "O Lord God, who brought me out of Egypt, out of the exile," etc., I would be like a sow entering a synagogue,[27] for God never performed such a work for me. God would punish me as a liar; I would be making an imaginary god out of him. Yet I must recite and keep all the other words of the first commandment. I may also say, "You are my God, the God and also the Creator of us all, who, to be sure, led the children of Israel out of Egypt, but not me; however, you did lead me out of *my* Egypt and *my* exile." Thus the first commandment remains common to both Jews and Gentiles. It is especially adapted and suited to the Jews with reference to the exodus from Egypt, just as everyone after his own exile

---

[27] A proverbial expression.

can and should name and praise the God of all as his own God and Helper.

Let me suggest an analogy. It is as if a prince or the head of a household wished to establish an ordinance for his country or his house because God had rescued him from great need and he wanted to show his gratitude, as perhaps Naaman the Syrian did or might have done.[28] He also would begin by teaching first about God, how he alone should be worshiped and regarded as the true God, able and willing to deliver from every need all who trust and believe in him, whatever nation it may be, just as the first commandment teaches and makes no distinction, but declares that God punishes all who hate him and helps all who love him, etc. After that the prince or the head of a household would continue by enunciating the ordinances for his country or his house.

In this way the prince would not have imposed the ordinances of his country on all the other countries which did not experience this help, nor would he have had the authority to do this, even if he at the outset first commanded that they should worship and honor the true God of all countries. That is what Moses also does. When he is supposed to organize his people, who have been delivered from Egypt, he first lets God himself issue his Ten Commandments, which pertain to all of mankind. Subsequently, and still at God's command, he gives his people the peculiar laws of their country, which do not concern other nations. As Moses' people were obligated to obey these ordinances because God had given him this command, so each country and each household is duty-bound to observe the ordinances of its prince and head of a household. For these also are the commandments of God, who ordained all the governments of the world.[29]

Similarly, the third commandment concerning the Sabbath, of which the Jews make so much, is per se a commandment that applies to the whole world; but the form in which Moses frames it and adapts it to his people was imposed only on the Jews, just as with regard to the first commandment none but the Jews must believe and confess that the common God of all the world led

---

[28] Cf. I Kings 5.
[29] An application of the Pauline principle expressed in Rom. 13:1.

them out of Egypt. For the true meaning of the third commandment is that we on that day should teach and hear the word of
God, thereby sanctifying both the day and ourselves. And in accord
with this, ever after to the present day, Moses and the prophets are
read and preached on the Sabbath day among the Jews. Wherever
God's word is preached it follows naturally that one must necessarily celebrate at the same hour or time and be quiet, and without any other preoccupation only speak and hear what God declares, what he teaches us and tells us.

Therefore everything depends completely on this, that we sanctify the day. This is more important than celebrating it.[30] For God
does not say: You shall celebrate the holy day or make it a Sabbath
—that will take care of itself. No, you shall sanctify the holy day or
the Sabbath. He is far more concerned about the sanctifying than
about the celebrating of it. And where one or the other might be or
must be neglected, it would be far better to neglect the celebrating
than the sanctifying, since the commandment places the greater
emphasis on the sanctifying and does not institute the Sabbath for
its own sake, but for the sake of its being sanctified. The Jews, however, lay greater emphasis on the celebrating than on the sanctifying (which God and Moses do not do) because of the additions
they have made.

Moses' mention of the seventh day, and of how God created
the world in six days, which is why they are to do no work—all this
is a temporal adaptation with which Moses suits this commandment to his people, especially at that time. We find nothing written
about this previously, either by Abraham or at the time of the old
fathers. This is a temporary addendum and adaptation intended
solely for this people which was brought out of Egypt. Nor was it
to endure forever, any more than was the whole law of Moses. But
the sanctifying—that is, the teaching and preaching of God's word,
which is the true, genuine, and sole meaning of this commandment
—has been from the beginning and pertains to all the world forever.
Therefore the seventh day does not concern us Gentiles, nor did it

---

[30] The German terms are *heiligen* ("sanctify") and *feiern* ("celebrate"). A
similar distinction is made in Luther's interpretation of the third commandment
in his *Large Catechism*; see Theodore G. Tappert (ed.), *The Book of Concord*
(Philadelphia: Fortress, 1959), pp. 375-379.

concern the Jews beyond the advent of the Messiah, although by
the very nature of things one must, as already said, rest, celebrate,
and keep the Sabbath on whatever day or at whatever hour God's
word is preached. For God's word cannot be heard or taught when
one is preoccupied with something else or when one is not quiet.

Therefore Isaiah, too, declares in chapter 66 [:23] that the
seventh day, or, as I call it, Moses' adaptation of it, will cease at
the time of the Messiah when true sanctification and the word of
God will appear richly. He says that there will be one Sabbath after
another and one new moon after another, that is, that all will be
sheer Sabbath, and there will no longer be any particular seventh
day with six days in between. For the sanctifying or the word of
God will enjoy full scope daily and abundantly, and every day will
be a Sabbath.[31]

I am well aware of what the Jews say about this and how they
interpret this saying of Isaiah. However, I cannot include everything in the present letter that I have in mind against the Jews, who
so shamefully distort and pervert the prophets. But in brief, no
Jew can tell me how it is possible for all flesh to worship before the
Lord in Jerusalem every new moon and every Sabbath, as the text,
translated most accurately and exactly into German according to
their understanding, conveys. Some people or flesh live so far from
Jerusalem that they could not get there within twenty, thirty, or a
hundred Sabbaths, and the Jews themselves have not worshiped in
Jerusalem for fifteen hundred years, that is, in twelve times fifteen
hundred new moons—I will say nothing of the Sabbaths. However,
I cannot enlarge on all of this in the course of a letter.

Jeremiah comments on the first commandment's qualifying
phrase, "who brought you out of the land of Egypt," in chapter
23 [:5]: "Behold, the days are coming, says the Lord, when I will
raise up for David a righteous Branch, and he shall reign as king
and deal wisely, and shall execute justice and righteousness in the
land," etc. And he adds immediately: "Behold, the days are coming, says the Lord, when men shall no longer say, 'As the Lord lives
who brought up the people of Israel out of the land of Egypt,' but

---

[31] With these paragraphs, Luther has reached the heart of his argument
against the Sabbatarians as such, as distinguished from his broader polemic
against the Jews.

'As the Lord lives who brought up and led the descendants of the house of Israel (note that not the entire house of Israel but the descendants of it are mentioned here) out of the north country and out of all the countries where he had driven them.' Then they shall dwell in their own land" [vv. 7-8].

There are many important matters in this passage which would be dealt with. But let us stay with our subject. Wherever the Jews hold to their old teachers,[32] they are agreed with us that Jeremiah is here speaking about the time of the Messiah. When this time comes, the prophet states plainly, that part of the first commandment which was given by Moses, where it says, "who brought you out of the land of Egypt," will cease to apply. For the text says that one must no longer swear by the God who brought them up out of Egypt, but by the God who gathered them from all the lands unto the Branch of David. Now, if this phrase in the first commandment does not pertain beyond the time of the Messiah, then Moses' law is not eternal but terminates with the Messiah, and there remains only the law of the Ten Commandments, which was in force prior to Moses from the beginning of the world and also among all the Gentiles: namely, that one must not have more than one God, etc. So far as the Ten Commandments are concerned, there is no difference between Jews and Gentiles, for God is the God not only of the Jews but also of the Gentiles, as St. Paul declares [Rom. 3:29] and as the aforementioned examples of the kings of Egypt, Assyria, Babylon, Persia, etc., prove.[33]

Nor can we Gentiles join in the words of the fourth commandment, "that your days may be long in the land which the Lord your God gives you." And yet all of us must obey the first part, namely, the words, "Honor your father and your mother." Moses, or rather God himself, is here speaking with the people of Israel whom he had led from Egypt into the land of Canaan. In this commandment he refers to the same country of Canaan, which he gave them at that time in order that they should live long in it and experience good times if they would observe the fourth commandment concerning obedience to parents. So here again the general

---

[32] Presumably Jewish exegetes who dealt with the passage before it became a focus of controversy with the Christians.
[33] Cf. above, p. 87.

commandment implanted into the hearts of all people is adapted and applied especially to the Jews with reference to the land of Canaan. We Gentiles, of course, are not able to say or believe— nor could God tolerate our doing so—that he brought us out of Egypt or led us into the land of Canaan, in which we will prosper if we honor father and mother. No, we have to take this in a general sense, that God would give happiness and well-being to anyone in his own country who honors father and mother. We also observe that countries and governments, yes, also families and estates, decline or survive so remarkably according to their obedience or disobedience; and it has never happened otherwise than that he fares badly and dies an evil death who dishonors father and mother.

Therefore this fourth commandment cannot be eternal, that is, it cannot, as the blindness of the Jews would have it, be applied to us Gentiles in the sense that we will possess the land of Canaan and prosper in it, when they themselves have had to live outside of this country in all sorts of misery for fifteen hundred years as people who despised, dishonored, and persecuted their fathers and prophets. They do not cease from persecuting them; therefore the punishment, too, does not cease. For they reject the Messiah, whom their fathers and prophets proclaimed and foretold and commanded and enjoined them to accept. They remain their fathers' disobedient children.

I should here like to point to similar circumstances that attend the ninth and tenth commandments, which forbid the coveting of another man's wife and house. For among the Jews a letter of divorce had to be recognized as legal; but this cannot be the case among us Gentiles, much less the cunning and the trickery employed in alienating wife and house which were practiced so willfully among the Jews, as the prophet Malachi laments [2:14-16].

And finally, to bring this letter to a close, I hope, my dear friend, that you will at lease have been supplied with enough material to defend yourself against the Sabbatarians and to preserve the purity of your Christian faith.[34] If you are unable to con-

---

[34] A reiteration of the purposes of the letter as occasioned by Count Schlick's request. Cf. above, p. 65.

vert the Jews, then consider that you are no better than all the prophets, who were always slain and persecuted by this base people who glory solely in the boast that they are Abraham's seed, though they surely know that there have always been many desperate, lost souls also among them, so that they might well recognize that it requires more to be a child of God than just to be the seed of Abraham. Therefore neither does the law of Moses do them any good, for they have never kept it, as is shown by the aforementioned verse from Jeremiah 31, where God himself states this and bemoans it. Rather their disobedience does them harm. Even today they do not keep this law, nor can they keep it so long as Jerusalem does not become the seat of the Jews' kingdom and priesthood.

It is a known fact—and this they also admit in part—that they themselves no longer understand the law of Moses, especially certain passages in Leviticus and in other books. How, then, could they keep it even if they were now in Jerusalem? In brief, since these fifteen hundred years of exile, of which there is no end in sight, nor can there be, do not humble the Jews or bring them to awareness, you may with a good conscience despair of them.[35] For it is impossible that God would leave his people, if they truly were his people, without comfort and prophecy so long. He never did this before. Moreover, he promised that he would do nothing without a prophecy preceding the event, as Amos says, "Surely the Lord God does nothing without revealing his secret to his servants the prophets" [Amos 3:7]. All estates, all governments, all the works of man must exist, occur, and continue in the word of God so that his people may know how they stand with God and what they are to do, to suffer, and to expect. This God has done from the beginning, and this he will do forever.

Because God for fifteen hundred years has failed to do this with the Jews but lets them live on and on in exile without any

---

[35] Luther's advice reflects the despairing attitude that he himself had adopted on the question, as evidenced also in his lectures, *Table Talk*, and correspondence during this period. Cf. Reinhold Lewin, *Luthers Stellung zu den Juden: Ein Beitrag zur Geschichte der Juden in Deutschland während des Reformationszeitalters* (Berlin, 1911), pp. 72 ff., and Heinrich Bornkamm, *Luther and the Old Testament,* trans. by Eric W. and Ruth C. Gritsch, ed. by Victor I. Gruhn (Philadelphia: Fortress, 1969), pp. 77 ff.

word or prophecy to them regarding it, it is evident that he has forsaken them, that they can no longer be God's people, and that the true Lord, the Messiah, must have come fifteen hundred years ago.[36] What, do you suppose, might be the sin that continues to provoke such a terrible penalty and such silence of God other than their rejection, past and present, of the true Seed of Abraham and David, the dear Lord Messiah? They committed more terrible sins before the Babylonian captivity—the murdering of the prophets, etc.—than they can point to subsequently.

It does not make sense that they should suffer such misery for fifteen hundred years for unknown sins—sins which they cannot name—whereas they did not have to suffer more than seventy years for sins that were more obvious, terrible, murderous, and idolatrous. Furthermore, at that time they were not without prophets and without comfort, while in their present exile not even a fly flicks a wing for their consolation. If this is not being forsaken by God, then the devil, too, may boast that he is not forsaken by God.

If we reckon the time exactly, we find that their present exile under the Roman Empire is lasting longer than their former state and government in the land of Canaan. Anyone may figure the time from the exodus from Egypt to the final destruction of Jerusalem, under which they still live, and he will arrive at the sum of approximately fifteen hundred and ten years.[37] At present they have not lived many fewer years in exile; and in the end this will become a far longer period of time, since they neither have had nor will they have any prophet or prophecy regarding their exile's end. Is it credible that God should let his people live longer devoid of their dominion than in possession of it, longer without the law, temple, divine worship, Jerusalem, priesthood, kingdom, and country than with them?

This letter has grown in the writing. I was quite unaware of it, so quickly did my pen skim over the paper. For I have more thoughts on this subject than I have managed to express. Please

---

[36] In his closing paragraphs, Luther reiterates the argument that he had developed earlier in the letter, reinforcing it with further chronological computations. Cf. above, pp. 66 ff.

[37] Luther assumes the traditional date of 1430 B.C. for the Exodus. Modern scholars, working on the basis of archaeological research as well as a critical analysis of the literary sources, generally prefer a later date.

be content with this for the time being, for the subject is far too big to be disposed of in a letter.[38] I commend you to God. Amen.

---

[38] Five years later, Luther published three substantial treatises on the subject. Cf. above, p. 65, n. 1.

AGAINST THE ANTINOMIANS

1539

Translated by Martin H. Bertram

INTRODUCTION

The present treatise, published in early 1539, is one of the chief documents in the controversy over the relationship of law and gospel that racked the Lutheran movement in general, and the town of Wittenberg in particular, during the years 1537-1540. Focus of this dispute, as he had been of the earlier "Antinomian controversy" dating from the year 1527, was Luther's younger colleague, John Agricola (*ca.* 1494-1566). A native of Luther's own birthplace, Eisleben, Agricola matriculated at the University of Wittenberg in 1515 and, like his contemporary Philip Melanchthon, soon became both an ardent follower and a close personal friend of Luther. He studied medicine for a time, served as catechist to the youth of Wittenberg, and then in 1525, having been disappointed in his hope of obtaining a chair on the Wittenberg theological faculty, accepted the position of director of the newly founded Latin School in Eisleben, where in subsequent years he also gained a widespread following as a preacher.

Melanchthon's *Articles of Visitation*,[1] prepared for the guidance of those who fanned out from Wittenberg to inspect the condition of the churches in Electoral Saxony in 1527, gave the occasion for the first controversy. In the conviction that Luther's doctrine of "the freedom of a Christian" was being grossly misinterpreted in some quarters as a charter for moral laxity, Melanchthon laid great stress, in the *Articles*, on the necessity for a continued preaching of the law as well as the gospel. "Many," he noted, "now talk only about the forgiveness of sins and say little or nothing about repentance."[2] But true repentance and contrition for sin—which are to be instilled by the rigorous preaching of the law—are the necessary preconditions of genuine faith. Furthermore, the preaching of the law, e.g., the Ten Commandments, is useful and necessary, he insisted, as a guide to the good works which are to follow true faith.

---

[1] See *Instructions for the Visitors of Parish Pastors in Electoral Saxony*, 1528. *LW* 40, 263–320 (a revised version of the *Articles*).
[2] *LW* 40, 274.

To this emphasis on the law Agricola objected, claiming that it was unfaithful to the basic insights of evangelical faith. Contrition and repentance for sin, he stated, are not so much a precondition of faith as a consequence of it. What can best induce genuine sorrow over one's sin and a turning from it is not the preaching of the law, but the preaching of the gospel of God's immeasurable grace in Christ. And as to guidance for the Christian life, it is to be derived not from the Ten Commandments or other aspects of the law in the usual sense, but from the apostolic admonitions which follow from the gospel.[3]

Agricola here was undoubtedly picking up authentic elements in Luther's own teaching, yet without the counterbalance of Luther's realism concerning the Christian's situation as *simul justus et peccator*. For the moment, the disagreement was patched over with a compromise formula worked out in conference between Agricola, Melanchthon, Luther, and Bugenhagen, a formula which is reflected in the text of the *Instructions* as published in 1528. In one sense, it is said, faith precedes repentance; but here faith refers only to a general faith in God as judge. Truly justifying faith in the God of grace and mercy must be preceded by repentance.[4]

During his years at Eisleben, Agricola further developed his distinctive views, spurred in part by his running dialog with the local Romanist preacher, Witzel, who laid special stress upon the role of the law. Nevertheless, when Agricola returned to Wittenberg in 1536 with a view to assuming a professorship which Luther was now in process of arranging for him,[5] the relationship between the two men was at first cordial. Luther appointed Agricola his substitute, both in his pulpit duties and in his university lecturing, during his absence from Wittenberg to attend the conference at Smalcald in early 1537. By the summer of that year, however, Luther had again become disturbed with the heterodoxy of Agricola's views on the subject of the law, as revealed in three of his sermons published at that time, as well as in a set of anonymous theses that were circulating in the town, which Luther attributed to Agricola

---

[3] For a full presentation of Agricola's views, see the monographs by Gustav Kawerau, *Johann Agricola von Eisleben* (Berlin, 1881), and Joachim Rogge, *Johann Agricolas Lutherverständnis* (Berlin, n.d. [1960]). Rogge, pp. 296 ff., gives a complete list of Agricola's forty-five extant publications.
[4] Cf. *LW* 40, 275.
[5] Apparently there was a misunderstanding concerning whether the appointment had in fact been tendered him; cf. Rogge, *op. cit.*, pp. 132 ff.

or his disciples. In these theses not only was Agricola's old polemic against the preaching of the law repeated, but also explicit citations of errors on this topic were given from the writings of both Luther and Melanchthon. Their views, the theses boldly assert, amount to a distortion of the plain meaning of Scripture.[6]

Luther, naturally, was incensed, and in two sermons preached in July and September, 1537, warned against both the theological error and the danger of moral laxity which he saw contained in the "Antinomian" position. Although the two theologians shortly thereafter seemed to have come to terms, the controversy was fueled again by Agricola's submission to the press, without Luther's approval, of a work which attempted to summarize, in thesis form, the Gospel texts for the church year. In a lengthy introduction and preface Agricola developed his argument that repentance and forgiveness should only be preached on the basis of the gospel. Acting in his capacity as dean of the theological faculty, Luther ordered the printed sheets confiscated. Then Luther insisted on publishing the anonymous theses and holding a public disputation with Agricola on their contents.[7] This "First Antinomian Disputation" took place on December 18, 1537, although Agricola failed to appear. After still further negotiations, Agricola agreed to another meeting at which he should publicly admit his errors and declare his agreement with Luther's views. This he did at the Second Disputation, held on January 12, 1538. Luther, in his remarks prepared for these two disputations,[8] holds firmly to the necessity for humbling the sin-

---

[6] The theses were later printed at Luther's initiative, together with his set of countertheses, as a basis for discussion at the disputation of December 18, 1537. See WA 39I, 343 ff.

[7] Cf. above, n. 6.

[8] The text of the documents connected with the controversy, including six sets of theses prepared at various times by Luther as well as the three full-scale disputations, may be found in WA 39I, 360-584. The text of the third disputation has been shown by modern scholars to have suffered emendation, probably by insertion of Melanchthonian material. See Werner Elert, *Law and Gospel*, trans. by Edward H. Schroeder ("Facet Books, Social Ethics Series," No. 16; Philadelphia: Fortress, 1967), pp. 38 ff., and, in addition to the other works there referred to, Gerhard Ebeling's further comments on the textual question in his essay, "On the Doctrine of the *Triplex Usus Legis* in the Theology of the Reformation," *Word and Faith*, trans. by James W. Leitch (Philadelphia: Fortress, 1963), pp. 62-78, especially p. 62, n. 2. From among the extensive further literature on the question of a twofold or threefold function of the law in Luther's thought, the study by Wilfried Joest, *Gesetz und Freiheit: Das Problem des Tertius usus legis bei Luther und die neutestamentliche Parainese* (Göttingen, 3rd ed., 1961), deserves special mention in the present context for its clear presentation of Agricola's views (pp. 46 ff.).

ner through the preaching of the law before the greatness of the redemption accomplished in Christ can be realized. The law is not superseded by the gospel; rather it serves continually as God's instrument in bringing men to the gospel. Even the Christian, Luther points out, constantly needs the law's rebuke.

Despite their public reconciliation, Luther once more became suspicious of Agricola's views during the succeeding months, perhaps incited, as Agricola later complained, by accusations made by his enemies that his assertions of agreement with Luther were insincere.[9] The *Table Talk* during this period contains several harsh comments about Agricola; Luther ranges him with Münzer, Karlstadt, Zwingli, and other such antagonists.[10] On September 6, 1538, yet another disputation was held, the third in the series, from which Agricola once again, however, absented himself. Here Luther shows himself very concerned to defend himself against the charge of unfaithfulness to his own earlier teaching, and in a passage of unusual autobiographical as well as doctrinal interest, he speaks as follows: "True it is that at the early stage of this movement we began strenuously to teach the gospel and made use of these words which the Antinomians now quote. But the circumstances of that time were very different from those of the present day. Then the world was terrorized enough when the pope or the visage of a single priest shook the whole of Olympus, not to mention earth and hell, over all which that man of sin had usurped the power to himself. To the consciences of men so oppressed, terrified, miserable, anxious, and afflicted, there was no need to inculcate the law. The clamant need then was to present the other part of the teaching of Christ in which he commands us to preach the remission of sin in his name, so that those who were already sufficiently terrified might learn not to despair, but to take refuge in the grace and mercy offered in Christ. Now, however, when the times are very dissimilar from those under the pope, our Antinomians—those suave theologians—retain our words, our doctrine, the joyful tidings concerning Christ, and wish to preach this alone, not observing that

---

[9] Cf. below, p. 108, where reference is made to the charge that Agricola was only awaiting Luther's death to reveal his true views, while claiming fidelity to Luther.
[10] WA, TR 4, 97.

men are other than they were under that hangman, the pope, and have become secure, froward, wicked violators—yea, Epicureans who neither fear God nor men. Such men they confirm and comfort by their doctrine. In those days we were terrorized so that we trembled even at the fall of a leaf. . . . But now our softly singing Antinomians, paying no attention to the change of the times, make men secure who are of themselves already so secure that they fall away from grace. . . . Our view hitherto has been and ought to be this salutary one—if you see the afflicted and contrite, preach grace as much as you can. But not to the secure, the slothful, the harlots, adulterers, and blasphemers."[11]

In December, 1538, Agricola approached Luther once more for a reconciliation, motivated partly, no doubt, by anxiety lest his stipend be cut off by the elector. To avoid any possibility of a miscarriage of the arrangement, he asked Luther himself to prepare the text of a recantation which he, Agricola, would sign. In response, Luther set about to prepare the text of the present treatise, wherein, much to Agricola's dismay, he embedded the one sentence which could be considered to constitute such a recantation (see below, p. 108) in the context of a harsh and satirical polemic, casting the whole in the form of an open letter to one of Agricola's arch-antagonists.[12]

The fact that Agricola was not alone in feeling that he was being treated unfairly is shown by the fact that at this very time his academic colleagues rallied to his side and proposed to elect him dean of the faculty of arts in the university. Only Luther's vehement objections stymied the project. As the controversy continued, Agricola appealed first to the rector of the university and then, on March 31, 1540, to the elector for an impartial investigation of the matter. This drew from Luther the angry reply, *Against the Eislebener*.[13] Now Agricola was depicted as not only misleading but positively dangerous to the social and ethical order; Antino-

---

[11] WA 39I, 571 ff.; English translation as given in James Mackinnon, *Luther and the Reformation* (4 vols.; London, 1930), IV, 171-172. Mackinnon's chapter on "Luther and Theological Dissent" (*ibid.*, pp. 161 ff.), gives a thorough review of the Antinomian controversy.
[12] Caspar Güttel; see below, p. 107, n. 1.
[13] *Wider den Eisleben.* WA 51, 429 ff.

mianism is a scourge the spread of which cannot be tolerated. The elector, in finally initiating an inquiry, ordered Agricola confined to the town of Wittenberg until the dispute should be settled. The latter, however, weary of the controversy, took flight in mid-August, 1540, for Berlin, where he had been offered the position of preacher to the court of Elector Joachim II of Brandenburg. Subsequently he formally withdrew his complaint against Luther, submitted a theological retraction (based on a draft prepared earlier by Melanchthon), and was reinstated—at least formally—in the good graces of both the political and theological authorities of Electoral Saxony.[14]

Against the Antinomians has not hitherto appeared in English. Our translation is based on the text, *Wider die Antinomer*, as it is given in *WA* 50, 468-477. A modern German version appears in the third Munich edition of Luther's works (H. H. Borchert and Georg Merz [eds.], *Martin Luther: Ausgewählte Werke*, Vol. IV [Munich, 1957], pp. 192-201), and, with certain revisions and omissions, in Kurt Aland (ed.), *Luther Deutsch*, Vol. IV (2nd rev. ed.; Stuttgart and Göttingen, 1964), pp. 224-231.

---

[14] The Antinomian question is dealt with in Articles IV-VI of the *Formula of Concord*. Recent monographs on the subject include Lauri Haikola, *Usus Legis* (Uppsala, 1958); Robert C. Schultz, *Gesetz und Evangelium in der lutherischen Theologie des 19. Jahrhunderts* (Berlin, 1958); and Gerhard O. Forde, *The Law-Gospel Debate: An Interpretation of Its Development* (Minneapolis: Augsburg, 1969).

AGAINST THE ANTINOMIANS

To the reverend and learned Dr. Caspar Güttel,[1] pastor in Eisleben, my especially good friend in Christ: Grace and peace in Christ, dear Doctor. I assume that you received some time ago a copy of the disputations against the new spirits who have dared to expel the law of God or the Ten Commandments from the church and to assign them to city hall.[2] I never expected that such false spirituality would occur to the mind of man, much less that anyone would support it. However, God warns us through such instances to be on our guard and not to assume that the devil is as far from us as these secure, impudent spirits suppose. We must, indeed, constantly call upon God for help and protection with awe, humility, and earnest prayer; otherwise the devil will soon conjure up a phantom before our eyes, so that we are ready to swear that it is the Holy Spirit himself. Of this we are warned not only by the heretics of the past but also by great and terrible examples from our own time.

I would probably have been willing to forget all the hurts I endured if I could have rested in the hope that I had clarified my position and defended myself sufficiently in the disputation. But Satan would not tolerate this. He is always trying to get me involved and giving the impression that things are not so bad between me and them. I am afraid that if I had died at Smalcald,[3]

---

[1] Caspar Güttel (1471-1542), like Luther, was originally an Augustinian monk. An early convert to the cause of the Reformation, he became a good friend of Luther and had a distinguished career as pastor and preacher in Eisleben. Agricola counted him among his foremost opponents. See Gustav Kawerau, *Kaspar Güttel, ein Lebensbild aus Luthers Freundeskreise* (Halle/Salle, 1882).
[2] Among the theses attributed to Agricola or his disciples that Luther had published in December, 1537 (cf. above, p. 103), there was one which stated that the place for the Decalogue is in the city hall, not in the pulpit (*Decalogus gehort auff das Ratthaus, nicht auff den Predigstuel*). WA 39I, 344. This statement cannot be located in any of Agricola's writings, but he was said to have made a remark to this effect to Melanchthon in the earlier debate over the *Articles of Visitation* (see above, pp. 101-102).
[3] Luther had suffered from a severe attack of kidney stones at Smalcald and had been unable to attend the conference.

I would forever have been called the patron of such spirits, since they appeal to my books. In fact, they did all this behind my back, without my knowledge and against my will. They did not have enough consideration to show me so much as a word or a letter of all this, nor did they question me at all about this matter. Thus I was forced to take Master John Agricola to task more than once, beyond what he experienced in the disputation, and I said to him in the presence of our doctors and theologians all that had to be said. For he is the instigator and the master of this game. I did this so that it would become very clear to him what a favor he did me and my spirit in this—a spirit for which I also, by the way, have some regard![4]

His words and actions indicated that he yielded humbly, and he promised to desist where he had carried things too far, and to hold with us. I had to take his word for this and be content. But when the same things continued to appear, and they even boasted (as in writings which arrived here), that Dr. Martin and Master Eisleben were in hearty accord with one another, I pressed him to issue a public disavowal in print. Otherwise there would be no prospect of rooting out the poison in Eisleben and the surrounding area. He declared himself willing to do this; but since he feared that he could not compose a statement that would command sufficient respect, he urged me to do it. He also said that I should do it as I saw fit and he would be entirely satisfied.[5] I accepted the offer and am herewith complying with the request, chiefly to prevent Master Eisleben or anyone else from stating after my death that I did nothing about this matter but that I ignored the whole thing and went along with it.

The matter stands thus: Master John Eisleben wishes to withdraw what he taught or wrote against the law or the Ten Commandments and to stand with us here in Wittenberg, as the *Confession* and the *Apology* did before the emperor at Augsburg; and if he should later depart from this or teach otherwise, it will be

---

[4] A satirical reference to Agricola's claim to be more faithful to the spirit of the early Luther than Luther himself; cf. above, pp. 103-105.

[5] To be sure of satisfying Luther with his retraction, Agricola had asked Luther to prepare the text of it; see above, p. 105. The first sentence of the next paragraph below constitutes, in effect, the direct statement of recantation.

worthless and will stand condemned. I would like to praise him for humbling himself in this way. But since it is generally known that he was one of my best and closest friends, I shall leave this to someone else, so that no one will suspect that I am not in earnest about it. If he remains humble, God can and will surely exalt him; but if he departs from this, God can certainly also debase him again.

Therefore, dear Doctor, I ask you not to regard this as simply a personal letter, but to proclaim and publicize it wherever you can, especially to those who are unable to read. For it is being printed to make it available to all who will or can read, so it must not be viewed as addressed solely to you. I have no other way of opposing the devil. In various writings he constantly presents a false picture of me and my views.

It is most surprising to me that anyone can claim that I reject the law or the Ten Commandments, since there is available, in more than one edition, my exposition of the Ten Commandments, which furthermore are daily preached and practiced in our churches. (I am not even mentioning the *Confession* and the *Apology* and our other books). Furthermore, the commandments are sung in two versions, as well as painted, printed, carved, and recited by the children morning, noon, and night.[6] I know of no manner in which we do not use them, unless it be that we unfortunately do not practice and paint them with our deeds and our life as we should. I myself, as old and as learned as I am, recite the commandments daily word for word like a child. So if anyone perchance gained some other impression from my writings and yet saw and perceived that I stressed the catechism so greatly, he might in all fairness have addressed me and said, "Dear Dr. Luther, how is it that you emphasize the Ten Commandments so much, though your teaching is that they are to be discarded?" That is what they should have done, and not worked secretly behind my back and waited for my death, after which they could

---

[6] Between 1520 and 1529 Luther published a number of studies of the Ten Commandments which later served as a basis for his treatment of them in the *Large Catechism* and *Small Catechism* of 1529. His *Treatise on Good Works* of 1520 (*LW* 44, 15-114) also follows the structure of the Decalogue. The two sung versions mentioned here are no doubt Luther's two hymns based on the Ten Commandments: "These Are the Holy Ten Commands" (1524), *LW* 53, 278–279; and "Man, Wouldst Thou Live All Blissfully" (1524), *LW* 53, 281.

make of me what they would.[7] Ah well, let them be forgiven who cease doing this.

To be sure, I did teach, and still teach, that sinners shall be stirred to repentance through the preaching or the contemplation of the passion of Christ, so that they might see the enormity of God's wrath over sin, and learn that there is no other remedy for this than the death of God's Son. This doctrine is not mine, but St. Bernard's.[8] What am I saying? St. Bernard's? It is the message of all of Christendom, of all the prophets and apostles. But how can you deduce from this that the law is to be cast aside? I cannot find such a deduction in my logic textbook. I should like to see or hear the master who could demonstrate it.

When Isaiah 53 [:8] declares that God has "stricken him for the transgression of my people," tell me, my dear fellow, does this proclamation of Christ's suffering and of his being stricken for our sin imply that the law is cast away? What does this expression, "for the transgression of my people," mean? Does it not mean "because my people sinned against my law and did not keep my law"? Or does anyone imagine that there can be sin where there is no law? Whoever abolishes the law must simultaneously abolish sin. If he permits sin to stand, he must most certainly permit the law to stand; for according to Romans 5 [:13], where there is no law there is no sin. And if there is no sin, then Christ is nothing. Why should he die if there were no sin or law for which he must die? It is apparent from this that the devil's purpose in this fanaticism is not to remove the law but to remove Christ, the fulfiller of the law.

For he is well aware that Christ can quickly and readily be removed, but that the law is written in the depth of the heart and cannot be erased. This is clearly seen in the psalms of lamentation.

---

[7] A charge that had been leveled at Agricola by his opponents in the controversy; see above, p. 108. Already in the summer of 1538 Luther spoke of the Antinomians as a "new sect" and discussed them in the same context as he does here: "I have survived three terrible storms: Münzer, the Sacramentarians, and the Anabaptists. When these were quieted others arose." WA, TR 4, 30-32.
[8] Bernard of Clairvaux (ca. 1091–1153). Luther felt that Bernard, although he misinterpreted the Christian faith on some matters, was essentially in agreement with him in the doctrine of justification. Cf. John M. Headley, Luther's View of Church History (New Haven: Yale University Press, 1963), pp. 101-103.

For here the dear saints are unable to bear the wrath of God. This is nothing but the law's perceptible preaching in man's conscience. The devil knows very well too that it is impossible to remove the law from the heart. In Romans 2 [:14-15] St. Paul testifies that the Gentiles who did not receive the law from Moses and thus have no law are nevertheless a law to themselves, being obliged to witness that what the law requires is written in their hearts, etc. But the devil devotes himself to making men secure, teaching them to heed neither law nor sin, so that if sometime they are suddenly overtaken by death or by a bad conscience, they have grown so accustomed to nothing but sweet security that they sink helplessly into hell. For they have learned to perceive nothing in Christ but sweet security. Therefore such terror must be a sure sign that Christ (whom they understand as sheer sweetness) has rejected and forsaken them. That is what the devil strives for, and that is what he would like to see.

It seems to me that these spirits think that all who are listening to the message are pure Christians, without sin—though in reality they are dejected and downcast hearts who feel their sin and fear God and who therefore must be comforted. To such, the dear Jesus can never be portrayed sweetly enough.[9] They need much more of this, as I discovered in many of them—to say nothing of myself. But these spirits themselves are not such Christians, for they are so secure and confident. Neither are their listeners, who also are secure and happy. In one passage a fine, beautiful young woman, a splendid singer, sings thus: "He feeds the hungry so that they rejoice, and sends the rich empty away. He humbles the mighty and exalts the lowly, and his grace is with those who fear him" [Luke 1:50-53]. If the Magnificat speaks the truth, then God must be the foe of the secure spirits who are unafraid, as such spirits who do away with law and sin are sure to be.

Therefore I ask you, dear Doctor, to keep to the pure doctrine as you have always done. Preach that sinners must be roused to repentance not only by the sweet grace and suffering of Christ, by the message that he died for us, but also by the terrors of the law.

---

[9] Cf. the quotation from Luther cited above, pp. 104-105, for his view of the need for preaching grace or judgment depending on the condition of the hearer.

For they are wrong in maintaining that one must follow only one method of preaching repentance, namely, to point to Christ's suffering on our behalf, claiming as they do that Christendom might otherwise become confused and be at a loss to know which is the true and only way. No, one must preach in all sorts of ways—God's threats, his promises, his punishment, his help, and anything else—in order that we may be brought to repentance, that is, to a knowledge of sin and the law through the use of all the examples in the Scriptures. This is in accord with all the prophets and the apostles and St. Paul, who writes in Romans 2 [:4]: "Do you not know that God's kindness is meant to lead you to repentance?"[10]

But suppose I had taught or declared that the law should not be taught in the church, though all my writings prove the opposite and from the beginning have always stressed the catechism. Why should people adhere to me so tenaciously, and thus at the same time oppose me (since my teaching has always been quite the opposite)? I would thus have defected from myself, as I did from the doctrine of the pope. For I will and may truthfully and boastfully say that there is not alive today as sincere and ardent a papist as I once was. These who pass as papists today are not motivated by the fear of God, as I, poor wretch, had to be; they have some other interest, as can readily be seen and as they well know. I had to experience the truth of St. Peter's words: "Grow in the knowledge of our Lord" [II Pet. 3:18]. I see no doctor, no council, no fathers—even if I were able to distill their books and reduce them to the veriest essence—who carried out this "growing" instantly in the beginning and were able to develop it to a state of perfection. By way of proof, even St. Peter had to learn his "growing" from St. Paul (Galatians 2 [:11-14]), and St. Paul learned it from Christ himself, who had to tell him, "My grace is sufficient for you" [II Cor. 12:9].

Dear God, should it be unbearable that the holy church con-

---

[10] A favorite text of the Antinomians. Luther accepts its validity; repentance, in his view, is to be induced by the preaching of both the law *and* the gospel. Indeed, the preaching of Christ's sacrifice on the cross can be the most effective means of humbling the sinner, since it demonstrates how serious is the guilt for which atonement had to be made, as Luther points out two paragraphs below. However, Agricola is mistaken in relying on this alone, apart from the direct preaching of the law.

fesses itself a sinner, believes in the forgiveness of sins, and asks for remission of sin in the Lord's Prayer? How can one know what sin is without the law and conscience? And how will we learn what Christ is, what he did for us, if we do not know what the law is that he fulfilled for us and what sin is, for which he made satisfaction? And even if we did not require the law for ourselves, or if we could tear it out of our hearts (which is impossible), we would have to preach it for Christ's sake, as is done and as has to be done, so that we might know what he did and what he suffered for us. For who could know what and why Christ suffered for us without knowing what sin or law is? Therefore the law must be preached wherever Christ is to be preached, even if the word "law" is not mentioned, so that the conscience is nevertheless frightened by the law when it hears that Christ had to fulfill the law for us at so great a price. Why, then, should one wish to abolish the law, which cannot be abolished, yes, which is only intensified by such an attempt? For the law terrifies me more when I hear that Christ, the Son of God, had to fulfill it for me than it would were it preached to me without the mention of Christ and of such great torment suffered by God's Son, but were accompanied only by threats. For in the Son of God I behold the wrath of God in action, while the law of God shows it to me with words and with lesser deeds.

Good heavens, I should at least be left in peace by my own people! It is enough to be harassed by the papists. One is tempted to say with Job and Jeremiah, "I wish I had never been born."[11] Similarly, I am tempted to say that I wish I had never published my books, and I would not be greatly concerned or hurt if all my books had already disappeared and the books of these fine spirits were offered for sale in all bookstores, as they would like. Then they would get their fill of this great honor. But on the other hand, I dare not regard myself as better than our dear Lord Jesus Christ, who also laments from time to time, "I have labored in vain, and all my pains are for nought."[12] For the devil is lord of the world. I myself could never believe this, that the devil should be the lord and god of the world. But I experienced often enough that this too

[11] Cf. Job 3:1-10; Jer. 20:14-18.
[12] A reference, perhaps, to a text such as Luke 13:34.

is an article of faith: He is "prince of the world, god of this age." However—God be praised—this is not believed by the children of men, and I myself do not fully believe it. For everyone thinks he knows best and hopes that the devil is beyond the ocean and God is tucked in our pocket.

But it is for the sake of the godly who wish to be saved that we must live, preach, write, do, and suffer all. Otherwise, if one contemplates the devil and the false brethren, it seems better not to preach, to write, or to do anything, but only to die early and be buried. For they pervert and revile all things and convert them into objects of offense and damage, just as the devil drives and leads them to do. It is inevitable that we struggle and suffer. We cannot be any better than the dear prophets and apostles who also had the same experience.

They have devised for themselves a new method whereby one is to preach grace first and then the revelation of wrath. The word "law" is not to be heard or spoken. This is a nice little toy[13] from which they derive much pleasure. They claim they can fit the entire Scripture into this pattern and thus they become the light of the world. That is the meaning they foist on St. Paul in Romans 1 [:18]. But they fail to see that he teaches just the opposite. First he calls attention to the wrath of God from heaven and makes all the world sinners and guilty before God; then, after they have become sinners, he teaches them how to obtain mercy and be justified. That is what the first three chapters powerfully and clearly demonstrate. It is also indicative of a particular blindness and stupidity when they claim that the revelation of God's wrath is something different from the law. This is, of course, impossible, for the manifestation of wrath is the law when it is acknowledged and felt, just as St. Paul says, "The law brings wrath" [Rom. 4:15]. So haven't they fixed things smartly when they abolish the law and yet teach it by proclaiming the revelation of wrath? But they reverse the order of things and teach the law after they teach the gospel, and wrath after grace. I can indeed see some of the shameful errors the devil has in mind with this little toy; but I cannot

---

[13] *Katzenstülgen*, a toy chair for dolls.

enlarge on these at present. Moreover, this is unnecessary, because I hope that they will cease.

It also reflected extraordinary arrogance and presumption that they wanted to unearth something novel and uncommon, so that people would say, "I really believe that he is a great man, a second Paul." Why should those in Wittenberg[14] have a monopoly on wisdom? I, too, have a brain, etc. Yes, of course you have a brain, but one that is bent on its own honor and that exposes itself to ridicule with its wisdom. For they want to do away with the law and yet teach wrath, which is the function of the law alone. Thus they merely discard the few letters that compose the word "law," meanwhile affirming the wrath of God, which is indicated and understood by these letters. It is only that they reverse the order fixed by St. Paul and try to place the last first. Isn't this a fine piece of work, before which all the world should stand in amazement? But let this suffice for the time being; for I hope that since Master Eisleben is changing his mind and recanting, the others who derived their views from him will also desist. May God help them to that end. Amen.

In just these terms we could easily, if we wanted, trace the history of the church from its inception. We should perceive that such was at all times the course of events: when God's word flourished somewhere and his little flock was gathered, the devil became aware of the light, and he breathed and blew and stormed against it with strong, mighty winds from every nook and corner in an attempt to extinguish this divine light. And even if one or two winds were brought under control and were successfully resisted, he constantly stormed and blew forth from a different hole against the light. There was no letup or end to it, nor will there be until the Last Day.

I believe that I alone—not to mention the ancients—have suffered more than twenty blasts and rabbles which the devil has blown up against me. First there was the papacy. Indeed, I believe that the whole world must know with how many storms, bulls,

---

[14] Although Agricola was at this time resident in Wittenberg, Luther here still identifies him with Eisleben, where his teachings had gained considerable currency; cf. Luther's comment above, p. 108.

THE CHRISTIAN IN SOCIETY

and books the devil raged against me through these men, how wretchedly they tore me to pieces, devoured and destroyed me. At times I, too, breathed on them a little, but accomplished no more with it than to enrage and incite them all the more to blow and blast me without ceasing to the present day. And then when I had practically stopped fearing such blasts of the devil, he began to blow at me from a different hole by Münzer and the revolt,[15] by which he almost succeeded in extinguishing the light. When Christ had nearly stuffed up this hole, he broke a few panes in the window by means of Karlstadt,[16] and rushed and roared so vehemently that I feared he would carry light and wax and wick away. But God again helped his poor candle and kept it from being snuffed out. Then came the Anabaptists,[17] who flung door and windows open as they tried to extinguish the light. They did create a dangerous situation, but they did not achieve their aim.

Several also raged against the old teachers, both the pope and Luther together: for example, Servetus,[18] Campanus,[19] and others like them. I will not mention here the others who did not attack

[15] The reference is to Thomas Münzer and the Peasants' Revolt of 1524-1525. See above, p. 14, n. 5.
[16] Andreas Bodenstein von Karlstadt (ca. 1480-1541), former colleague of Luther at Wittenberg who broke with him in the early 1520's and wrote numerous treatises challenging particularly Luther's interpretation of the sacraments. See the Introduction to Luther's *Against the Heavenly Prophets*. LW 40, 75-77.
[17] In Luther's mind the Anabaptists were always associated with the Zwickau prophets who created an uproar in Wittenberg in 1521-1522, with Thomas Münzer and the Peasants' Revolt of 1524-1525, and with Karlstadt. Recent scholarship has disputed this interpretation of Anabaptism. Cf. Franklin H. Littell, *The Origins of Sectarian Protestantism* (New York: Macmillan, 1964), pp. 3-11.
[18] Michael Servetus (ca. 1511-1553), Spanish physician and theologian whose anti-Trinitarian views were rejected by Roman Catholics and mainline Protestants alike. Early in 1553 he was interrogated by the inquisitor-general of Lyons, but managed to escape. On his way to Naples he stopped in Geneva, was arrested, tried, and finally burned as a heretic on October 27, 1553. Cf. Roland H. Bainton, *Hunted Heretic: The Life and Death of Michael Servetus, 1511-1553* (Boston: Beacon Press, 1960).
[19] John Campanus (1500-ca. 1575) had studied at Wittenberg between 1527 and 1530. However, he rejected Luther's interpretation of the Lord's Supper and the Trinity. His views corresponded with those Melanchthon condemned in Article I of the *Augsburg Confession* as the heresy of the "Samosatenes, old and new." Tappert (ed.), *The Book of Concord*, p. 28. Cf. also George H. Williams, *The Radical Reformation* (Philadelphia: Westminster Press, 1962), p. 272 *et passim*.

116

me openly in print, whose venomous and base writings and words I personally had to endure. I only wish to say that since I paid history no heed, I had to learn from my own experience that the church, because of the precious word, indeed, because of the cheering, blessed light, cannot live in tranquillity, but must forever live in expectation of new gales from the devil. That is the way it has been from the beginning, as you read in the *Tripartite Ecclesiastical History*[20] as well as in the books of the holy fathers.

And even if I were to live another hundred years and should succeed by the grace of God not only in allaying the past and present storms and rabbles but also all future ones, I realize that this would still not procure peace for our descendants so long as the devil lives and rules. Therefore I am also praying for a gracious hour of death; I care no more for this life.[21] I exhort you, our posterity, to pray and to pursue the word of God with diligence. Keep God's poor candle burning. Be warned and be on the alert, watching lest at any hour the devil try to break a pane or window or fling open a door or tear the roof off in order to extinguish the light; for he will not die before the Last Day. You and I have to die, but after our death he still remains the same as he always has been, unable to desist from his raging.

I can see there in the distance how the devil is puffing out his cheeks so vigorously that he is turning all red as he prepares to blow and rage. But our Lord Christ from the beginning (even when he was in the flesh) struck these puffed cheeks with his fist, so that they emitted nothing but the devil's stinking wind. He still does this today and will ever continue to do so. For Christ does not lie when he declares, "I am with you always, to the close of the age" [Matt. 28:20], and when he assures us that the gates of hell shall not prevail against the church [Matt. 16:18]. At the same time we are enjoined to remain awake and to do our part in preserving the light. We read, "Be watchful," for the devil is called a "roaring lion"

---

[20] The *Historia ecclesiastica tripartita,* a compilation of extracts from Socrates, Sozomenus, and Theodoret, was the principal handbook of church history used in the Middle Ages. Its author and compiler, Cassiodorus (d. *ca.* 570), wished to augment the reworking of Eusebius' church history by Rufinus.
[21] In his later years Luther's thought turned frequently to his own death, especially in times of illness or discouragement. Cf. his remarks concerning his sojourn at Smalcald, above, pp. 107-108.

who "prowls around, seeking some one to devour" [I Pet. 5:8], and this he did not only in the days of the apostles when St. Peter uttered these words; he does so to the end of time. Let us be guided by this. God help us as he helped our forefathers, and as he will help our heirs, to the honor and glory of his divine name forever. For after all, we are not the ones who can preserve the church, nor were our forefathers able to do so. Nor will our successors have this power. No, it was, is, and will be he who says, "I am with you always, to the close of the age." As it says in Hebrews 13 [:8], "Jesus Christ is the same yesterday, and today, and forever," and in Revelation 1 [:8], "He who is and who was and who is to come." This is his name and no one else's; nor may anyone else be called by that name.

A thousand years ago you and I were nothing, and yet the church was preserved at that time without us. He who is called "who was" and "yesterday" had to accomplish this. Even during our lifetime we are not the church's guardians. It is not preserved by us, for we are unable to drive off the devil in the persons of the pope, the sects, and evil men. If it were up to us, the church would perish before our very eyes, and we together with it (as we experience daily). For it is another Man who obviously preserves both the church and us. He does this so plainly that we could touch and feel it, if we did not want to believe it. We must leave this to him who is called "who is" and "today." Likewise we will contribute nothing toward the preservation of the church after our death. He who is called "who is to come" and "forever" will accomplish it. What we are now saying about ourselves in this respect, our ancestors also had to say, as is borne out by the psalms and the Scriptures. And our descendants will make the same discovery, prompting them to join us and the entire church in singing Psalm 124: "If it had not been the Lord who was on our side, let Israel now say," etc.

It is a tragic thing that there are so many examples before us of those who thought they had to preserve the church, as though it were built on them. In the end they perished miserably. Yet such fierce judgment of God cannot break, humble, or check our pride and wickedness. What was Münzer's fate in our day (to say nothing of old and former times), who imagined that the church could not exist without him and that he had to bear it up and rule it? Recently the Anabaptists reminded us forcefully enough how mighty and how close to us the lovely devil is, and how dangerous our pretty thoughts are, impelling us to pause and reflect (according to the advice of Isaiah) before any undertaking, to determine whether it is God or an idol, whether gold or clay. But it is no use —we are so secure, without fear and concern; the devil is far from us, and we have none of that flesh in us that was in St. Paul and of which he complains in Romans 7 [:23], exclaiming that he cannot deliver himself from it as he would like, but that he is captive to it. No, we are the heroes who need not worry about our flesh and our thoughts. We are sheer spirit, we have taken captive our own flesh together with the devil, so that all our thoughts and ideas are surely and certainly inspired by the Holy Spirit, and how can he be found wanting?[22] Therefore it all has such a nice ending—namely, that both steed and rider break their necks.

But this is enough of such lamentations. May our dear Lord Christ be and remain our dear Lord Christ, praised forever. Amen.

---

[22] Luther's ironical résumé of the position he attributes to the Antinomians.

ON THE JEWS AND THEIR LIES

1543

Translated by Martin H. Bertram

INTRODUCTION

The fact that Luther, during the last years of his life, wrote treatises harshly condemnatory of the Jews and Judaism is rather widely known. The treatises themselves, however, have not previously been available in English. The publication here of the longest and most infamous of them, *On the Jews and Their Lies,* will no doubt prove dismaying to many readers, not only because it shows Luther at his least attractive, but also because of the potential misuse of this material. The risk to Luther's reputation is gladly borne, since the exposure of a broader range of his writings to modern critical judgment is an inherent purpose of this American edition. However, the thought of possible misuse of this material, to the detriment either of the Jewish people or of Jewish-Christian relations today, has occasioned great misgivings. Both editor and publisher, therefore, wish to make clear at the very outset that publication of this treatise is being undertaken only to make available the necessary documents for scholarly study of this aspect of Luther's thought, which has played so fateful a role in the development of anti-Semitism in Western culture. Such publication is in no way intended as an endorsement of the distorted views of Jewish faith and practice or the defamation of the Jewish people which this treatise contains.

Already upon its first appearance in the year 1543, Luther's treatise caused widespread dismay, not only among contemporary Jews but also in Protestant circles. Melanchthon and Osiander are known to have been unhappy with its severity. Henry Bullinger, in correspondence with Martin Bucer, remarked that Luther's views reminded him of those of the Inquisitors. And a subsequent document prepared by the churches of Zurich declared (speaking specifically of the treatise *Vom Schem Hamphoras,* published later in 1543), that "if it had been written by a swineherd, rather than by a celebrated shepherd of souls, it might have some—but very little—justification."[1]

---

[1] The Zurich document is cited in WA 53, 574. For the views of Melanchthon, Osiander, Bullinger, and other Reformers, see Lewin, *Luthers Stellung zu den Juden* (cited above, p. 96, n. 35), pp. 97 ff.

The negative attitudes expressed in these late treatises struck Luther's contemporaries with special force, as they do us, in view of the fact that earlier in his career he had shown marked sympathy toward the Jews. In the great controversy over the banning of Hebrew books that had rocked Europe in the 1510's, the young Luther had sided with the great Hebraist John Reuchlin (uncle of Philip Melanchthon) over against the Dominican, John Pfefferkorn.[2] And in 1523, when Luther's treatise *That Jesus Christ Was Born a Jew* was published, it was greeted with joy by Jewish readers throughout Europe. Employing his gifts of satire in this instance on the Jews' behalf, he had written: "Our fools, the popes, bishops, sophists, and monks—the crude asses' heads—have hitherto so treated the Jews that anyone who wished to be a good Christian would almost have had to become a Jew. If I had been a Jew and had seen such dolts and blockheads govern and teach the Christian faith, I would sooner have become a hog than a Christian. . . . I hope that if one deals in a kindly way with the Jews and instructs them carefully from Holy Scripture, many of them will become genuine Christians and turn again to the faith of their fathers, the prophets and patriarchs. They will only be frightened further away from it if their Judaism is so utterly rejected that nothing is allowed to remain, and they are treated only with arrogance and scorn." We Gentiles, Luther adds, should remember that it is not we but the Jews, who, humanly speaking, are closest to Christ: "We are aliens and in-laws; they are blood relatives, cousins, and brothers of our Lord."[3]

In 1523, Luther's concluding comments and practical recommendations concerning the Jews had been as follows: "Therefore, I would request and advise that one deal gently with them and instruct them from Scripture; then some of them may come along. Instead of this we are trying only to drive them by force, slandering them, accusing them of having Christian blood if they don't

---

[2] See Luther's letter to Spalatin of August 5, 1514 (*LW* 48, 9 ff.), and further index references in *LW* 48 to Reuchlin. For details, see Armas K. E. Holmio, *The Lutheran Reformation and the Jews* (Hancock, Mich.: Finnish Lutheran Book Concern, 1949), ch. 3, together with Marvin Lowenthal, *The Jews of Germany: The Story of Sixteen Centuries* (Philadelphia: Jewish Publication Society, 1936), ch. 10.

[3] *LW* 45, 200-201.

stink, and I know not what other foolishness. So long as we thus treat them like dogs, how can we expect to work any good among them? Again, when we forbid them to labor and do business and have any human fellowship with us, thereby forcing them into usury, how is that supposed to do them any good? If we really want to help them, we must be guided in our dealings with them not by papal law but by the law of Christian love. . . . If some of them should prove stiff-necked, what of it? After all, we ourselves are not all good Christians either."[4]

Compared to the foregoing, Luther's treatise *On the Jews and Their Lies* exhibits quite a different attitude. Here we find Luther treating the Jews with the "arrogance and scorn" that he had condemned in 1523. Rather than "dealing gently" with them, he advocates exceedingly harsh measures. As to the Jews' economic role, he overlooks the fact that the restrictions which a Christian society had placed on them may have forced them into usury; he now blames solely their avarice and cunning. In short, his image of the Jews and his recommendations concerning them are almost wholly negative.

How is this transformation to be explained? A variety of theories have been propounded to account for it. Reference has been made to Luther's declining health in his later years; to his frustration over the obstacles being met by the Reformation and the splintering of the movement; and to certain untoward experiences with the Jews, such as the encounter that he mentions in the present treatise.[5] The significance of such factors, however, is difficult to estimate.

More clearly influential was the point on which he himself lays repeated emphasis—namely, what he terms Jewish "obstinacy," that is, the Jews' refusal to accept conversion. His hopes for such conversions had been running high in the 1520's and are clearly reflected in the treatise *That Jesus Christ Was Born a Jew*. The motive for the kindly treatment that he recommends is, as he frankly admits, "that we might convert some of them"; and the treatise ends on an expectant note: "Here I will let the matter rest

---

[4] *Ibid.*, 229.
[5] Cf. below, pp. 191-192.

for the present, until I see what I have accomplished."[6] The response among Jews in Germany and elsewhere to the work of Luther at this time was indeed quite positive. They welcomed the return to Hebraic sources which the Reformation encouraged, as well as the breakup of the monolithic power of the medieval church which it was effecting, and which seemed to promise greater freedom for minority groups. Some Jewish people even hailed Luther's work as presaging the coming of the Messiah.[7] The number of actual conversions, however, was very small. On the contrary, Luther subsequently began to hear of Jewish efforts to convert Christians; it was such reports that led to the writing of his treatise *Against the Sabbatarians*. Both there and in the present treatise he refers several times to the disappointment of his hopes in this respect.[8]

Yet another theory, propounded by Newman, Lowenthal, and others, refers to Luther's attitude to the Judiac elements within Christian theology. Although his own reformatory work may be viewed as an expression of the prophetic spirit, he later grew fearful of what he regarded as a misinterpretation and exaggeration of Old Testament motifs on the part of chiliastic radicals, Sabbatarians, anti-Trinitarians, and other such groups. He therefore (according to this view) turned in anger both against these "Judaizers" and against the Jews as such.

It may be, however, that there was not so great a change in Luther's attitude toward the Jews as has commonly been thought. A closer inspection of his utterances on the question throughout his career reveals that he was never so unambiguously positive toward them as a reading of his 1523 treatise in isolation would suggest. Wilhelm Maurer has demonstrated, in fact, that Luther's earliest lectures—those on the Psalms, delivered in 1513-1515—already contained in essence the whole burden of his later charges against the Jews.[9] The Jews, Luther asserts in these lectures, suffer continually

---

[6] *LW* 45, 229.
[7] Newman, *Jewish Influence on Christian Reform Movements* (cited above, p. 60, n. 5), p. 628; Lewin, *op. cit.*, pp 18 f.
[8] Cf. below, pp. 137, 177, 253.
[9] Maurer, *"Die Zeit der Reformation,"* in Rengstorf and von Kortzfleisch (eds.), *Kirche und Synagoge* (cited above, p. 61, n. 7), pp. 378 ff.

under God's wrath; they are paying the penalty for their rejection of Christ. They spend all their efforts in self-justification, but God will not hear their prayers. Neither kindness nor severity will improve them. They become constantly more stubborn and more vain. Moreover, they are active enemies of Christ; they blaspheme and defame him, spreading their evil influence even into Christian hearts. As for Jewish efforts to interpret Scripture, these, Luther asserts, are simply lies. They forsake the word of God and follow the imaginations of their hearts. It would be quite wrong, he concludes, for Christians to extend tolerance to those who hold such views.

Similar sentiments are expressed in Luther's *Lectures on Romans* of 1515-1516; and as for Luther's role in the Reuchlin controversy, it appears that he, like most of his contemporaries, regarded the chief issues as being freedom of inquiry, the role of ecclesiastical authority, and the preservation of Hebrew literature for scholarly purposes, rather than the merits of Judaism or the Jews as such.

In short, the evidence indicates that the Luther of these earlier years shared to the full in the medieval prejudices against the Jews. From this perspective, his more favorable attitude toward the Jews as expressed in the early 1520's is to be understood as a temporary modification of the underlying negative stereotype which characterized his earliest statements, and to which he returned in his later treatises. That underlying stereotype, in turn, can be understood only in terms of the medieval background.[10]

The place of the Jew in a culture as dominated by the Christian faith and by Christian institutions as was medieval Europe had long been problematic. Already in the patristic period, the church's polemic against Judaism had produced a highly negative image of the Jew. As a modern Jewish thinker has written, speaking of the new religion's daughter-relationship to the old: "The children did

---

[10] See further, for a survey of alternative interpretations of Luther's writings on the Jews, Kurt Meier, "*Zur Interpretation von Luthers Judenschriften,*" in James Atkinson *et al., Vierhundertfünfzig Jahre lutherische Reformation, 1517–1967, Festschrift für Franz Lau zum 60. Geburtstag* (Göttingen: Vandenhoeck & Ruprecht, 1967), pp. 233-251.

not arise and call the mother blessed; instead, they called the mother blind."[11] Probably the most virulent of anti-Jewish spokesmen in the ancient church was John Chrysostom. In the year 387 he preached a series of sermons against the Jews, concerning which the historian James Parkes comments: "In these discourses there is no sneer too mean, no gibe too bitter for him to fling at the Jewish people. No text is too remote to be able to be twisted to their confusion, no argument is too casuistical, no argument too startling for him to employ. . . ."[12]

The so-called "dark ages," marked by relative social disorganization in Europe, were on the whole a period of respite for the Jews. But the more Western culture moved toward the unity of the "medieval synthesis," the more the Jews appeared as an anomaly, a rent in the otherwise seamless robe of Christendom. The First Crusade, organized to combat the Muslim occupiers of the Holy Land, turned against "the infidel at home," and from this year, 1096, medieval history is marked by a never-ending series of persecutions, pogroms, and expulsions of the Jews. All this comes to a climax in what Israel Abrahams, in his classic study of *Jewish Life in the Middle Ages*,[13] calls "that black age in Jewish life, the sixteenth century, the century of the ghetto and degradation." It dawned with the forced dissolution of the most substantial and most learned Jewish community in Europe, that of Spain, from which Jews were expelled by decree of Ferdinand and Isabella in 1492. Meanwhile the Inquisition had been employed to ferret out those of dubious faith among the Marranos, Spanish Jews who had been forcibly converted. Already in 1290 Jews had been entirely expelled from England, in 1394 from France. Now, as the sixteenth century proceeded, the disparate German principalities and cities followed suit.

The full story of Christian-Jewish relations during this period cannot be recounted here;[14] suffice it to say that Luther lived in an

---

[11] Abraham Joshua Heschel, *The Insecurity of Freedom: Essays on Human Existence* (New York: Farrar, Straus & Giroux, 1966), p. 169.
[12] *The Conflict of the Church and the Synagogue: A Study in the Origins of Antisemitism* (New York: Atheneum, 1969), p. 163.
[13] New York: Atheneum, 1969 (reprinted from the edition of 1896), p. 64.
[14] A comprehensive survey is provided by Salo W. Baron in his *A Social and Religious History of the Jews*, Vol. XIII, *Inquisition, Renaissance, and Reformation* (New York: Columbia University Press, 1969). See also Guido Kisch,

atmosphere surcharged with anti-Judaism. Moreover, he had specific models on which to draw when composing his own anti-Jewish tracts. Not only were there the documents of the Reuchlin-Pfefferkorn controversy earlier in the century; more recently, key figures in both the Protestant and the Roman Catholic camps had issued blasts against the Jews. The Strassburg Reformer Martin Bucer published a treatise *On the Jews* in 1539 which caused him to be regarded by the Jews, for the time being, as their chief antagonist among the Protestants. Compared with Luther's subsequent proposals, however, Bucer's program for dealing with the Jews was relatively moderate, though the area of overlap is obvious. No new synagogues were to be built. The Jews were to refrain from "insulting" Christianity, and were to be compelled to attend Christian sermons. They were to abjure whatever the Talmud had added to the Scriptures, to be barred from all business activity, and to be assigned to menial tasks. The Jews, Bucer declared, are implacable foes of the true faith, just like the papists and the Turks.[15]

Two years later Luther's arch-antagonist John Eck published a similar treatise entitled *Refutation of a Jew-Book* (*Ains Judenbuechlins Verlegung*). Fulminating against the "cunning, false, perjured, thievish, vindictive, and traitorous Jews," he decries the security and freedom they had hitherto been granted and recommends new and more stringent anti-Jewish laws.[16] As the historian Heinrich Graetz comments, noting the similarity of Eck's treatise to Luther's published two years later, "These two passionate opponents were of one heart and soul in their hatred of Jews."[17]

The Jews in Medieval Germany: A Study of Their Legal and Social Status (Chicago: University of Chicago Press, 1949).
[15] Bucer's views are summarized in Stern, *Josel of Rosheim* (cited above, p 61, n. 7), p. 165. This volume offers invaluable background information for the study of Luther's writings on the Jews.
[16] *Ibid.*, p. 183.
[17] Graetz, *History of the Jews* (Philadelphia: Jewish Publication Society, 1946 [reprinted from the edition of 1893–1894]), IV, 546 f. The "Jew-Book" which Eck set himself to refute was, significantly, the work of the Lutheran pastor and theologian Andreas Osiander, who unlike Luther had remained sympathetic to the Jews. Osiander's tract defended the Jews against the charge of ritual murder, shrewdly analyzing some of the possible causes for the making of such accusations, e.g., the effort of parents whose children had died of neglect or of unknown causes to shift the blame to Jews. Cf. Stern, *op. cit.*, pp. 181 ff.

Further grist for Luther's mill was provided by works written by Jewish converts to provide both an explanation and an exposé of the practices of their former co-religionists. One such work whose influence is detectable in the present treatise dates from the period of the Reuchlin controversy. Entitled *On the Life and Customs of the Jews* (*De Vita et Moribus Iudeorum Liberus*), it was written by the former rabbi Victor of Carben, and published in Paris in 1511. Most fully utilized by Luther was a book published at Augsburg in 1530 by Anthony Margaritha entitled *The Whole Jewish Faith* (*Der gantz Jüdisch glaub*).[18] Descendant of an eminent rabbinic family, Margaritha became a convert to Christianity in 1522, and subsequently embraced Lutheranism. His book so appealed to Luther that he had it read to him at table.[18a] The Jewish community, however, considered it inaccurate and slanderous and petitioned the emperor to bar its circulation. Their complaints resulted in Margaritha's imprisonment and eventual expulsion from Augsburg.

For much of the biblical interpretation in the present treatise, Luther was dependent on his medieval predecessors in the chain of Christian polemicists against the Jews. He himself mentions two of his mentors in this respect within the very first paragraphs of the treatise, referring to "those two excellent men, Lyra and Burgensis." Both of these eminent exegetes, whose work dates from the fourteenth and fifteenth centuries respectively, have already been briefly identified in our comments on the treatise *Against the Sabbatarians*.[19] Underlying this work, in turn, was that of Raymund

---

[18] The full title, as it appears on a copy of the first edition of the book, gives a vivid idea of its contents: *Der gantz Jüdisch glaub / mit sampt ainer grundtlichen und war-/hafften anzaygunge Aller Satzungen Ceremonien / Gebetten Haymliche und offentliche Gebreuch deren sich dye / Juden halten durch das gantz Jar Mit schoenen und ge-/gründten Argumenten wyder jren Glauben.* ("The whole Jewish faith, together with a thorough and truthful account of all the regulations, ceremonies, and prayers both for family and public worship, as observed by the Jews throughout the year, with excellent and well-founded arguments against their faith.")

[18a] Cf. *LW* 54, 436 (No. 5504).

[19] Cf. above, p. 66, n. 3, and p. 68, n. 5. Nicholas of Lyra's apologetic treatise *Pulcherrimae quaestiones Iudaicam perfidam in catholicam fide improbantes* will be referred to below as *Pulcherrimae quaestiones*; in *WA* 53, it is cited as *Contra Iudaeos*. Paul of Burgos' *Scrutinium Scripturarum* will be referred to as *Scrutinium*.

Martin, thirteenth-century Dominican scholar (d. 1285) whose anti-Jewish apologetic treatise *Dagger of Faith* (*Pugio fidei*) Luther may also have consulted directly. Another authority whose influence is shown by Luther's text is the early fourteenth-century Genoan, Salvagus Porchetus, whose *Victory Against the Impious Jews* (*Victoria adversus impios Hebraeos*) was brought out in a printed edition at Paris in 1520. This same treatise by Porchetus was to serve as the chief source for Luther's *Vom Schem Hamphoras*, published later in 1543.[20]

Yet another source of Luther's attitude toward the Jews was the undercurrent of superstition in the Middle Ages, in which the Jew figured as the embodiment of all that was uncanny or subversive of established order. Sorcery and magic, poisoning of wells and blighting of crops, desecration of the host and the ritual murder of Christian children—these and all other sorts of evils were charged against them.[21] It appears that Luther accepted this aspect of the popular culture at face value. Moreover, the intensity of his own sense of the demonic lent special vividness to these images in Luther's mind.

It is, indeed, difficult to determine to what extent Luther's anti-Semitism, as expressed in the treatises of 1543, represents merely a distillation and concentration of the traditional Christian enmity toward the Jews, and to what extent it was fed by special elements of his own theology or by the dynamics of his own personality. A psychological analysis is difficult at this historical dis-

---

The prominence especially of Lyra in the received tradition is evidenced by the fact that in the great "Basel Bible" printed in six folio volumes by Frober in 1498 (an edition that Luther himself may well have used), not only does Lyra's *Postilla* or Commentary accompany the biblical text on every page, but also the treatise *Pulcherrimae quaestiones* is reprinted in the final volume—an illustration of how closely biblical exegesis and anti-Jewish polemics were interrelated.

A copy of the Basel Bible owned by the Newberry Library of Chicago was used for checking and amplifying the references in the apparatus of WA 53 for the purposes of the present edition. The Weimar editors themselves used a printed Bible of 1634, *Biblia sacra cum glossa ordinaria,* which contains also Paul of Burgos' *Scrutinium Scripturarum.* Cf. WA 53, 9 f., n. 3, and 413, n. 1.

[20] Cf. WA 53, 579, 609. Porchetus' treatise will be referred to below as *Victoria.*

[21] For details, see Joshua Trachtenberg, *The Devil and the Jews: The Medieval Conception of the Jew and Its Relation to Modern Antisemitism* (New Haven: Yale University Press, 1943).

tance, though it is clear that Luther harbored an immense capacity for hatred, which could be directed variously at Jews, papists, *Schwärmer*, or other adversaries, and which in each case quite obscured the human countenance of the opponent. Equally clear is Luther's gift of language; this in itself lent special intensity to the anti-Jewish commonplaces he repeated.

As to theological factors, it can be said quite firmly that Luther's negativity toward the Jews was in no way due to a Marcionite attitude which would disparage the role of the Hebrew Scriptures or postulate a disjunction between the God of Abraham, Isaac, and Jacob and the God and Father of Jesus Christ. As strongly as he might insist on the distinction between law and gospel, Luther never equated these directly with the Old and the New Testaments as such. The God of wrath and mercy has been at work since the days of Adam, and the Old Testament, like the New, testifies both to his judgment and to his grace. The Hebrew Bible, therefore, is for Luther in every sense Holy Scripture.

This very fact, however—Luther's profound respect for the Old Testament—might well be seen as a factor contributing to the sharpness of his polemic against the Jews. The question at issue in large portions of the present treatise is: Whose interpretation of these sacred Scriptures—that of the Jews or that of the Christians—is correct? For Luther, their proper meaning is Christological. But this in turn raised for him—as it had for earlier participants in the age-old Jewish-Christian controversy—the question of who should be regarded as the legitimate heirs of ancient Israel, the Christian church or postbiblical Judaism. Has the new covenant so entirely replaced the old that the Jews no longer have any claim to the title "people of God"?

These questions have remained under discussion between Jews and Christians down to our own day,[22] although since the unspeakable sufferings visited upon the Jews in the twentieth century in the midst of a "Christian civilization," Christians are perhaps less inclined to press their claims of superiority in an uncritical manner. It is hoped that publication of the present treatise, un-

---

[22] Cf. Hans Joachim Schoeps, *The Jewish-Christian Argument: A History of Theologies in Conflict,* trans. by David E. Green (New York: Holt, Rinehart and Winston, 1963).

pleasant as its contents are, will contribute to greater candor concerning the role which Christians have played in this dark story. As Aarne Siirala has written, "The way in which the often suppressed facts of the history of the persecution of and discrimination against the Jews are brought into the consciousness of Christians will be one decisive element in our being a church of repentance and faith in our generation."[23]

Luther's intent to write something like the present treatise had been intimated at the conclusion of his letter *Against the Sabbatarians*.[24] Later he apparently had a change of heart and resolved "to write no more either about the Jews or against them."[25] However, when in May, 1542, he received from his Moravian friend Count Schlick a copy of a Jewish apologetic pamphlet[26] together with a request that he refute it, Luther decided to break his silence; and once he put pen to paper, the full force of his accumulated wrath burst forth.

The treatise falls into four major parts plus an addendum. In the first, extending to p. 176 below, Luther considers what he calls the "false boasts" of the Jews: their pride of lineage and homeland and their reliance on the covenant of circumcision and on the law. All these Luther considers to be forms of "works-righteousness," and hence contrary to the fundamental principle not only of the Reformation, but also, in his view, of the entire Scriptures. It is only through God's grace, received through faith, Luther insists, that a man—or a people—can be justified.

The second and lengthiest portion of the treatise, extending

---

[23] Siirala, "Luther and the Jews," *Lutheran World: Publication of the Lutheran World Federation*, XI, No. 3 (July, 1964), pp. 337-357; the citation is from p. 337. The entire content of this issue of *Lutheran World*, as well as that of October, 1963 (X, No. 4), was devoted to the theme of Jewish-Christian relations and offers valuable insight into the present state of the question in Lutheran circles. Cf. also the impressive work by a Roman Catholic scholar, Alan T. Davies, *Anti-Semitism and the Christian Mind: The Crisis of Conscience after Auschwitz* (New York: Herder and Herder, 1969).
[24] Cf. above, pp. 97-98.
[25] Cf. below, p. 137.
[26] *Ibid.* The pamphlet has never been identified. It may well have been the source for some of the statements about Jewish teaching and practice which are cited by Luther in his treatise and which are not traceable to other authorities.

from p. 176 to p. 254 below, is devoted to a debate over the exegesis of key biblical passages. In this section of the treatise Luther is most heavily dependent on his predecessors. He may be understood as standing in the centuries-old tradition of apologetically oriented, christological exegesis of the Old Testament that began in the New Testament itself, was further developed by the apostolic fathers and the apologists, and continued to be refined during the patristic and medieval periods down to Luther's own day. His choice of texts (especially the classic four from Genesis 49, II Samuel 23, Haggai 2, and Daniel 9),[27] as well as the manner of his treatment of them, all reflect such precedents. Here his dependence on Nicholas of Lyra and Paul of Burgos is especially close.

If Luther had any quarrel with Lyra, it was at the point of the latter's indebtedness to rabbinic exegesis. Lyra himself had been closely dependent on the commentaries of the great Jewish scholar of the eleventh century, Rabbi Solomon ben Isaac, known as Rashi.[28] Lyra insisted on the primacy of the "literal" sense of Scripture over against the allegorical and other modes of medieval interpretation, and in this Luther agreed with him. For Luther, however, the "literal" sense—also of the Old Testament—was at the same time the "christological" sense. This, of course, the Jewish interpreters disallowed, either denying that the key passages at issue were messianic at all, or demurring at their particular application to Jesus as the Christ. To Luther, however, such rabbinic views were but another species of the "lies" of the Jews. So clear to him is the christological meaning that he can attribute their nonacceptance of it only to willful blindness.[29]

The abusiveness of Luther's critique of the Jews increases measurably as the treatise proceeds. In the third section (pp. 254-267 below), after dealing with their reputed calumnies against the persons of Jesus and of Mary, he recounts some of the grossest

---

[27] Cf. below, p. 176, n. 36.
[28] Cf. Hailperin, *Rashi and the Christian Scholars* (cited above, p. 66, n. 3).
[29] On Luther's methods of biblical interpretation, see Heinrich Bornkamm, *Luther and the Old Testament,* trans. by Eric W. and Ruth C. Gritsch, ed. by Victor I. Gruhn (Philadelphia: Fortress, 1969); Jaroslav Pelikan, *Luther the Expositor (Luther's Works,* Companion Volume [St. Louis: Concordia, 1959]); Willem Jan Kooiman, *Luther and the Bible,* trans. by John Schmidt (Philadelphia: Muhlenberg, 1961).

elements of medieval superstition concerning the Jews. It is with all this behind him that he arrives at the fourth and final main section of the treatise (pp. 267-292 below, the remainder being an addendum). Here he presents to both secular and ecclesiastical authorities his recommendations for action concerning the Jews. This is the section which has been most often quoted in subsequent anti-Semitic literature and which, above all, is responsible for the notoriety of the treatise.

Indeed, one hardly knows whether to be more astonished at the crudity of Luther's language here or at the cruelty of his proposals: let their synagogues be burnt, their houses razed, their prayer books seized, let them be reduced to a condition of agrarian servitude, and—as a "final solution"—let them be expelled from the country. It is no wonder that Rabbi Josel of Rosheim, the great Jewish leader who in 1537 had tried in vain to secure an interview with Luther, was moved to say, upon reading the present treatise: "Never before has a *Gelehrter,* a scholar, advocated such tyrannical and outrageous treatment of our poor people."[30]

Fortunately, Luther's proposals did not meet with a widespread response among the authorities. The treatise itself apparently did not have a large sale, as contrasted to his treatise *That Jesus Christ Was Born a Jew* of twenty years before. In no case were his suggestions for the burning of synagogues, the razing of houses, and the seizure of books followed. In Neumark, however, the right of safe-conduct of Jews was withdrawn. The same occurred in Electoral Saxony, where Elector John Frederick revoked certain concessions he had made to the Jews in 1539 (following his earlier repressive edict of 1537).[31] In so doing, the elector specifically cited Luther's treatises as having alerted him to the Jews' nefarious designs. Philip of Hesse also introduced new measures prohibiting Jews from engaging in money-lending and requiring them to attend Christian sermons. In Brandenburg, on the other hand, Elector Joachim followed a tolerant policy, and when accusations were made against local Jews, Luther's old antagonist

---

[30] From his petition to the magistrates of Strassburg asking that circulation of the treatise be forbidden. Quoted in Lowenthal, *op. cit.,* p. 163, and summarized in Stern, *op. cit.,* pp. 196 ff.

[31] Cf. above, p. 61.

Agricola[32] stepped forward to defend them. The immediate effect of Luther's proposals thus was small;[33] it remained for a later century to refine and systematize them and apply them on a massive scale.

Our translation is based on the text, *Von den Jüden und jren Lügen,* as found in *WA* 53, 417-552. Like *Against the Sabbatarians,* the present treatise was reprinted in the second Munich edition (1934-1940) of Luther's works (H. H. Borchert and Georg Merz [eds.], *Martin Luther: Ausgewählte Werke,* Vol. III of the *Ergänzungsreihe* [Munich, 1936], pp. 61-228), though it had not been included in the first edition (1922 ff.) and was again omitted from the third edition (1948 ff.). Translation of the treatise into English hitherto has been limited to brief excerpts published in fugitive pamphlets.

---

[32] Cf. above, pp. 102-106.
[33] For further details, see Lewin, *op. cit.,* pp. 97 ff., and Maurer, *op. cit.,* pp. 416 ff.

ON THE JEWS AND THEIR LIES

I had made up my mind to write no more either about the Jews or against them.[1] But since I learned that these miserable and accursed people do not cease to lure to themselves even us, that is, the Christians, I have published this little book, so that I might be found among those who opposed such poisonous activities of the Jews and who warned the Christians to be on their guard against them. I would not have believed that a Christian could be duped by the Jews into taking their exile and wretchedness upon himself.[2] However, the devil is the god of the world, and wherever God's word is absent he has an easy task, not only with the weak but also with the strong. May God help us. Amen.

Grace and peace in the Lord. Dear sir and good friend,[3] I have received a treatise in which a Jew engages in dialog with a Christian. He dares to pervert the scriptural passages which we cite in testimony to our faith, concerning our Lord Christ and Mary his mother, and to interpret them quite differently.[4] With this argument he thinks he can destroy the basis of our faith.

This is my reply to you and to him. It is not my purpose to quarrel with the Jews, nor to learn from them how they interpret or understand Scripture; I know all of that very well already. Much less do I propose to convert the Jews, for that is impossible.

---

[1] Luther's chief earlier writings on the subject were his treatise of 1523, *That Jesus Christ Was Born a Jew* (*LW* 45, 199-229), and the open letter of 1538, *Against the Sabbatarians* (cf. above, pp. 57-98). He had promised at the conclusion of *Sabbatarians* to deal with the matter further, but apparently the resolve mentioned above intervened. Five years later, however, came the publication in quick succession of three treatises on the Jewish question: *On the Jews and Their Lies, Vom Schem Hamphoras* ("On the Ineffable Name"), and *The Last Words of David.* Cf. above, p. 65, n. 1.

[2] A reference to the conversions to Judaism of which Luther had received reports.

[3] Luther's correspondent Count Schlick; cf. above, pp. 59, 65.

[4] I.e., in other than christological or trinitarian terms, or without reference to messianic prediction and fulfillment. The Jewish apologetic treatise to which Luther refers has not been identified.

Those two excellent men, Lyra and Burgensis,[5] together with others, truthfully described the Jews' vile interpretation for us two hundred and one hundred years ago respectively. Indeed they refuted it thoroughly. However, this was no help at all to the Jews, and they have grown steadily worse.

They have failed to learn any lesson from the terrible distress that has been theirs for over fourteen hundred years in exile.[6] Nor can they obtain any end or definite terminus of this, as they suppose, by means of the vehement cries and laments to God. If these blows do not help, it is resonable to assume that our talking and explaining will help even less.

Therefore a Christian should be content and not argue with the Jews. But if you have to or want to talk with them, do not say any more than this: "Listen, Jew, are you aware that Jerusalem and your sovereignty, together with your temple and priesthood, have been destroyed for over 1,460 years?" For this year, which we Christians write as the year 1542 since the birth of Christ, is exactly 1,468 years, going on fifteen hundred years, since Vespasian and Titus destroyed Jerusalem and expelled the Jews from the city.[7] Let the Jews bite on this nut and dispute this question as long as they wish.

For such ruthless wrath of God is sufficient evidence that they assuredly have erred and gone astray. Even a child can comprehend this. For one dare not regard God as so cruel that he would punish his own people so long, so terribly, so unmercifully, and in addition keep silent, comforting them neither with words nor with deeds, and fixing no time limit and no end to it. Who would have

---

[5] Famed medieval exegetes and authors of anti-Jewish treatises. Cf. above, pp. 66, 68 n. 5, 130. ("Burgensis" is a Latinate reference to Paul of Burgos.)
[6] A theme that Luther had already developed in *Sabbatarians*. The lesson they should have learned, according to Luther, was that they were being punished for their rejection of the Messiah.
[7] Luther assumes the date of A.D. 74 for the destruction of Jerusalem, rather than the year 70 accepted by modern scholars. For this and other aspects of Luther's chronology as related to the present treatise, see his *Supputatio annorum mundi* (literally, "Reckoning of the Years of the World"), a tabular outline of world history from the creation down to the year 1540 (WA 53, 21-182). Prepared by Luther originally only for his own use, it was published in 1541, with a revised edition in 1545. For the sections dealing with biblical times Luther was heavily dependent on Lyra and Paul of Burgos.

faith, hope, or love toward such a God? Therefore this work of wrath is proof that the Jews, surely rejected by God, are no longer his people, and neither is he any longer their God.[8] This is in accord with Hosea 1 [:9], "Call his name Not my people, for you are not my people and I am not your God." Yes, unfortunately, this is their lot, truly a terrible one. They may interpret this as they will; we see the facts before our eyes, and these do not deceive us.

If there were but a spark of reason or understanding in them, they would surely say to themselves: "O Lord God, something has gone wrong with us. Our misery is too great, too long, too severe; God has forgotten us!" etc. To be sure, I am not a Jew, but I really do not like to contemplate God's awful wrath toward this people. It sends a shudder of fear through body and soul, for I ask, What will the eternal wrath of God in hell be like toward false Christians and all unbelievers? Well, let the Jews regard our Lord Jesus as they will. We behold the fulfillment of the words spoken by him in Luke 21 [:20, 22 f.]: "But when you see Jerusalem surrounded by armies, then know that its desolation has come near . . . for these are days of vengeance. For great distress shall be upon the earth and wrath upon this people."

In short, as has already been said, do not engage much in debate with Jews about the articles of our faith. From their youth they have been so nurtured with venom and rancor against our Lord that there is no hope until they reach the point where their misery finally makes them pliable and they are forced to confess that the Messiah has come, and that he is our Jesus. Until such a time it is much too early, yes, it is useless to argue with them about how God is triune, how he became man, and how Mary is the mother of God. No human reason nor any human heart will ever grant these things, much less the embittered, venomous, blind heart of the Jews. As has already been said, what God cannot reform with such cruel blows, we will be unable to change with words and works. Moses was unable to reform the Pharaoh by means of

---

[8] See above, p. 67, n. 4, for a summary of Luther's reasoning on this point, as set forth already in *Sabbatarians*. A critical examination of this commonplace of Christian apologetics is provided in Jules Isaac, *The Teaching of Contempt: Christian Roots of Anti-Semitism*, trans. by Helen Weaver (New York: Holt, Rinehart and Winston, 1964), pp. 39 ff.

plagues, miracles, pleas, or threats; he had to let him drown in the sea.

Now, in order to strengthen our faith, we want to deal with a few crass follies of the Jews in their belief and their exegesis of the Scriptures, since they so maliciously revile our faith. If this should move any Jew to reform and repent, so much the better. We are now not talking with the Jews but about the Jews and their dealings, so that our Germans, too, might be informed.[9]

There is one thing about which they boast and pride themselves beyond measure, and that is their descent from the foremost people on earth, from Abraham, Sarah, Isaac, Rebekah, Jacob, and from the twelve patriarchs, and thus from the holy people of Israel. St. Paul himself admits this when he says in Romans 9 [:5]: *Quorum patres,* that is, "To them belong the patriarchs, and of their race is the Christ," etc. And Christ himself declares in John 4 [:22], "Salvation is from the Jews." Therefore they boast of being the noblest, yes, the only noble people on earth. In comparison with them and in their eyes we Gentiles (Goyim) are not human; in fact we hardly deserve to be considered poor worms by them. For we are not of that high and noble blood, lineage, birth, and descent. This is their argument, and indeed I think it is the greatest and strongest reason for their pride and boasting.

Therefore, God has to endure that in their synagogues, their prayers, songs, doctrines, and their whole life, they come and stand before him and plague him grievously (if I may speak of God in such a human fashion). Thus he must listen to their boasts and their praises to him for setting them apart from the Gentiles, for letting them be descended from the holy patriarchs, and for selecting them to be his holy and peculiar people, etc. And there is no limit and no end to this boasting about their descent and their physical birth from the fathers.

And to fill the measure of their raving, mad, and stupid folly, they boast and they thank God, in the first place, because they were created as human beings and not as animals; in the second place,

---

[9] Already by the time of writing *Sabbatarians,* Luther had given up his earlier hope of converting large numbers of Jews; he wrote chiefly in order "to fortify the Christians" (see above, p. 66). The same is true in the present treatise. On his remark concerning the need to inform "our Germans," cf. below, p. 190, n. 61.

because they are Israelites and not Goyim (Gentiles); in the third place because they were created as males and not as females.[10] They did not learn such tomfoolery from Israel, but from the Goyim. For history records that the Greek Plato daily accorded God such praise and thanksgiving—if such arrogance and blasphemy may be termed praise of God. This man, too, praised his gods for these three items: that he was a human being and not an animal; a male and not a female; a Greek and not a non-Greek or barbarian.[11] This is a fool's boast, the gratitude of a barbarian who blasphemes God! Similarly, the Italians fancy themselves the only human beings; they imagine that all other people in the world are nonhumans, mere ducks or mice by comparison.

No one can take away from them their pride concerning their blood and their descent from Israel. In the Old Testament they lost many a battle in wars over this matter, though no Jew understands this. All the prophets censured them for it, for it betrays an arrogant, carnal presumption devoid of spirit and of faith. They were also slain and persecuted for this reason. St. John the Baptist took them to task severely because of it, saying, "Do not presume to say to yourselves, 'We have Abraham for our father'; for I tell you, God is able from these stones to raise up children to Abraham" [Matt. 3:9]. He did not call them Abraham's children, but a "brood of vipers" [Matt. 3:7]. Oh, that was too insulting for the noble blood and race of Israel, and they declared, "He has a demon" [Matt. 11:18]. Our Lord also calls them a "brood of vipers"; furthermore, in John 8 [:39, 44] he states: "If you were Abraham's children, you would do what Abraham did. . . . You are of your father the devil." It was intolerable to them to hear that they were not Abraham's but the devil's children, nor can they bear to hear this today. If they should surrender this boast and argument, their whole system which is built on it would topple and change.

I hold that if their Messiah, for whom they hope, should come

---

[10] Three such expressions do occur in the Jewish liturgy, though the first is quoted by Luther in garbled form. Thanks is given that God has not created one a bondman, a heathen (Goy), or a woman. Cf. Joseph H. Hertz (ed. and trans.), *The Authorized Daily Prayer Book* (rev. ed.; New York: Bloch, 1948), pp. 19-21. Luther owed much of his knowledge of such matters to the book *Der gantz Jüdisch glaub* (see above, p. 130, and n. 18).
[11] Cf. Moses Hadas, *Hellenistic Civilization: Fusion and Diffusion* (New York: Columbia University Press, 1959), p. 14.

THE CHRISTIAN IN SOCIETY

and do away with their boast and its basis they would crucify and blaspheme him seven times worse than they did our Messiah; and they would also say that he was not the true Messiah, but a deceiving devil. For they have portrayed their Messiah to themselves as one who would strengthen and increase such carnal and arrogant error regarding nobility of blood and lineage. That is the same as saying that he should assist them in blaspheming God and in viewing his creatures with disdain, including the women, who are also human beings and the image of God as well as we; moreover, they are our own flesh and blood, such as mother, sister, daughter, housewives, etc. For in accordance with the aforementioned threefold song of praise, they do not hold Sarah (as a woman) to be as noble as Abraham (as a man). Perhaps they wish to honor themselves for being born half noble, of a noble father, and half ignoble, of an ignoble mother. But enough of this tomfoolery and trickery.

We propose to discuss their argument and boast and prove convincingly before God and the world—not before the Jews, for, as already said, they would accept this neither from Moses nor from their Messiah himself—that their argument is quite empty and stands condemned. To this end we quote Moses in Genesis 17, whom they surely ought to believe if they are true Israelites. When God instituted circumcision, he said, among other things, "Any uncircumcised male shall be cut off from his people" [Gen. 17:14]. With these words God consigns to condemnation all who are born of flesh, no matter how noble, high, or how low their birth may have been. He does not even exempt from this judgment the seed of Abraham, although Abraham was not merely of high and noble birth from Noah, but was also adjudged holy (Genesis 15) and became Abraham instead of Abram (Genesis 17). Yet none of his children shall be numbered among God's people, but rather shall be rooted out, and God will not be his God, unless he, over and above his birth, is also circumcised and accepted into the covenant of God.

To be sure, before the world one person is properly accounted nobler than another by reason of his birth, or smarter than another because of his intelligence, or stronger and more handsome than

142

another because of his body, or richer and mightier than another in view of his possessions, or better than another on account of his special virtues. For this miserable, sinful, and mortal life must be marked by such differentiation and inequality; the requirements of daily life and the preservation of government make it indispensable.

But to strut before God and boast about being so noble, so exalted, and so rich compared to other people—that is devilish arrogance, since every birth according to the flesh is condemned before him without exception in the aforementioned verse, if his covenant and word do not come to the rescue once again and create a new and different birth, quite different from the old, first birth. So if the Jews boast in their prayer before God and glory in the fact that they are the patriarchs' noble blood, lineage, and children, and that he should regard them and be gracious to them in view of this, while they condemn the Gentiles as ignoble and not of their blood, my dear man, what do you suppose such a prayer will achieve? This is what it will achieve: Even if the Jews were as holy as their fathers Abraham, Isaac, and Jacob themselves, yes, even if they were angels in heaven, on account of such a prayer they would have to be hurled into the abyss of hell. How much less will such prayers deliver them from their exile and return them to Jerusalem!

For what does such devilish, arrogant prayer do other than to give God's word the lie, for God declares: Whoever is born and not circumcised shall not only be ignoble and worthless but shall also be damned and shall not be a part of my people, and I will not be his God. The Jews rage against this with their blasphemous prayer as if to say: "No, no, Lord God, that is not true; you must hear us, because we are of the noble lineage of the holy fathers. By reason of such noble birth you must establish us as lords over all the earth and in heaven too. If you fail to do this, you break your word and do us an injustice, since you have sworn to our fathers that you will accept their seed as your people forever."

This is just as though a king, a prince, a lord, or a rich, handsome, smart, pious, virtuous person among us Christians were to pray thus to God: "Lord God, see what a great king and lord I am! See how rich, smart, and pious I am! See what a handsome lad or lass I am in comparison to others! Be gracious to me, help me, and in view of all of this save me! The other people are not as deserving, because they are not so handsome, rich, smart, pious, noble, and high-born as I am." What, do you suppose, should such a prayer merit? It would merit that thunder and lightning strike down from heaven and that sulphur and hellfire strike from below. That would be just punishment; for flesh and blood must not boast before God. For as Moses says, whoever is born even from holy patriarchs and from Abraham himself stands condemned before God and must not boast before him. St. Paul says the same thing in Romans 3 [:27], as does John 3 [:6].

Such a prayer was also spoken by the Pharisee in the Gospel as he boasted about all his blessings, saying, "I am not like other men." Moreover, his prayer was beautifully adorned, since he said it with thanksgiving and fancied that he was sitting on God's lap as his pet child. But thunder and lightning from heaven cast him down to hell's abyss, as Christ himself declared, saying that the publican was justified but the Pharisee condemned. Oh, what do we poor muck-worms, maggots, stench, and filth presume to boast of before him who is the God and Creator of heaven and earth, who made us out of dirt and out of nothing! And as far as our nature, birth, and essence are concerned, we are but dirt and nothing in his eyes; all that we are and have comes from his grace and his rich mercy.

Abraham was no doubt even nobler than the Jews, since as we pointed out above, he was descended from the noblest patriarch, Noah—who in his day was the greatest and oldest lord, priest, and father of the entire world—and from the other nine succeeding patriarchs. Abraham saw, heard, and lived with all of them, and some of them (as for instance Shem, Shelah, Eber) outlived him by many years.[12] So Abraham obviously was not lacking in nobility of blood and birth; and yet this did not in the least aid him in being numbered among God's people. No, he was idolatrous, and he would have remained under condemnation if God's word had not called him, as Joshua in chapter 24 [:2 f.] informs us out of God's own mouth: "Your fathers lived of old beyond the Euphrates, Terah, the father of Abraham and Nahor; and they served other

---

[12] Cf. the genealogies in Gen. 10 and 11.

gods. Then I took your father Abraham from beyond the River and led him," etc.

Even later, after he had been called and sanctified through God's word and through faith, according to Genesis 15, Abraham did not boast of his birth or of his virtues. When he spoke with God (Genesis 18) he did not say: "Look how noble I am, born from Noah and the holy patriarchs, and descended from your holy nation," nor did he say, "How pious and holy I am in comparison with other people!" No, he said, "Behold, I have taken upon myself to speak to the Lord, I who am but dust and ashes" [Gen. 18:27]. This is, indeed, how a creature must speak to its Creator, not forgetting what it is before him and how it is regarded by him. For that is what God said of Adam and of all his children (Genesis 3 [:19]), "You are dust, and to dust you shall return," as death itself persuades us visibly and experientially, to counteract, if need be, any such foolish, vain, and vexatious presumption.

Now you can see what fine children of Abraham the Jews really are, how well they take after their father, yes, what a fine people of God they are. They boast before God of their physical birth and of the noble blood inherited from their fathers, despising all other people, although God regards them in all these respects as dust and ashes and damned by birth the same as all other heathen. And yet they give God the lie; they insist on being in the right, and with such blasphemous and damnable prayer they purpose to wrest God's grace from him and to regain Jerusalem.

Furthermore, even if the Jews were seven times blinder than they are—if that were possible—they would still have to see that Esau or Edom, as far as his physical birth is concerned, was as noble as Jacob, since he was not only the son of the same father, Isaac, and of the same mother, Rebekah, but he was also the firstborn; and primogeniture at that time conferred the highest nobility over against the other children. But what did his equal birth or even his primogeniture—by virtue of which he was far nobler than Jacob—benefit him? He was still not numbered among God's people, although he called Abraham his grandfather and Sarah his grandmother just as Jacob did, indeed, as has already been said, even more validly than did Jacob. Conversely, Abraham himself as well as Sarah had to regard him as their grandson, the son of Isaac and Rebekah; they even had to regard him as the firstborn and the nobler, and Jacob as the lesser. But tell me, what good did his physical birth and his noble blood inherited from Abraham do him?

Someone may interpose that Esau forfeited his honor because he became evil, etc. We must rejoin, first of all, that the question at issue is whether nobility of blood in itself is so valid before God that one could thereby be or become God's people. If it is not, why then do the Jews exalt this birth so highly before other children of men! But if it is valid, why then does God not guard it from falling? For if God regards physical birth as adequate for making the descendants of the holy patriarchs his people, he dare not let them become evil, thereby losing his people and becoming a non-God. If he does, however, let them become evil, it is certain that he does not regard birth as a means of yielding or producing a people for him.

In the second place, Esau was not ejected from the people of God because he became evil later on, nor was Jacob counted among the people of God in view of his subsequent good life. No, while they were both still in their mother's womb the word of God distinguishd between the two: Jacob was called Esau was not, in accordance with the words, "The elder shall serve the younger" [Gen. 25:23]. This was not at all affected by the fact that they were both carried under the same mother's heart; that they were both nourished with the same milk and blood of one and the same mother, Rebekah; that they were born of her at the same time. So one must say that no matter how identical flesh, blood, milk, body, and mother were in this instance, they could not help Esau, nor could they hinder Jacob from acquiring the grace by which people become God's children or his people; decisive here are the word and calling, which ignore the birth.

Ishmael, too, can say that he is equally a true and natural son of Abraham. But what does his physical birth avail him? Despite this, he has to yield up the home and heritage of Abraham and leave it to his brother Isaac. You may say that Ishmael was born of Hagar while Isaac was born of Sarah. If anything, this strengthens our argument. For Isaac's birth from Sarah was effected by the word of God and not by flesh and blood, since Sarah was past the natural age for bearing children. To discuss the question of birth a bit further, although Ishmael is Abraham's flesh and blood and his natural son, still the flesh and blood of such a holy father does not help him. It rather harms him, because he has no more than flesh and blood from Abraham and does not also have God's word in his favor. The fact that Isaac is descended from the blood of Abraham does not handicap him—even though it was useless to Ishmael —because he has the word of God which distinguishes him from his brother Ishmael, who is of the flesh and blood of the same Abraham.

Why should so much ado be made of this? After all, if birth counts before God, I can claim to be just as noble as any Jew, yes, just as noble as Abraham himself, as David, as all the holy prophets and apostles. Nor will I owe them any thanks if they consider me just as noble as themselves before God by reason of my birth. And if God refuses to acknowledge my nobility and birth as the equal to that of Isaac, Abraham, David, and all the saints, I maintain that he is doing me an injustice and that he is not a fair judge. For I will not give it up and neither Abraham, David, prophets, apostles nor even an angel in heaven, shall deny me the right to boast that Noah, so far as physical birth or flesh and blood is concerned, is my true, natural ancestor, and that his wife (whoever she may have been) is my true, natural ancestress; for we are all descended, since the Deluge, from that one Noah. We did not descend from Cain, for his family perished forever in the flood together with many of the cousins, brothers-in-law, and friends of Noah.

I also boast that Japheth, Noah's firstborn son,[13] is my true, natural ancestor and his wife (whoever she may have been) is my true, natural ancestress; for as Moses informs us in Genesis 10, he is the progenitor of all of us Gentiles. Thus Shem, the second son of Noah, and all of his descendants have no grounds to boast over against his older brother Japheth because of their birth. Indeed, if birth is to play a role, then Japheth as the oldest son and the true

---

[13] Japheth is listed third in the enumeration of Noah's sons in Gen. 9:18, but in the further tables of lineage in 10:2 ff., his offspring are listed first.

heir has reason for boasting over against Shem, his younger brother, and Shem's descendants, whether these be called Jews or Ishmaelites or Edomites. But what does physical primogeniture help the good Japheth, our ancestor? Nothing at all. Shem enjoys precedence—not by reason of birth, which would accord precedence to Japheth, but because God's word and calling are the arbiter here.

I could go back to the beginning of the world and trace our common ancestry from Adam and Eve, later from Shem, Enoch, Kenan, Mahalalel, Jared, Enoch, Methuselah, Lamech; for all of these are our ancestors just as well as the Jews', and we share equally in the honor, nobility, and fame of descent from them as do the Jews. We are their flesh and blood just the same as Abraham and all his seed are. For we were in the loins of the same holy fathers in the same measure as they were, and there is no difference whatsover with regard to birth or flesh and blood, as reason must tell us. Therefore the blind Jews are truly stupid fools, much more absurd than the Gentiles, to boast so before God of their physical birth, though they are by reason of it no better than the Gentiles, since we both partake of one birth, one flesh and blood, from the very first, best, and holiest ancestors. Neither one can reproach or upbraid the other about some peculiarity without implicating himself at the same time.

But let us move on.[14] David lumps us all together nicely and convincingly when he declares in Psalm 51 [:5]: "Behold, I was brought forth in iniquity, and in sin did my mother conceive me." Now go, whether you are Jew or Gentile, born of Adam or Abraham, of Enoch or David, and boast before God of your fine nobility, of your exalted lineage, your ancient ancestry! Here you learn that we all are conceived and born in sin, by father and mother, and no human being is excluded.

But what does it mean to be born in sin other than to be born under God's wrath and condemnation, so that by nature or birth we are unable to be God's people or children, and our birth, glory, and nobility, our honor and praise denote nothing more and can denote nothing else than that, in default of anything to our credit other

---

[14] Here Luther is countering the Jews' claim to special birth with the doctrine of the universality of sin; then he goes on to discuss circumcision.

than our physical birth, we are condemned sinners, enemies of God, and in his disfavor? There, Jew, you have your boast, and we Gentiles have ours together with you, as well as you with us. Now go ahead and pray that God might respect your nobility, your race, your flesh and blood.

This I wanted to say for the strengthening of our faith; for the Jews will not give up their pride and boasting about their nobility and lineage. As was said above, their hearts are hardened. Our people, however, must be on their guard against them, lest they be misled by this impenitent, accursed people who give God the lie and haughtily despise all the world. For the Jews would like to entice us Christians to their faith, and they do this wherever they can. If God is to become gracious also to them, the Jews, they must first of all banish such blasphemous prayers and songs, that boast so arrogantly about their lineage, from their synagogues, from their hearts, and from their lips, for such prayers ever increase and sharpen God's wrath toward them. However, they will not do this, nor will they humble themselves abjectly, except for a few individuals whom God draws unto himself particularly and delivers from their terrible ruin.

The other boast and nobility over which the Jews gloat and because of which they haughtily and vainly despise all mankind is their circumcision, which they received from Abraham. My God, what we Gentiles have to put up with in their synagogues, prayers, songs, and doctrines! What a stench we poor people are in their nostrils because we are not circumcised! Indeed, God himself must again submit to miserable torment—if I may put it thus—as they confront him with inexpressible presumption, and boast: "Praised be Thou, King of the world, who singled us out from all the nations and sanctified us by the covenant of circumcision!"[15] And similarly with many other words, the tenor of all of which is that God should esteem them above all the rest of the world because they in compliance with his decree are circumcised, and that he should condemn all other people, just as they do and wish to do.

In this boast of nobility they glory as much as they do in their

---

[15] A paraphrase rather than a direct quotation from Luther's source, *Der gantz Jüdisch glaub*, the section on circumcision.

physical birth. Consequently I believe that if Moses himself would appear together with Elijah and their Messiah and would try to deprive them of this boast or forbid such prayers and doctrine, they would probably consider all three of them to be the three worst devils in hell, and they would be at a loss to know how to curse and damn them adequately, to say nothing of believing them. For they have decided among themselves that Moses, together with Elijah and the Messiah, should endorse circumcision, yes, rather that they should help to strengthen and praise such arrogance and pride in circumcision, that these should, like themselves, look upon all Gentiles as awful filth and stench because they are not circumcised. Moses, Elijah, and the Messiah must do all that they prescribe, think, and wish. They insist that they are right, and if God himself were to do other than they think, he would be in the wrong.

Now just behold these miserable, blind, and senseless people. In the first place (as I said previously in regard to physical birth), if I were to concede that circumcision is sufficient to make them a people of God, or to sanctify and set them apart before God from all other nations, then the conclusion would have to be this: Whoever was circumcised could not be evil nor could he be damned. Nor would God permit this to happen, if he regarded circumcision as imbued with such holiness and power. Just as we Christians say: Whoever has faith cannot be evil and cannot be damned so long as faith endures. For God regards faith as so precious, valuable, and powerful that it will surely sanctify and prevent him who has faith and retains his faith from being lost or becoming evil. But I shall let this go for now.

In the second place, we note here again how the Jews provoke God's anger more and more with such prayer. For there they stand and defame God with a blasphemous, shameful, and impudent lie. They are so blind and stupid that they see neither the words found in Genesis 17 nor the whole of Scripture, which mightily and explicitly condemns this lie. For in Genesis 17 [:12 f.] Moses states that Abraham was ordered to circumcise not only his son Isaac—who at the time was not yet born—but all the males born in his house, whether sons or servants, including the slaves. All of these were circumcised on one day together with Abraham; Ishmael too, who at the time was thirteen years of age, as the text informs us. Thus the covenant or decree of circumcision encompasses the entire seed of all the descendants of Abraham, particularly Ishmael, who was the first seed of Abraham to be circumcised. Accordingly, Ishmael is not only the equal of his brother Isaac, but he might even—if this were to be esteemed before God—be entitled to boast of his circumcision more than Isaac, since he was circumcised one year sooner. In view of this, the Ishmaelites might well enjoy a higher repute than the Israelites, for their forefather Ishmael was circumcised before Isaac, the progenitor of the Israelites, was born.

Why then do the Jews lie so shamefully before God in their prayer and preaching, as though circumcision were theirs alone, through which they were set apart from all other nations and thus they alone are God's holy people? They should really (if they were capable of it) be a bit ashamed before the Ishmaelites, the Edomites, and other nations when they consider that they were at all times a small nation, scarcely a handful of people in comparison with others who were also Abraham's seed and were also circumcised, and who indubitably transmitted such a command of their father Abraham to their descendants; and that the circumcision transmitted to the one son Isaac is rather insignificant when compared with the circumcision transmitted to Abraham's other sons. For Scripture records that Ishmael, Abraham's son, became a great nation, that he begot twelve princes, also that the six sons of Keturah (Genesis 25 [:1 ff.]), possessed much greater areas of land than Israel. And undoubtedly these observed the rite of circumcision handed down to them by their fathers.

Now since circumcision, as decreed by God in Genesis 17, is practiced by so many nations, beginning with Abraham (whose seed they all are the same as Isaac and Jacob), and since there is no difference in this regard between them and the children of Israel,[16] what are the Jews really doing when they praise and thank God in their prayers for singling them out by circumcision

---

[16] Circumcision is a widespread practice among the Semitic peoples, and was customary in ancient times among the Egyptians and the Canaanites as well as the Jews.

from all other nations, for sanctifying them, and for making them his own people? This is what they are doing: they are blaspheming God and giving him the lie concerning his commandment and his words where he says (Genesis 17 [:12 f.] that circumcision shall not be prescribed for Isaac and his descendants alone, but for all the seed of Abraham. The Jews have no favored position exalting them above Ishmael by reason of circumcision, or above Edom, Midian, Ephah, Epher, etc., all of whom are reckoned in Genesis as Abraham's seed. For they were all circumcised and made heirs of circumcision, the same as Israel.

Now, what does it benefit Ishmael that he is circumcised? What does it benefit Edom that he is circumcised—Edom who, moreover, is descended from Isaac, who was set apart, and not from Ishmael? What does it benefit Midian and his brothers, born of Keturah, that they are circumcised? They are, for all of that, not God's people; neither their descent from Abraham nor their circumcision, commanded by God, helps them. If circumcision does not help them in becoming God's people, how can it help the Jews. For it is one and the same circumcision, decreed by one and the same God, and there is one and the same father, flesh and blood or descent that is common to all. There is absolute equality; there is no difference, no distinction among them all so far as circumcision and birth are concerned.

Therefore it is not a clever and ingenious, but a clumsy, foolish, and stupid lie when the Jews boast of their circumcision before God, presuming that God should regard them graciously for that reason, though they should certainly know from Scripture that they are not the only race circumcised in compliance with God's decree, and that they cannot on that account be God's special people. Something more, different, and greater is necessary for that, since the Ishmaelites, the Edomites, the Midianites, and other descendants of Abraham may equally comfort themselves with this glory, even before God himself. For with regard to birth and circumcision these are, as already said, their equals.

Perhaps the Jews will declare that the Ishmaelites and Edomites, etc., do not observe the rite of circumcision as strictly as they do. In addition to cutting off the foreskin of a male child, the Jews force the skin back on the little penis and tear it open with sharp fingernails, as one reads in their books.[17] Thus they cause extraordinary pain to the child, without and against the command of God, so that the father, who should really be happy over the circumcision, stands there and weeps as his child's cries pierce his heart. We answer roundly that such an addendum is their own invention, yes, it was inspired by the accursed devil, and is in contradiction to God's command, since Moses says in Deuteronomy 4 [:2] and 12 [:32]: "You shall not add to the word which I command you, nor take from it." With such a devilish supplement they ruin their circumcision, so that in the sight of God no other nation practices circumcision less than they, since with such wanton disobedience they append and practice this damnable supplement.

Now let us see what Moses himself says about circumcision. In Deuteronomy 10 [:16] he says: "Circumcise therefore the foreskin of your heart, and be no longer stubborn," etc. Dear Moses, what do you mean? Does it not suffice that they are circumcised physically? They are set apart from all other nations by this holy circumcision and made a holy people of God. And you rebuke them for stubbornness against God? You belittle their holy circumcision? You revile the holy, circumcised people of God? You should venture to talk like that today in their synagogues! If there were not stones conveniently near, they would resort to mud and dirt to drive you from their midst, even if you were worth ten Moseses.

He also chides them in Leviticus 26 [:41], saying: "If then their uncircumcised heart is humbled," etc. Be careful, Moses! Do you know whom you are speaking to? You are talking to a noble, chosen, holy, circumcised people of God. And you dare to say that they have uncircumcised hearts? That is much worse than having a seven-times-uncircumcised flesh; for an uncircumcised heart can have no God. And to such the circumcision of the flesh is of no avail. Only a circumcised heart can produce a people of God, and it can do this even when physical circumcision is absent or is impossible, as it was for the children of Israel during their forty years in the wilderness.

---

[17] Margaritha describes the procedure in *Der gantz Jüdisch glaub*; Raymund Martin and Paul of Burgos also had already referred to it. On these source materials employed by Luther, cf. above, pp. 130-131.

Thus Jeremiah also takes them to task, saying in chapter 4 [:4]: "Circumcise yourselves to the Lord, remove the foreskin of your hearts, O men of Judah and inhabitants of Jerusalem; lest my wrath go forth like fire, and burn with none to quench it. . . ." Jeremiah, you wretched heretic, you seducer and false prophet, how dare you tell that holy, circumcised people of God to circumcise themselves to the Lord? Do you mean to imply that they were hitherto circumcised physically to the devil, as if God did not esteem their holy, physical circumcision? And are you furthermore threatening them with God's wrath, as an eternal fire, if they do not circumcise their hearts? But they do not mention such circumcision of the heart in their prayer, nor do they praise or thank God for it with as much as a single letter. And you dare to invalidate their holy circumcision of the flesh, making it liable to God's wrath and the eternal fire? I advise you not to enter their synagogue; all devils might dismember and devour you there.

In Jeremiah 6 [:10] we read, further, "Their ears are uncircumcised, they cannot listen." Well, well, my dear Jeremiah, you are surely dealing roughly and inconsiderately with the noble, chosen, holy, circumcised people of God. Do you mean to say that such a holy nation has uncircumcised ears? And, what is far worse, that they are unable to hear? Is that not tantamount to saying that they are not God's people? For he who cannot hear or bear to hear God's word is not of God's people. And if they are not God's people, then they are the devil's people; and then neither circumcising nor skinning nor scraping will avail. For God's sake, Jeremiah, stop talking like that! How can you despise and condemn holy circumcision so horribly that you separate the chosen, circumcised, holy people from God and consign them to the devil as banished and damned? Do they not praise God for having set them apart through circumcision both from the devil and from all the other nations and for making them a holy and peculiar people? Yea, "He has spoken blasphemy! Crucify him, crucify him!"

In chapter 9 [:25 f.] Jeremiah says further: "Behold, the days are coming, says the Lord, when I will punish all those who are circumcised but yet uncircumcised—Egypt, Judah, Edom, the sons of Ammon, Moab, and all who dwell in the desert . . . for all these

154

nations are uncircumcised, and all the house of Israel is uncircumcised in heart. . . ."

In the face of this, what becomes of the arrogant boast of circumcision by reason of which the Jews claim to be a holy nation, set apart from other peoples? Here God's word lumps them together with the heathen and uncircumcised, and threatens the same visitation for both. Moreover, the best part of Israel, the noble, royal tribe of Judah, is mentioned here, and after that the entire house of Israel. Worst of all, he declares that the heathen are, to be sure, uncircumcised according to the flesh, but that Judah, Edom, and Israel, who are circumcised according to the flesh, are much viler than the heathen, since they have an uncircumcised heart; and this, as said before, is far worse than uncircumcised flesh.

These and similar passages prove irrefutably that the Jews' arrogance and boast of circumcision over against the uncircumcised Gentiles are null and void, and, unless accompanied by something else, deserves nothing but God's wrath. God says that they have an uncircumcised heart. But the Jews do not pay attention to such a foreskin of the heart; rather they think that God should behold their proud circumcision in the flesh and hear their arrogant boasts over against all Gentiles, who are unable to boast of such circumcision. These blind, miserable people do not see that God condemns their uncircumcised heart so clearly and explicitly in these verses, and thereby condemns their physical circumcision together with their boasting and their prayer. They go their way like fools, making the foreskins of their heart steadily thicker with such haughty boasts before God and their contempt for all other people. By virtue of such futile, arrogant circumcision in the flesh they presume to be God's only people, until the foreskin of their heart has become thicker than an iron mountain and they can no longer hear, see, or feel their own clear Scripture, which they read daily with blind eyes overgrown with a pelt thicker than the bark of an oak tree.[18]

---

[18] Luther's picturesque version of the traditional doctrine of the "veil" which prevents the Jews from understanding the true (christological) meaning of their Scriptures. Cf. also below, pp. 170-171.

If God is to give ear to their prayers and praises and accept them, they must surely first purge their synagogues, mouths and hearts of such blasphemous, shameful, false, and deceitful boasting and arrogance. Otherwise they will only go from bad to worse and arouse God's anger ever more against themselves. For he who would pray before God dare not confront him with haughtiness and lying, he dare not praise only himself, condemn all others, claim to be God's only people, and execrate all the others, as they do. As David says in Psalm 5 [:4 ff.]: "For thou are not a God who delights in wickedness; evil may not sojourn with thee. The boastful may not stand before thy eyes; thou hatest all evildoers. Thou destroyest those who speak lies; the Lord abhors bloodthirsty and deceitful men." But rather, as verse 7 tells us: "I through the abundance of thy steadfast love will enter thy house, I will worship toward thy holy temple in the fear of thee."

This psalm applies to all men, whether circumcised or not, but particularly and especially to the Jews, for whom it was especially given and composed—as was all the rest of Scripture also. And they are more masterfully portrayed in it than all other heathen. For they are the ones who constantly have pursued godless ways, idolatry, false doctrine, and who have had uncircumcised hearts, as Moses himself and all the prophets cry out and lament. But in all this they always claimed to be pleasing to God and they slew all the prophets on this account. They are the malicious, stiff-necked people that would not be converted from evil to good works by the preaching, reproof, and teaching of the prophets. The Scriptures bear witness to this everywhere. And still they claim to be God's servants and to stand before him. They are the boastful, arrogant rascals who to the present day can do no more than boast of their race and lineage, praise only themselves, and disdain and curse all the world in their synagogues, prayers, and doctrines. Despite this, they imagine that in God's eyes they rank as his dearest children.

They are real liars and bloodhounds who have not only continually perverted and falsified all of Scripture with their mendacious glosses from the beginning until the present day. Their heart's most ardent sighing and yearning and hoping is set on the day on which they can deal with us Gentiles as they did with the

Gentiles in Persia at the time of Esther.[19] Oh, how fond they are of the book of Esther, which is so beautifully attuned to their bloodthirsty, vengeful, murderous yearning and hope. The sun has never shone on a more bloodthirsty and vengeful people than they are who imagine that they are God's people who have been commissioned and commanded to murder and to slay the Gentiles. In fact, the most important thing that they expect of their Messiah is that he will murder and kill the entire world with their sword. They treated us Christians in this manner at the very beginning throughout all the world. They would still like to do this if they had the power, and often enough have made the attempt, for which they have got their snouts boxed lustily.[20]

We can perhaps enlarge on this subject later; but let us now return to their false, lying boast regarding circumcision. These shameful liars are well aware that they are not the exclusive people of God, even if they did possess circumcision to the exclusion of all other nations. They also know that the foreskin is no obstacle to being a people of God. And still they brazenly strut before God, lie and boast about being God's only people by reason of their physical circumcision, unmindful of the circumcision of the heart. Against this there are weighty scriptural examples. In the first place, we adduce Job, who, as they say, descended from Nahor.[21] God did not impose circumcision on him and his heirs. And yet his book shows clearly that there were very few great saints in Israel who were the equal of him and of his people. Nor did the prophet Elisha oblige Naaman of Syria[22] to become circumcised; and yet he was sanctified and became a child of God, and undoubtedly many others with him.

Furthermore, there stands the whole of the prophet Jonah, who converted Nineveh to God and preserved it together with kings, princes, lords, land, and people, yet did not circumcise these

---

[19] Cf. Esther 9:5 ff.
[20] It is not clear what basis, if any, Luther may have had for this assertion.
[21] The brother of Abraham; cf. Gen. 11:26. Luther alludes to a rabbinic tradition based on the occurrence of the name "Uz" in Genesis 22:21 and Job 1:1.
[22] Cf. II Kings 5. Luther's list of Gentiles who were accepted by God without being required to be circumcised—Job, Naaman, etc.—is similar to that employed in Sabbatarians. Cf. above, pp. 85 ff.

people. Similarly, Daniel converted the great kings and peoples of Babylon and Persia, such as Nebuchadnezzar, Cyrus, Darius, etc., and yet they remained Gentiles, uncircumcised, and did not become Jews. Earlier, Joseph instructed Pharaoh the king, his princes, and his people, as Psalm 105 [:22] informs us, yet he left them uncircumcised. This, I say, these hardened and inveterate liars know, and yet they stress circumcision so greatly, as though no uncircumcised person could be a child of God. And whenever they seduce a Christian they try to alarm him so that he will be circumcised. Subsequently they approach God and exult in their prayer that they have brought us to the people of God through circumcision—as though this were a precious deed. They disdain, despise, and curse the foreskin on us as an ugly abomination which prevents us from becoming God's people, while their circumcision, they claim, effects all.

What is God to do with such prayer and praise which they bring forth together with their coarse, blasphemous lying, contrary to all Scripture (as already stated)? He will indeed hear them and bring them back to their country! I mean that if they were dwelling in heaven, such boasts, prayers, praise, and lies about circumcision alone would hurl them instantly into the abyss of hell. I have already written about this against the Sabbatarians.[23] Therefore, dear Christian, be on your guard against such damnable people whom God has permitted to sink into such profound abominations and lies, for all they do and say must be sheer lying, blasphemy, and malice, however fine it may look.

But you may ask: Of what use then is circumcision? Or why did God command it so strictly? We answer: Let the Jews fret about that! What does that matter to us Gentiles? It was not imposed on us, as you have heard, nor do we stand in need of it, but we can be God's people without it, just as the people in Nineveh, in Babylon, in Persia, and in Egypt were. And no one can prove that God ever commanded a prophet or a Jew to circumcise the Gentiles. Therefore they should not harass us with their lies and idolatry. If they claim to be so smart and wise as to instruct and circumcise us Gentiles, let them first tell us what purpose circum-

---

[23] Cf. above, pp. 85-87.

cision serves, and why God commanded it so strictly. This they owe us; but they will not do it until they return to their home in Jerusalem again—that is to say, when the devil ascends into heaven. For when they assert that God enjoined circumcision for the purpose of sanctifying them, saving them, making them God's people, they are lying atrociously, as you have heard. For Moses and all the prophets testify that circumcision did not help even those for whom it was commanded, since they were of uncircumcised hearts. How, then, should it help us for whom it was not commanded?

But to speak for us Christians—we know very well why it was given or what purpose it served. However, no Jew knows this, and even when we tell him it is just like addressing a stump or a stone. They will not desist from their boasting and their pride, that is, from their lies. They insist that they are in the right; God must be the liar and he must be in error. Therefore, let them go their way and lie as their fathers have done from the beginning. But St. Paul teaches us in Romans 3 that when circumcision is performed as a kind of work it cannot make holy or save, nor was it meant to do so. Nor does it damn the uncircumcised Gentiles, as the Jews mendaciously and blasphemously say. Rather, he says, "circumcision is of great value in this way—that they were entrusted with the word of God" [cf. Rom. 3:1 ff.]. That is the point, there it is said, there it is found! Circumcision was given and instituted to enfold and to preserve God's word and his promise. This means that circumcision should not be useful or sufficient as a work in itself, but those who possess circumcision should be bound by this sign, covenant, or sacrament to obey and to believe God in his words and to transmit all this to their descendants.

But where such a final cause or reason for circumcision no longer obtained, circumcision as a mere work no longer was to enjoy validity or value, all the more so if the Jews should patch or attach another final cause or explanation to it. This is also borne out by the words in Genesis 17: "I will be your God, and in token of this you shall bear my sign upon your flesh" [cf. Gen. 17:8, 11]. This expresses the same thought found in St. Paul's statement that circumcision was given so that one should hear or obey God's word. For when God's word is no longer heard or kept, then he is surely no longer our God, since we in this life must comprehend and have God solely through his word. This wretched life cannot bear and endure him in his brilliant majesty, as he says in Exodus 36 [33:20]: "Man shall not see me and live."[24]

There are innumerable examples throughout all of Scripture which show what cause or purpose the Jews assigned to circumcision. For as often as God wanted to speak with them through the prophets—whether about the Ten Commandments, in which he reproved them, or about the promise of future help—they were always obdurate, or as the quoted verses from Moses and Jeremiah testify, they were of uncircumcised heart and ears. They always claimed to do the right and proper thing, while the prophets (that is, God himself whose word they preached) always did the wrong and evil thing. Therefore the Jews slew them all, and they have never yet allowed any to die unpersecuted and uncondemned, with the exception of a few at the time of David, Hezekiah, and Josiah. The entire course of the history of Israel and Judah is pervaded by blasphemy of God's word, by persecution, derision, and murder of the prophets. Judging them by history, these people must be called wanton murderers of the prophets and enemies of God's word. Whoever reads the Bible cannot draw any other conclusion.

As we said, God did not institute circumcision nor did he accept the Jews as his people in order that they might persecute, mock, and murder his word and his prophets, and thereby render a service to justice and to God. Rather, as Moses says in the words dealing with circumcision in Genesis 17, this was done in order that they might hear God and his word; that is, that they might let him be their God. Apart from this circumcision in itself would not help them, since it would then no longer be God's circumcision, for it would be without God, contending against his word; it would have become merely a human work. For he had bound himself, or his word, to circumcision. Where these two part company, circumcision remains a hollow husk or empty shell devoid of nut or kernel.

The following is an analogous situation for us Christians: God

---

[24] A succinct statement of Luther's distinction between "God in himself" and "God in his revelation." Cf. Paul Althaus, *The Theology of Martin Luther*, trans. by Robert C. Schultz (Philadelphia: Fortress, 1966), ch. 4.

gave us baptism, the sacrament of his body and blood, and the keys for the ultimate purpose or final cause that we should hear his word in them and exercise our faith therein. That is, he intends to be our God through them, and through them we are to be his people. However, what did we do? We proceeded to separate the word and faith from the sacrament (that is, from God and his ultimate purpose) and converted it into a mere *opus legis*, a work of the law, or as the papists call it, an *opus operatum*—merely a human work, which the priests offered to God and the laity performed as a work of obedience as often as they received it. What is left of the sacrament? Only the empty husk, the mere ceremony, *opus vanum*, divested of everything divine. Yes, it is a hideous abomination in which we perverted God's truth into lies and worshiped the veritable calf of Aaron. Therefore God also delivered us into all sorts of terrible blindness and innumerable false doctrines, and, furthermore, he permitted Muhammad and the pope together with all devils to come upon us.

The people of Israel fared similarly. They always divorced circumcision as an *opus operatum*, their own work, from the word of God, and persecuted all the prophets through whom God wished to speak with them, according to the terms on which circumcision was instituted. Yet despite this, they constantly and proudly boasted of being God's people by virtue of their circumcision. Thus they are in conflict with God. God wants them to hear him and to observe circumcision properly and fully; but they refuse and insist that God respect their work of circumcision, that is, half of circumcision, indeed, the husk of circumcision. God, in turn, refuses to do this; and so they move farther and farther apart, and it is impossible to reunite or reconcile them.

Now, who wishes to accuse God of an injustice? Tell me, anyone who is reasonable, whether it is fitting that God regard the works of those who refuse to hear his word, or if he should consider them to be his people when they do not want to regard him as their God? With all justice and good reason God may say, as the psalm declares [Ps. 81:11 f.]: "Israel would have none of me. So I gave them over to their stubborn hearts, to follow their own counsels." And in Deuteronomy 32 [:21], Moses states, "They have stirred me to jealously with what is no god. . . . So I will stir them to jealousy with those who are no people."

Similarly among us Christians[25] the papists can no longer pass for the church. For they will not let God be their God, because they refuse to listen to his word, but rather persecute it most terribly, then come along with their empty husks, chaff, and refuse, as they hold mass and practice their ceremonies. And God is supposed to recognize them and look upon them as his true church, ignoring the fact that they do not acknowledge him as the true God, that is, they do not want him to speak to them through his preachers. His word must be accounted heresy, the devil, and every evil. This he will indeed do, as they surely will experience, far worse than did the Jews.

Now we can readily gather from all this that circumcision was very useful and good, as St. Paul declares—not indeed on its own account but on account of the word of God. For we are convinced, and it is the truth, that the children who were circumcised on the eighth day became children of God, as the words state, "I will be their God" [Gen. 17:7], for they received the perfect and full circumcision, the word with the sign, and did not separate the two. God is present, saying to them, "I will be their God"; and this completed the circumcision in them. Similarly, our children receive the complete, true, and full baptism, the word with the sign, and do not separate one from the other; they receive the kernel in the shell. God is present; he baptizes and speaks with them, and thereby saves them.

But now that we have grown old, the pope comes along—and the devil with him—and teaches us to convert this into an *opus legis* or *opus operatum*. He severs word and sign from each other, teaching that we are saved by our own contrition, work, and satisfaction. We share the experience related by St. Peter in II Peter 2 [:22]: "The dog turns back to his own vomit, and the sow is washed only to wallow in the mire." Thus our sacrament has become a work, and we eat our vomit again. Likewise the Jews, as they grew old, ruined their good circumcision performed on the

---

[25] Luther considers the Jews a prototype of legalism and self-righteousness; he therefore can turn his polemic without further ado against the occurrence of the same type within the church.

eighth day, separated the word from the sign, and made a human or even a swinish work out of it. In this way they lost God and his word and now no longer have any understanding of the Scriptures.

God truly honored them highly by circumcision, speaking to them above all other nations on earth and entrusting his word to them. And in order to preserve this word among them, he gave them a special country; he performed great wonders through them, ordained kings and government, and lavished prophets upon them who not only apprised them of the best things pertaining to the present but also promised them the future Messiah, the Savior of the world. It was for his sake that God accorded them all of this, bidding them look for his coming, to expect him confidently and without delay. For God did all of this solely for his sake: for his sake Abraham was called, circumcision was instituted, and the people were thus exalted so that all the world might know from which people, from which country, at which time, yes, from which tribe, family, city, and person, he would come, lest he be reproached by devils and by men for coming from dark corner or from unknown ancestors. No, his ancestors had to be great patriarchs, excellent kings, and outstanding prophets, who bear witness to him.

We have already stated how the Jews, with few exceptions, viewed such promises and prophets. They were never able to tolerate a prophet, and always persecuted God's word and declined to give ear to God. That is the complaint and lament of all the prophets. And as their fathers did, so they still do today, nor will they ever mend their ways. If Isaiah, Jeremiah, or other prophets went about among them today and proclaimed what they proclaimed in their day, or declared that the Jews' present circumcision and hope for the Messiah are futile, they would again have to die at their hands as happened then. Let him who is endowed with reason, to say nothing of Christian understanding, note how arbitrarily they pervert and twist the prophets' books with their confounded glosses, in violation of their own conscience (on which we can perhaps say more later).[26] For now that they can no longer stone or kill the prophets physically or personally, they torment them spiritually,

---

[26] Cf. below, pp. 178, 184 ff., 200, 205.

mutilate, strangle, and maltreat their beautiful verses so that the human heart is vexed and pained. For this forces us to see how, because of God's wrath, they are wholly delivered into the devil's hands. In brief, they are a prophet-murdering people; since they can no longer murder the living ones, they must murder and torment the ones that are dead.

Subsequently, after they have scourged, crucified, spat upon, blasphemed, and cursed God in his word, as Isaiah 8 prophesies, they pretentiously trot out their circumcision and other vain, blasphemous, invented, and meaningless works. They presume to be God's only people, to condemn all the world, and they expect that their arrogance and boasting will please God, that he should repay them with a Messiah of their own choosing and prescription. Therefore, dear Christian, be on your guard against such accursed, incorrigible people, from whom you can learn no more than to give God and his word the lie, to blaspheme, to pervert, to murder prophets, and haughtily and proudly to despise all people on earth. Even if God would be willing to disregard all their other sins—which, of course, is impossible—he could not condone such ineffable (although poor and wretched)pride. For he is called a God of the humble, as Isaiah 66 [:2] states: "But this is the man to whom I will look, he that is humble and contrite in spirit, and trembles at my word." I have said enough about the second false boast of the Jews, namely, their false and futile circumcision, which did not avail them when they were taken to task by Moses and by Jeremiah because of their uncircumcised heart. How much less is it useful now when it is nothing more than the devil's trickery with which he mocks and fools them, as he also does the Turks. For wherever God's word is no longer present, circumcision is null and void.

In the third place, they are very conceited because God spoke with them and issued them the law of Moses on Mount Sinai. Here we arrive at the right spot, here God really has to let himself be tortured, here he must listen as they tire him with their songs and praises because he hallowed them with his holy law, set them apart from other nations, and led them out of Egypt. Here we poor Goyim are really despised, and are mere ciphers compared to the holy, chosen, noble, and highly exalted people which is in possession of God's word! They state, as I myself heard:[27] "Indeed, what do you have to say to this—that God himself spoke with us on Mount Sinai and that he did this with no other people?" We have nothing with which to refute that, for we cannot deny them this glory. The books of Moses are ready to give proof of it, and David, too, testifies to it, saying in Psalm 147 [:19 f.]: "He declares his word to Jacob, his statutes and ordinances to Israel. He has not dealt thus with any other nation; they do not know his ordinances." And in Psalm 103 [:7]: "He made known his ways to Moses, his acts to the people of Israel."

They relate that the chiefs of the people wore wreaths at Mount Sinai at that time as a symbol that they had contracted a marriage with God through the law, that they had become his bride, and that the two had wedded one another.[28] Later we read in all the prophets how God appears and talks with the children of Israel as a husband with his wife. From this also sprang the peculiar worship of Baal; for "Baal" denotes a man of the house or a master of the house, "Beulah" denotes a housewife. The latter also has taken a German form,[29] as when we say "My dear *Buhle*" [sweetheart], and "I must have a *Buhle*." Formerly this was an inoffensive term, designating a young lass. It was said that a young man courted [*buhlte*] a young girl with a view to marriage. Now the word has assumed a different connotation.

Now we challenge you, Isaiah, Jeremiah, and all the prophets, and whoever will, to come and to be bold enough to say that such a noble nation with whom God himself converses and with whom he himself enters into marriage through the law, and to whom he joins himself as to a bride, is not God's people. Anyone doing that, I know, would make himself ridiculous and come to grief. In default of any other weapons, they would tear and bite him to pieces with their teeth for trying to dispossess them of such glory, praise,

---

[27] Luther had had several face-to-face colloquies with Jews who had visited him in Wittenberg. Cf. his own account of one such incident below, p. 191.
[28] A Jewish tradition reflected in the festivities of *Simhath Torah* ("Rejoicing in the Law"), the day which marks the conclusion and re-commencement of the yearly cycle of readings from the Torah. Cf. in Isaac Landman (ed.), *The Universal Jewish Encyclopedia* (New York: Universal Jewish Encyclopedia Co., 1939 ff.).
[29] A derivation not supported by modern etymological research.

and honor. One can neither express nor understand the obstinate, unbridled, incorrigible arrogance of this people, springing from this advantage—that God himself spoke to them. No prophet has ever been able to raise his voice in protest or stand up against them, not even Moses. For in Numbers 16, Korah arose and asserted that they were all holy people of God, and asked why Moses alone should rule and teach. Since that time, the majority of them have been genuine Korahites; there have been very few true Israelites. For just as Korah persecuted Moses, they have never subsequently left a prophet alive or unpersecuted, much less have they obeyed him.

So it became apparent that they were a defiled bride, yes, an incorrigible whore and an evil slut with whom God ever had to wrangle, scuffle, and fight. If he chastised and struck them with his word through the prophets, they contradicted him, killed his prophets, or, like a mad dog, bit the stick with which they were struck.. Thus Psalm 95 [:10] declares: "For forty years I loathed that generation and said, 'They are a people who err in heart, and they do not regard my ways.'" And Moses himself says in Deuteronomy 31 [:27]: "For I know how rebellious and stubborn you are; behold, while I am yet alive with you, today you have been rebellious against the Lord; how much more after my death!" And Isaiah 48 [:4]: "Because I know that you are obstinate, and your neck is an iron sinew and your forehead brass. . . ." And so on; anyone who is interested may read more of this. The Jews are well aware that the prophets upbraided the children of Israel from beginning to end as a disobedient, evil people and as the vilest whore, although they boasted so much of the law of Moses, or circumcision, and of their ancestry.

But it might be objected: Surely, this is said about the wicked Jews, not about the pious ones as they are today. Well and good, for the present I will be content if they confess, as they must confess, that the wicked Jews cannot be God's people, and that their lineage, circumcision, and law of Moses cannot help them. Why, then, do they all, the most wicked as well as the pious, boast of circumcision, lineage, and law? The worse a Jew is, the more arrogant he is, solely because he is a Jew—that is, a person de-

166

scended from Abraham's seed, circumcised, and under the law of Moses. David and other pious Jews were not as conceited as the present-day, incorrigible Jews. However wicked they may be, they presume to be the noblest lords over against us Gentiles, just by virtue of their lineage and law. Yet the law rebukes them as the vilest whores and rogues under the sun.

Furthermore, if they are pious Jews and not the whoring people, as the prophets call them, how does it happen that their piety is so concealed that God himself is not aware of it, and they are not aware of it either? For they have, as we said, prayed, cried, and suffered almost fifteen hundred years already, and yet God refuses to listen to them. We know from Scripture that God will hear the prayers or sighing of the righteous, as the Psalter says [Ps. 145:19]: "He fulfills the desire of all who fear him, he also hears their cry." And Psalm 34 [:17]: "When the righteous cry for help, the Lord hears." As he promised in Psalm 50 [:15]: "Call upon me in the day of trouble; I will deliver you." The same is found in many more verses of the Scripture. If it were not for these, who would or could pray? In brief, he says in the first commandment that he will be their God. Then, how do you explain that he will not listen to these Jews? They must assuredly be the base, whoring people, that is, no people of God, and their boast of lineage, circumcision, and law must be accounted as filth. If there were a single pious Jew among them who observed these, he would have to be heard; for God cannot let his saints pray in vain, as Scripture demonstrates by many examples. This is conclusive evidence that they cannot be pious Jews, but must be the multitude of the whoring and murderous people.

Such piety is, as already has been said, so concealed among them that they themselves also can know nothing of it. How then shall God know of it? For they are full of malice, greed, envy, hatred toward one another, pride, usury, conceit, and curses against us Gentiles. Therefore, a Jew would have to have very sharp eyes to recognize a pious Jew, to say nothing of the fact that they all should be God's people as they claim. For they surely hide their piety effectively under their manifest vices; and yet they all, without exception, claim to be Abraham's blood, the people of the circumcision and of Moses, that is, God's nation, compared with whom the Gentiles must surely be sheer stench. Although they know that God cannot tolerate this, nor did he tolerate it among the angels, yet he should and must listen to their lies and blasphemies to the effect that they are his people by virtue of the law he gave them and because he conversed with their forefathers at Mount Sinai.

Why should one make many words about this? If the boast that God spoke with them and that they possess his word or commandment were sufficient so that God would on this basis regard them as his people, then the devils in hell would be much worthier of being God's people than the Jews, yes, than any people. For the devils have God's word and know far better than the Jews that there is a God who created them, whom they are obliged to love with all their heart, to honor, fear, and serve, whose name they dare not misuse, whose word they must hear on the Sabbath and at all times; they know that they are forbidden to murder or to inflict harm on any creature.[30] But what good does it do them to know and to possess God's commandment? Let them boast that this makes them God's own special, dear angels, in comparison with whom other angels are nothing! How much better off they would be if they did not have God's commandment or if they were ignorant of it. For if they did not have it, they would not be condemned. The very reason for their condemnation is that they possess his commandment and yet do not keep it, but violate it constantly.

In the same manner murderers and whores, thieves and rogues and all evil men might boast that they are God's holy, peculiar people; for they, too, have his word and know that they must fear and obey him, love and serve him, honor his name, refrain from murder, adultery, theft, and every other evil deed. If they did not have God's holy and true word, they could not sin. But since they do sin and are condemned, it is certain that they do have the holy, true word of God, against which they sin. Let them boast, like the Jews, that God has sanctified them through his law and chosen them above all other men as a peculiar people!

It is the same kind of boasting when the Jews boast in their

---

[30] A recurrence of Luther's natural-law doctrine; cf. above pp. 89-95.

synagogues, praising and thanking God for sanctifying them through his law and setting them apart as a peculiar people, although they know full well that they are not at all observing this law, that they are full of conceit, envy, usury, greed, and all sorts of malice. The worst offenders are those who pretend to be very devout and holy in their prayers. They are so blind that they not only practice usury—not to mention the other vices—but they teach that it is a right which God conferred on them through Moses.[31] Thereby, as in all the other matters, they slander God most infamously. However, we lack the time to dwell on that now.

But when they declare that even if they are not holy because of the Ten Commandments (since all Gentiles and devils are also duty-bound to keep these, or else are polluted and condemned on account of them) they still have the other laws of Moses, besides the Ten Commandments, which were given exclusively to them and not also to the Gentiles, and by which they are sanctified and singled out from all other nations—O Lord God, what a lame, loose, and vain excuse and pretext this is! If the Ten Commandments are not obeyed, what does the keeping of the other laws amount to other than mere jugglery and mummery, indeed, a veritable mockery which treats God as a fool. It is just as if an evil, devilish fellow among us were to parade about in the garb of a pope, cardinal, bishop, or pastor and observe all the precepts and the ways of these persons, but underneath this spiritual dress would be a genuine devil, a wolf, an enemy of the church, a blasphemer who trampled both the gospel and the Ten Commandments under foot and cursed and damned them. What a fine saint he would be in God's sight!

---

[31] The practice of usury, in the simple sense of the taking of interest on loans (without any connotation of exorbitant rates), is prohibited in such texts as Exod. 22:25, Lev. 25:35 ff., and Deut. 23:19 f., but only with respect to fellow Israelites. The Deuteronomy text is the most explicit with regard to dealings with others: "To a foreigner you may lend upon interest, but to your brother you shall not lend upon interest" (23:20).

The practice of usury was strictly forbidden to Christians by the medieval church, but permitted to Jews. The prohibition began to break down during the Reformation period; Luther himself, however, steadfastly maintained the medieval position. See his *Trade and Usury* (LW 45, 245-310), wherein, however, in contrast to his argument in the present treatise, he makes no mention of the Jews as special offenders in this respect. His polemic is directed chiefly against the Fuggers and other (Christian) bankers and entrepreneurs.

Or let us suppose that somewhere a pretty girl came along, adorned with a wreath, and observed all the manners, the duties, the deportment and discipline of a chaste virgin, but underneath was a vile, shameful whore, violating the Ten Commandments. What good would her fine obedience in observing outwardly all the duties and customs of a virgin's station do her? It would help her this much—that one would be seven times more hostile to her than to an impudent, public whore. Thus God constantly chided the children of Israel through the prophets, calling them a vile whore because, under the guise and decor of external laws and sanctity, they practiced all sorts of idolatry and villainy, as especially Hosea laments in chapter 2.

To be sure, it is commendable when a pious virgin or woman is decently and cleanly dressed and adorned and outwardly conducts herself with modesty. But if she is a whore, her garments, adornments, wreath, and jewels would better befit a sow that wallows in the mire. As Solomon says [Prov. 11:22]: "Like a gold ring in a swine's snout is a beautiful woman without discretion." That is to say, she is a whore. Therefore, this boast about the external laws of Moses, apart from obedience to the Ten Commandments, should be silenced; indeed, this boast makes the Jews seven times more unworthy to be God's people than the Gentiles are. For the external laws were not given to make a nation the people of God, but to adorn and enhance God's people externally. Just as the Ten Commandments were not given that any might boast of them and haughtily despise all the world because of them, as if they were holy and God's people because of them; rather they were given to be observed, and that obedience to God might be shown in them, as Moses and all the prophets most earnestly teach. Not he who has them shall glory, as we saw in the instance of the devils and of evil men, but he who keeps them.[32] He who has them and fails to keep them must be ashamed and terrified because he will surely be condemned by them.

But this subject is beyond the ken of the blind and hardened Jews. Speaking to them about it is much the same as preaching the gospel to a sow. They cannot know what God's commandment

[32] Cf. Rom. 2:13 ff.

really is, much less do they know how to keep it. After all, they could not listen to Moses, nor look into his face; he had to cover it with a veil. This veil is there to the present day, and they still do not behold Moses' face, that is, his doctrine. It is still veiled to them [cf. II Cor. 3:13 ff.; Exod. 34:33 ff.]. Thus they could not hear God's word on Mount Sinai when he talked to them, but they retreated, saying to Moses: "You speak to us, and we will hear; but let not God speak to us, lest we die" [Exod. 20:19]. To know God's commandment and to know how to keep it requires a high prophetic understanding.

Moses was well aware of that when he said in Exodus 34 that God forgives sin and that no one is guiltless before him, which is to say that no one keeps his commandments but he whose sins God forgives. As David also testifies in Psalm 32 [:1 f.], "Blessed is he whose transgression is forgiven, . . . to whom the Lord imputes no iniquity." And in the same psalm [cf. v. 6]: "Therefore let every one who is godly offer prayer to thee for forgiveness," which means that no saint keeps God's commandments. But if the saints fail to keep them, how will the ungodly, the unbelievers, the evil people keep them? Again we read in Psalm 143 [:2]: "O Lord, enter not into judgment with thy servant; for no man living is righteous before thee." That attests clearly enough that even the holy servants of God are not justified before him unless he sets aside his judgment and deals with them in his mercy; that is, they do not keep his commandments and stand in need of forgiveness of sins.

This calls for a Man who will assist us in this, who bears our sin for us, as Isaiah 53 [:6] says: "The Lord has laid on him the iniquity of us all." Indeed, that is truly to understand God's law and its observance—when we know, recognize, yes, and feel that we have it, but do not keep it and cannot keep it; that in view of this, we are poor sinners and guilty before God; and that it is only out of pure grace and mercy that we receive forgiveness for such guilt and disobedience through the Man on whom God has laid this sin. Of this we Christians speak and this we teach, and of this the prophets and apostles speak to us and teach us. They are the ones who were and still are our God's bride and pure virgin; and yet they boast of no law or holiness as the Jews do in their synagogues. They rather wail over the law and cry for mercy and forgiveness of sins. The Jews, on the other hand, are as holy as the barefoot friars who possess so much excess holiness that they can use it to help others to get to heaven, and still retain a rich and abundant supply to sell. It is of no use to speak to any of them about these matters, for their blindness and arrogance are as solid as an iron mountain. They are in the right; God is in the wrong. Let them go their way, and let us remain with those who pray the *Miserere,* Psalm 51, that is, with those who know and understand what the law is, and what it means to keep and not to keep it.

Learn from this, dear Christian, what you are doing if you permit the blind Jews to mislead you. Then the saying will truly apply, "When a blind man leads a blind man, both will fall into the pit" [cf. Luke 6:39]. You cannot learn anything from them except how to misunderstand the divine commandments, and, despite this, boast haughtily over against the Gentiles—who really are much better before God than they, since they do not have such pride of holiness and yet keep far more of the law than these arrogant saints and damned blasphemers and liars.

Therefore be on your guard against the Jews, knowing that wherever they have their synagogues, nothing is found but a den of devils in which sheer self-glory, conceit, lies, blasphemy, and defaming of God and men are practiced most maliciously and vehe-ing his eyes on them. God's wrath has consigned them to the presumption that their boasting, their conceit, their slander of God, their cursing of all people are a true and a great service rendered to God—all of which is very fitting and becoming to such noble blood of the fathers and circumcised saints. This they believe despite the fact that they know they are steeped in manifest vices. mently, just as the devils themselves do. And where you see or hear a Jew teaching, remember that you are hearing nothing but a venomous basilisk[33] who poisons and kills people merely by fasten-And with all this, they claim to be doing right. Be on your guard against them!

In the fourth place,[34] they pride themselves tremendously on

---

[33] A legendary beast credited with the power to kill with its breath or look.
[34] The first three points have dealt with the Jews' claims resting on their lineage (above, pp. 140 ff.), on the covenant of circumcision (pp. 149 ff.), and on their possession of the law (pp. 164 ff.).

having received the land of Canaan, the city of Jerusalem, and the temple from God. God has often squashed such boasting and arrogance, especially through the king of Babylon, who led them away into captivity and destroyed everything (just as the king of Assyria earlier had led all of Israel away and had laid everything low). Finally they were exterminated and devastated by the Romans over fourteen hundred years ago—so that they might well perceive that God did not regard, nor will regard, their country, city, temple, priesthood, or principality, and view them on account of these as his own peculiar people. Yet their iron neck, as Isaiah calls it [Isa. 48:4] is not bent, nor is their brass forehead [*ibid.*] red with shame. They remain stone-blind, obdurate, immovable, ever hoping that God will restore their homeland to them and give everything back to them.

Moses had informed them a great many times, first, that they were not occupying the land because their righteousness exceeded that of other heathen—for they were a stubborn, evil, disobedient people—and second, that they would soon be expelled from the land and perish if they did not keep God's commandments. And when God chose the city of Jerusalem he added very clearly in the writings of all the prophets that he would utterly destroy this city of Jerusalem, his seat and throne, if they would not keep his commandments. Furthermore, when Solomon had built the temple, had sacrificed and prayed to God, God said to him (I Kings 9 [:3]), "I have heard your prayer and your supplications . . . I have consecrated this house," etc.; but then he added shortly thereafter [vv. 6 f.]: "But if you turn aside from following me . . . and do not keep my commandments . . . then I will cut off Israel from the land which I have given them; and the house which I have consecrated for my name I will cast out of my sight; and Israel will become a proverb and a byword among all peoples." With an utter disregard for this, they stood, and still stand, firm as a rock or as an inert stone image, insisting that God gave them country, city, and temple, and that therefore they have to be God's people or church.[35]

---

[35] Luther's use here of the specific term "church" rests on his strong sense of the unity of the Old and New Testaments, and indicates one of the great underlying issues in the polemic between Jews and Christians: Which of them can claim to be the legitimate successor of ancient Israel as the "people of God"? Cf. above, pp. 132-133.

They neither hear nor see that God gave them all of this that they might keep his commandments, that is, regard him as their God, and thus be his people and church. They boast of their race and of their descent from the fathers, but they neither see nor pay attention to the fact that he chose their race that they should keep his commandments. They boast of their circumcision; but why they are circumcised—namely, that they should keep God's commandments—counts for nought. They are quick to boast of their law, temple, worship, city, land and government; but why they possess all of this, they disregard.

The devil with all his angels has taken possession of this people, so that they always exalt external things—their gifts, their deeds, their works—before God, which is tantamount to offering God the empty shells without the kernels. These they expect God to esteem and by reason of them accept them as his people, and exalt and bless them above all Gentiles. But that he wants his laws observed and wants to be honored by them as God, this they do not want to consider. Thus the words of Moses are fulfilled when he says [Deut. 32:21] that God will not regard them as his people, since they do not regard him as their God. Hosea 2 [cf. 1:9] expresses the same thought.

Indeed, if God had not allowed the city of Jerusalem to be destroyed and had them driven out of their country, but had permitted them to remain there, no one could have convinced them that they are not God's people, since they would still be in possession of temple, city, and country regardless of how base, disobedient, and stubborn they were. [They would not have believed it] even if it had snowed nothing but prophets daily and even if a thousand Moseses had stood up and shouted: "You are not God's people, because you are disobedient and rebellious to God." Why, even today they cannot refrain from their nonsensical, insane boasting that they are God's people, although they have been cast out, dispersed, and utterly rejected for almost fifteen hundred years. By virtue of their own merits they still hope to return there again. But they have no such promise with which they could console themselves other than what their false imagination smuggles into Scripture.

Our apostle St. Paul was right when he said of them that "they have a zeal for God, but it is not enlightened," etc. [Rom. 10:2]. They claim to be God's people by reason of their deeds, works, and external show, and not because of sheer grace and mercy, as all prophets and all true children of God have to be, as was said. Therefore they are beyond counsel and help. In the same way as our papists, bishops, monks, and priests, together with their following, who insist that they are God's people and church; they believe that God should esteem them because they are baptized, because they have the name, and because they rule the roost. There they stand like a rock. If a hundred thousand apostles came along and said: "You are not the church because of your behavior or your many doings and divine services, even though these were your best efforts; no, you must despair of all this and adhere simply and solely to the grace and mercy of Christ, etc. If you fail to do this, you are the devil's whore or a school of knaves and not the church," they would wish to murder, burn at the stake, or banish such apostles. As for believing them and abandoning their own devices, of this there is no hope; it will not happen.

The Turks follow the same pattern with their worship, as do all fanatics. Jews, Turks, papists, radicals abound everywhere. All of them claim to be the church and God's people in accord with their conceit and boast, regardless of the one true faith and the obedience to God's commandments through which alone people become and remain God's children. Even if they do not all pursue the same course, but one chooses this way, another that way, re-sulting in a variety of forms, they nonetheless all have the same intent and ultimate goal, namely, by means of their own deeds they want to manage to become God's people. And thus they boast and brag that they are the ones whom God will esteem. They are the foxes of Samson which are tied together tail to tail but whose heads turn away in different directions [cf. Judg. 15:4].

But as we noted earlier, that is beyond the comprehension of the Jews, as well as of the Turks and papists. As St. Paul says in I Corinthians 1, "The unspiritual man does not receive the gifts of the Spirit of God, because they are spiritually discerned" [I Cor. 2:14]. Thus the words of Isaiah 6 [:9] come true: "Hear and hear, but do not understand; see and see, but do not perceive." For they do not know what they hear, see, say, or do. And yet they do not concede that they are blind and deaf.

That shall be enough about the false boast and pride of the Jews, who would move God with sheer lies to regard them as his people. Now we come to the main subject, their asking God for the Messiah.[36] Here at last they show themselves as true saints and pious children. At this point they certainly do not want to be accounted liars and blasphemers but reliable prophets, asserting that the Messiah has not yet come but will still appear. Who will take them to task here for their error or mistake? Even if all the angels and God himself publicly declared on Mount Sinai or in the temple in Jerusalem that the Messiah had come long ago and that he was no longer to be expected, God himself and all the angels would have to be considered nothing but devils. So convinced are these most holy and truthful prophets that the Messiah has not yet appeared but will still come. Nor will they listen to us. They turned a deaf ear to us in the past and still do so, although many fine scholarly people, including some from their own race,[37] have refuted them so thoroughly that even stone and wood, if endowed with a particle of reason, would have to yield. Yet they rave consciously against recognized truth. Their accursed rabbis, who indeed know better, wantonly poison the minds of their poor youth and of the common man and divert them from the truth. For I

[36] The question of the nature and timing of the Messiah's coming will occupy Luther for the whole central portion of the treatise, down to p. 254 below. The argument turns upon the interpretation of four crucial passages from the Old Testament: (a) Gen. 49:10, the enigmatic prophecy concerning "Shiloh": (pp. 178-192, below); (b) II Sam. 23:5, the reference by David to an "everlasting covenant," further supported by II Sam. 7:12 ff. (pp. 192-209); (c) Hag. 2:6-9, the promise concerning the "consolation of the Gentiles" (pp. 209-229; and (d) Dan. 9:24, the prediction concerning the "seventy weeks of years" (pp. 229-253). In passing, pertinent passages from Hosea, Isaiah, and Jeremiah are also dealt with. All of these texts had figured prominently in Christian polemics against Judaism since the postapostolic period. The specific arguments offered by Luther here closely parallel those of Lyra and Paul of Burgos.
[37] Of the Christian polemicists against Judaism whose writings were current in Luther's day, at least four—Paul of Burgos, Anthony Margaritha, Victor of Carben, and John-Baptist de Gratia-Dei—were converted Jews. Cf., on Paul of Burgos, Luther's comment below, p. 228.

believe that if these writings were read by the common man and the youth they would stone all their rabbis and hate them more violently than they do us Christians. But these villains prevent our sincere views from coming to their attention.

If I had not had the experience with my papists, it would have seemed incredible to me that the earth should harbor such base people who knowingly fly in the face of open and manifest truth, that is, of God himself. For I never expected to encounter such hardened minds in any human breast, but only in that of the devil. However, I am no longer amazed by either the Turks' or the Jews' blindness, obduracy, and malice, since I have to witness the same thing in the most holy fathers of the church, in pope, cardinals, and bishops. O you terrible wrath and incomprehensible judgment of the sublime Divine Majesty! How can you be so despised by the children of men that we do not forthwith tremble to death before you? What an unbearable sight you are, also to the hearts and eyes of the holiest men, as we see in Moses and the prophets. Yet these stony hearts and iron souls mock you so defiantly.

However, although we perhaps labor in vain on the Jews— for I said earlier that I don't want to dispute with them[38]—we nonetheless want to discuss their senseless folly among ourselves, for the strengthening of our faith and as a warning to weak Christians against the Jews, and, chiefly, in honor of God, in order to prove that our faith is true and that they are entirely mistaken on the question of the Messiah. We Christians have our New Testament, which furnishes us reliable and adequate testimony concerning the Messiah. That the Jews do not believe it does not concern us; we believe their accursed glosses still less. We let them go their way and wait for their Messiah. Their unbelief does not harm us; but as to the help they derive and to date have derived from it, they may ask of their long-enduring exile. That will, indeed, supply the answer for us. Let him who will not follow lag behind. They act as though they were of great importance to us. Just to vex us, they corrupt the sayings of Scripture. We do not at all desire or require their conversion for any advantage, useful-

---

[38] Cf. above, p. 137.

ness, or help accruing to us therefrom. All that we do in this regard is prompted rather by a concern for their welfare. If they do
not want it, they can disregard it; we are excused and can easily
dispense with them, together with all that they are, have, and can
do for salvation. We have a better knowledge of Scripture, thanks
be to God; this we are certain of, and all the devils shall never
deprive us of it, much less the miserable Jews.

First we want to submit the verse found in Genesis 49 [:10]:
"The scepter shall not depart from Judah . . . until Shiloh comes,
and to him shall be the obedience of the peoples."[39] This saying of
the holy patriarch Jacob, spoken at the very end of his life, has
been tortured and crucified in many ways down to the present day
by the modern, strange Jews, in violation of their own conscience.
For they realize fully that their twisting and perverting is nothing
but wanton mischief. Their glosses remind me very much of an
evil, stubborn shrew who clamorously contradicts her husband and
insists on having the last word although she knows she is in the
wrong. Thus these blinded people also suppose that it suffices to
bark and to prattle against the text and its true meaning; they are
entirely indifferent to the fact that they are lying impudently. I
believe they would be happier if this verse had never been written
rather than that they should change their mind. This verse pains
them intensely, and they cannot ignore it.

The ancient, true Jews understood this verse correctly, as we
Christians do,[40] namely, that the government or scepter should

---

[39] This text had figured in anti-Jewish polemics since the time of Justin Martyr;
cf. his *Dialogue with Trypho*, ch. 52. Luther himself had already utilized it
in his treatise of 1523 *That Jesus Christ Was Born a Jew* (*LW* 45 199-229;
cf. pp. 213 ff.). See also p. 73, above, n. 11. The German scholar Adolf
Posnanski devoted a massive volume solely to the history of the exegesis of this
text down to the late Middle Ages; see his *Schiloh: Ein Beitrag zur Geschichte
der Messiaslehre* (Leipzig: J. C. Hinrichs, 1904).

Luther, in citing the text at this point, inexplicably omits the intervening
phrase (indicated above by the ellipsis) to which he subsequently devotes
much attention. The full text reads as follows in the RSV: "The scepter shall
not depart from Judah, nor the ruler's staff from between his feet, until he
comes to whom it belongs; and to him shall be the obedience of the peoples."
[40] In his *Addition* to Lyra's comment on Gen. 49:10, Paul of Burgos mentions
one Rabbi Moses who maintains that the passage is messianic in character.
"These are noteworthy words," Paul writes, "although they are often maliciously denied by the Jews." The present-day Jewish scholar Herman Hailperin, in his study of *Rashi and the Christian Scholars* (cf. above, p. 66,

remain with the tribe of Judah until the advent of the Messiah; then "to him shall be the obedience of the peoples," to him they will adhere. That is, the scepter shall then not be confined to the tribe of Judah, but, as the prophets later explain, it shall be extended to all peoples on earth at the time of the Messiah. However, until he appears, the scepter shall remain in that small nook and corner, Judah. That, I say, is the understanding of the prophets and of the ancient Jews; this they cannot deny. For also their Chaldaean Bible,[41] which they dare oppose as little as the Hebrew Bible itself, shows this clearly.

In translation it reads thus: "The *shultan* shall not be put away from the house of Judah nor the *saphra* from his children's children eternally until the Messiah comes, whose is the kingdom, and the peoples will make themselves obedient to him." This is a true and faithful translation of the Chaldaean text, as no Jew or devil can deny.

For Moses' Hebrew term *shebet* ["scepter"] we use the word *Zepter* in German, whereas the Chaldaean translator chooses the word *shultan*. Let us explain these words. The Hebrew *shebet* is the designation for a *virga*;[42] it is really not a rod in the usual sense, for this term suggests to the German the thought of birch switches with which children are punished. Nor is it a staff used by invalids and the aged for walking. But it designates a mace held upright, such as a judge holds in his hand when he acts in his official capacity. As luxury increased in the world, this mace was made of silver or of gold. Now it is called a scepter, that is, a royal rod. *Skeptron* is a Greek word, but it has now been taken up into the German language. In his first book,[43] Homer describes his King Achilles as having a wooden scepter adorned with small silver nails. From this we learn what scepters originally were and how

---

n. 3), acknowledges that "The Haggadah (Targum, Midrash) was the starting point of the line of the messianic interpretation of Gen. 49:10; the Church then adopted it formally" (p. 302, n 181).

[41] I.e., the Aramaic Targumim. Luther uses the common medieval term for these ancient versions. For his argument in the following pages he is very closely dependent on Porchetus, *Victoria* (cf. above, p. 131). Lyra and Paul of Burgos also had stressed the significance of the Aramaic text.

[42] The Latin term means simply "rod."

[43] *The Iliad*, Book 1, lines 245 f.

they gradually came to be made entirely of silver and gold. In brief, it is the rod, whether of silver, wood, or gold, carried by a king or his representative. It symbolizes nothing other than dominion or kingdom. Nobody questions this.

To make it very clear: the Chaldaean translator does not use the word *shebet*, mace or scepter; but he substitutes the person who bears this rod, saying *shultan*, indicating that a prince, lord, or king shall not depart from the house of Judah; there shall be a sultan in the house of Judah until the Messiah comes. "Sultan" is also a Hebrew term, and a word well known to us Christians, who have waged war for more than six hundred years against the sultan of Egypt, and have gained very little to show for it. For the Saracens call their king or prince "sultan," that is, lord or ruler or sovereign. From this the Hebrew word *schilt* is derived, which has become a thoroughly German word (*Schild* ["shield"]).[44] It is as though one wished to say that a prince or lord must be his subjects' shield, protection, and defense, if he is to be a true judge, sultan, or lord, etc. Some people even try to trace the German term *Schultheiss* ["village mayor"] back to the word "sultan"; I shall not enter into this.

Saphra is the same as the Hebrew *sopher* (for Chaldee and Hebrew are closely related, indeed they are almost identical, just as Saxons and Swabians both speak German, but still there is a great difference). The word *sopher* we commonly translate into the German by means of *Kanzler* ["chancellor"]. Everyone, including Burgensis, translates the word *saphra* with *scriba* or scribe. These people are called scribes in the Gospel. They are not ordinary scribes who write for wages or without official authority. They are sages, great rulers, doctors and professors, who teach, order, and preserve the law in the state. I suppose that it also encompasses the chancelleries, parliaments, councillors, and all who by wisdom and justice aid in governing. That is what Moses wishes to express with the word *mehoqeq*,[45] which designates one who teaches, composes, and executes commands and decrees. Among the Saracens, for instance, the sultan's scribes or secretaries, his doctors, teachers, and scholars, are those who teach, interpret, and preserve the

---

[44] A statement not supported by modern etymological research.
[45] Translated "the ruler's staff" by the RSV, though Luther (following the Aramaic) interprets it differently. See the following paragraph.

Koran as the law of the land. In the papacy the pope's scribes or *saphra* are the canonists or jackasses who teach and preserve his decretals and laws. In the empire the *doctores legum,* the secular jurists, are the emperor's *saphra* or scribes who teach, administer, and preserve the imperial laws.

Thus Judah, too, had scribes who taught and preserved the law of Moses, which was the law of the land. Therefore we have translated the word *mehoqeq* with "master," that is, doctor, teacher, etc. So this passage, "The *mehoqeq,* i.e., master, will not be taken from between his feet," means that teachers and listeners who sit at their feet will remain in an orderly government. For every country, if it is to endure, must have these two things: power and law. The country, as the saying goes, must have a lord, a head, a ruler. But it must also have a law by which the ruler is guided. These are the mace and the *mehoqeq,* or sultan and *saphra.* Solomon indicates this also, for when he had received the rod, that is, the kingdom, he prayed only for wisdom so that he might rule the people justly (I Kings 3). For wherever sheer power prevails without the law, where the sultan is guided by his arbitrary will and not by duty, there is no government, but tyranny, akin to that of Nero, Caligula, Dionysius, Henry of Brunswick, and their like.[46] Such does not endure long. On the other hand, where there is law but no power to enforce it, there the wild mob will also do its will and no government can survive. Therefore both must be present: law and power, sultan and *saphra,* to supplement one another.[47]

Thus the councillors who gathered in Jerusalem and who were to come from the tribe of Judah were the *saphra;* the Jews called them the Sanhedrin.[48] Herod, a foreigner, an Edomite, did away

---

[46] Along with three proverbially evil rulers, Luther names his contemporary Henry I, Duke of Brunswick-Wolfenbüttel (1489-1568), who had proved a tenacious opponent of the Lutheran cause. Further on Henry, see Luther's *Against Hanswurst, LW* 41, 185-256.

[47] A fundamental motif in Luther's conception of political dynamics, recurring frequently in his works. See, for example, his discussion of the role of "the law" and "the sword" in *Temporal Authority: To What Extent It Ought To Be Obeyed,* Part Three (*LW* 45, 118 ff.).

[48] Luther himself adds here the following marginal note: *Vide Burgen. Gen. 49. addi. 3* ("See Burgensis on Genesis 49, Addition 3"). The point made by Paul of Burgos, which is found also in Lyra and other medieval controversialists, is that under the Sanhedrin, since it was drawn from the house of Judah, the scepter had not yet "departed from Judah." Herod, however, was a foreigner; under his reign, therefore, the Messiah had to come.

with this, and he himself became both sultan and *saphra,* mace and *mehoqeq* in the house of Judah, lord and scribe. Then the saying of the patriarch began to be fulfilled that Judah was no longer to retain the government or the *saphra.* Now it was time for the Messiah to come and to occupy his kingdom and sit on the throne of David forever, as Isaiah 9 [:6 f.] prophesies. Therefore let us now study this saying of the patriarch.

"Judah," he declares, "your brothers shall praise you," etc. [Gen. 49:8]. This, it seems to me, requires no commentary; it states clearly enough that the tribe of Judah will be honored above all of his brothers and will enjoy the prerogative. The text continues: "Your hand shall be on the neck of your enemies," etc. This also declares plainly that the famous and prominent tribe of Judah must encounter enemies and opposition, but that all will end successfully and victoriously for it. We continue: "Your father's sons shall bow down before you," etc. Again it is clear that this does not refer to the captivity but to the rule over his brothers, all of which was fulfilled in David. But not only did the tribe of Judah, in David, become lord over his brothers; he also spread his rule beyond, like a lion, forcing other nations into submission; for instance the Philistines, the Syrians, the Moabites, the Ammonites, the Edomites.

This is what he praises in these beautiful words [Gen. 49:9]: "Judah is a lion's whelp; from the prey, my son, you have gone up. He stooped down, he crouched as a lion, and as a lioness; who dares to rise up against him?"[49] This is to say that he was enthroned and established a kingdom which no one could overwhelm, though the adjacent nations frequently and mightily tried to do so.

All right, up to this point the patriarch has established, ordained, and confirmed the kingdom, the sultan, the rod, the *saphra* in the tribe of Judah. There Judah, the sultan, sits enthroned for his rule. What is to happen now? This, he says: He shall remain thus until the Messiah comes; that is, many will oppose him, attempting to overthrow and destroy the kingdom and simply make it disappear from the earth. The histories of the kings and the

---

[49] Following Luther's German. The RSV has for the last phrase, "Who dares rouse him up?"

prophets amply testify that all the Gentile nations ever earnestly strove to do this. And the patriarch himself declares, as we heard before, that Judah must have its foes. For such is the course of events in the world that wherever a kingdom or principality rises to a position of might, envy will not rest until it is destroyed. All of history illustrates this with numerous examples.

However, in this instance the Holy Spirit states: This kingdom in the tribe of Judah is mine, and no one shall take it from me, no matter how angry and mighty he may be, even if the gates of hell should try. The words will still prove true: *Non auferetur*, "It shall not be taken away." You devils and Gentiles may say: *Auferetur*, we shall put an end to it, we shall devour it, we shall silence it, as Psalm 74 bemoans. But it shall remain undevoured, undevastated. "The *shebet* or sultan shall not depart from the house of Judah, nor the *saphra* from his children's children," until the *shiloh* or Messiah comes—no matter how you all rant and rage.

And when he does appear, the kingdom will become far different and still more glorious. For since you would not tolerate the tribe of Judah in a little, narrow corner, I shall change him into a truly strong lion who will become sultan and *saphra* in all the world. I will do this in such a way that he will not draw a sword nor shed a drop of blood, but the nations will voluntarily and gladly submit themselves to him and obey him. Such shall be his kingdom. For after all, the kingdom and all things are his.

Approach the text, both Chaldaean and Hebrew, with this understanding and this thought, and I wager that your heart together with the letters will surely tell you: By God! that is the truth, that is the patriarch's meaning. And then consult the histories to ascertain whether this has not happened and come to pass in this way and still continues to do so. Again you will be compelled to say: It is verily so. For it is undeniable that the sultan and *saphra* remained with the tribe of Judah until Herod's time, even if it was at times feeble and was not maintained without the opposition of mighty foes. Nevertheless, it was preserved. Under Herod and after Herod, however, it fell into ruin and came to an end. It was so completely destroyed that even Jerusalem, once the throne-seat of the tribe of Judah, and the land of Canaan were wiped out. Thus

183

the verse was fulfilled which said that the sultan has departed and the Messiah has come.

I do not have the time at present to demonstrate what a rich fountainhead this verse is and how the prophets drew so much information from it concerning the fall of the Jews and the election of the Gentiles, about which the modern Jews and bastards know nothing at all. But we have clearly and forcefully seen from this verse that the Messiah had to come at the time of Herod. The alternative would be to say that God failed to keep his promise and, consequently, lied. No one dare do that save the accursed devil and has servants, the false bastards and strange Jews. They do this incessantly. In their eyes God must be a liar. They claim that they are right when they assert that the Messiah has not yet come, despite the fact that God declared in very plain words that the Messiah would come before the scepter had entirely departed from Judah. And this scepter has been lost to Judah for almost fifteen hundred years now. The clear words of God vouch for this, and so do the visible effect and fulfillment of these same words.

What do you hope to accomplish by engaging an obstinate Jew in a long dispute on this? It is just as though you were to talk to an insane person and prove to him that God created heaven and earth, according to Genesis 1, pointing out heaven and earth to him with your hands, and he would nevertheless prattle that these are not the heaven and earth mentioned in Genesis 1, or that they were not heaven and earth at all, but were called something else, etc. For this verse, "The scepter shall not depart from Judah," etc., is as clear and plain as the verse, "God created heaven and earth." And the fact that this scepter has been removed from Judah for almost fifteen hundred years is as patent and manifest as heaven and earth are, so that one can readily perceive that the Jews are not simply erring and misled but that they are maliciously and willfully denying and blaspheming the recognized truth in violation of their conscience. Nobody should consider such a person worthy of wasting a single word on him, even if it dealt with Markolf the mockingbird,[50] much less if it deals with such exalted divine words and works.

---

[50] I.e., a swindler, an imposter.

184

But if anyone is tempted to become displeased with me, I will serve his purpose and give him the Jews' glosses on this text. First[51] I will present those who do not dismiss this text but adhere to it, particularly to the Chaldaean version, which no sensible Jew can deny. These twist and turn as follows: To be sure, they say, God's promise is certain; but our sins prevent the fulfillment of the promise. Therefore we still look forward to it until we have atoned, etc. Is this not an empty pretext, even a blasphemous one? As if God's promise rested on our righteousness, or fell with our sins! That is tantamount to saying that God would have to become a liar because of our sin, and conversely, that he would have to become truthful again by reason of our righteousness. How could one speak more shamefully of God than to imply that he is a shaking reed which is easily swayed back and forth either by our falling down or standing up?

If God were not to make a promise or keep a promise until we were rid of sin, he would have been unable to promise or do anything from the very beginning. As David says in Psalm 130 [:3]: "If thou, O Lord, shouldst mark iniquity, Lord, who could stand?" And in Psalm 102 [143:2]: "Enter not into judgment with thy servant; for no man living is righteous before thee." And there are many more such verses. The example of the children of Israel in the wilderness can be cited here. God led them into the land of Canaan without any righteousness on their part, in fact, with their great sins and shame, solely on account of his promise. In Deuteronomy 9 [:5] Moses says: "Know therefore that the Lord your God is not giving you this good land to possess because of your righteousness; for you are a stubborn and a disobedient people (it seems to me that this may indeed be called sin), but because of the promise which the Lord gave to your fathers," etc. By way of example he often wanted to exterminate them, but Moses interceded for them. So little was God's promise based upon their holiness.

It is true that wherever God promises anything conditionally, or with reservation, saying: "If you will do that, I will do this," then

---

[51] Luther presents various Jewish interpretations of the text, gleaned from his sources in the anti-Jewish literature. The first is found in Margaritha's *Der gantz Jüdisch glaub.*

the fulfillment is contingent on our action; for instance, when he declared to Solomon [I Kings 9], "If you will keep my statutes and my ordinances, then this house shall be consecrated to me; if not, I shall destroy it." However, the promise of the Messiah is not thus conditional.[52] For he does not say: "If you will do this or that, then the Messiah will come; if you fail to do it, he will not come." But he promises him unconditionally, saying: "The Messiah will come at the time when the scepter has departed from Judah." Such a promise is based only on divine truth and grace, which ignores and disregards our doings. That renders this subterfuge of the Jews inane, and, moreover, very blasphemous.

The others who depart from this text subject almost every single word of it to severe and violent misinterpretation. They really do not deserve to have their drivel and filth heard; still, in order to expose their disgrace we must exercise a bit of patience and also listen to their nonsense. For since they depart from the clear meaning of the text, they already stand condemned by their own conscience, which would constrain them to heed the text; but to vex us, they conjure up the Hebrew words before our eyes, as though we were not conversant with the Chaldaean text.

Some[53] engage in fantasies here and say that Shiloh refers to the city of that name, where the ark of the covenant was kept (Judges 21 [cf. I Sam. 4:3]), so that the meaning would be that the scepter shall not depart from Judah until Shiloh comes, that is, until Saul is anointed king of Shiloh. That is surely foolish prattle. Prior to King Saul not only did Judah have no scepter, but neither did all of Israel. How, then, can it have departed when Saul became king? The text declares that Judah had first been lord over his brothers and that he then became a lion, and therefore received the scepter. Likewise, before Saul's time no judge was lord or prince over the people of Israel, as we gather from Gideon's speech to the people in reply to their wish that he and his descendants rule over them: "I will not rule over you, and my son will not rule

---

[52] Luther here invokes a basic aspect of the distinction between law and gospel: the promises of the law are conditional upon man's performance, while the promises of the gospel (as found also in the Old Testament) are unconditional.

[53] As reported by Lyra in the *Postilla* on Gen. 49:10.

over you; the Lord will rule over you" (Judges 7 [8:23]). Nor was there a judge from the tribe of Judah, except perhaps for Othniel [Judg. 3:9], Joshua's immediate successor. All the others down to Saul were from the other tribes. And although Othniel is called Caleb's youngest brother, this does not prove that he was of the tribe of Judah, since he may have had a different father. And it does not make sense that Shiloh should here refer to a city or to Saul's coronation in Shiloh, for Saul was anointed by Samuel in Ramath (I Samuel 10) and confirmed at Gilgal.

In any case, what is the meaning of the Chaldaean text which says that the kingdom belongs to Shiloh and that nations shall be subject to it? When was the city of Shiloh or Saul ever accorded such an honor? Israel is one nation, not many, with one body of laws, one divine worship, one name. There are many nations, however, which have different and various laws, names, and gods. Now Jacob declares that not the one nation Israel—which was already his or was under Judah's scepter—but other nations would fall to Shiloh. Therefore this foolish talk reflects nothing other than the great stubbornness of the Jews, who will not submit to this saying of Jacob, although they stand convicted by their own conscience.

Others[54] indulge in the fancy that Shiloh refers to King Jeroboam, who was crowned in Shiloh, and to whom ten tribes of Israel had defected from Rehoboam, the king of Judah (I Kings 12). Therefore, they say, this is Jacob's meaning: The scepter shall not depart from Judah until Shiloh, that is, Jeroboam, comes. This is just as inane as the other interpretation; for Jeroboam was not crowned in Shiloh but in Shechem (I Kings 12). Thus the scepter did not depart from Judah, but the kingdom of Judah remained, together with the tribe of Benjamin and many of the children of Israel who dwelt in the cities of these two tribes, as we hear in I Kings 12. Moreover, the entire priesthood, worship, temple, and everything remained in Judah. Furthermore, Jeroboam never conquered the kingdom of Judah, nor did other nations fall to him, as they were to fall to Shiloh.

The third group[55] babbles thus: "Shiloh means 'sent,' and this

---

[54] Cf. Lyra, *ibid.*
[55] Lyra, *ibid,* and Porchetus, *Victoria,* I. 2, 4-6.

term applies to Nebuchadnezzar of Babylon." So the meaning is that the scepter shall not depart from Judah until Shiloh, that is, the king of Babylon, comes. He was to lead Judah into exile and destroy it. This also doesn't hold water, and a child learning his letters can disprove it. For Shiloh and *shiloch* are two different words. The latter may mean "sent." But that is not the word found here; it is Shiloh, and that, as the Chaldee says, means "Messiah." But the king of Babylon is not the Messiah who is to come from Judah, as the Jews and all the world know very well. Nor did the scepter depart from Judah even though the Jews were led captive into Babylon. That was just a punishment for seventy years. Also during this time great prophets—Jeremiah, Daniel, Ezekiel—appeared who upheld the scepter and said how long the exile would be. Furthermore, Jehoiachin, the king of Judah, was regarded as a king in Babylon. And many of those who were led away into captivity returned home again during their lifetime (Haggai 2). This cannot be viewed as loss of the scepter, but as a light flogging. Even if they were deprived of their country for a while by way of punishment, God nonetheless pledged his precious word that they could remain assured of their land.[56] But during the past fifteen hundred years not even a dog, much less a prophet, has any assurance concerning the land. Therefore the scepter has now definitely departed from Judah. I have written more about this against the Sabbatarians.[57]

The fourth group[58] twists the word *shebet* and interprets it to mean that the rod will not depart from Judah until Shiloh, that is, his son, will come, who will weaken the Gentiles. These regard the rod as the punishment and exile in which they now live. But the Messiah will come and slay all the Gentiles. That is humbug. It ignores the Chaldaean text entirely—something they may and dare not do—and is a completely arbitrary interpretation of the

---

[56] In the second edition of the treatise, published later in 1545, Luther adds at this point: "And what is promised, even though it is not yet present, is far more certain than what is present if it has not been promised. For the former must surely come, but the latter is never secure." Cf. WA 53, 459, footnote to line 16.

[57] Cf. above, pp. 59-98.

[58] Lyra, *Postilla* on Gen. 49:10; also reported by Raymund Martin, *Pugio Fidei*, II, 4.

word *shebet*. They overlook the preceding words in which Jacob makes Judah a prince and a lion or a king, adding immediately thereafter that the scepter, or *shebet*, shall not depart from Judah. How could such an odd meaning about punishment follow right on the heels of such glorious words about a principality or kingdom? The sins which provoked such a punishment would have to have been proclaimed first. But all that we find mentioned here are praise, honor, and glory to the tribe of Judah.

And even if the word *shebet* does designate a rod for punishment, how would that help them? For the judge's or the king's rod is also a rod of punishment for the evildoers. Indeed, the rod of punishment cannot be any but a judge's or sultan's rod, since the right to administer punishment belongs solely to the authority (Deuteronomy 32): *Mihi vindicatam*, "Vengeance is mine." In any event, this meaning remains unshaken—that the scepter or rod of Judah shall remain—even if this rod is one of punishment. But this arbitrary interpretation of the rabbis points to a foreign rod which does not rest in Judah's hand but on Judah's back and is wielded by a foreign hand. Even if this meaning were possible —which it is not—what would we do with the other passage that speaks of the *saphra* or *mehoqeq* at his feet? This would then also have to be a foreign lord's *mehoqeq* and a foreign nation's feet. But since Jacob declares that it is to be Judah and the *mehoqeq* of his feet, the other term, the rod, must also represent the rule of his tribe.

Some[59] twist the word *donec* ("until") and try to make "because" (*quia*) out of it. So they read: "The scepter of Judah will not depart *donec*, that is, because (*quia*) the Messiah will come." He who perpetrated this is a precious master, worthy of being crowned with thistles. He reverses the correct order of things in this manner: The Messiah will come, therefore the scepter will remain. Jacob, however, first makes Judah a prince and a lion to whom the scepter is assigned prior to the coming of the Messiah; he then, in turn, will give it to the Messiah. Thus Judah retains neither the principality nor the role of lion nor the scepter, which Jacob assigned to him. Furthermore, the fool arbitrarily makes out

---

[59] Sources for this and the following interpretation have not been identified.

of the term "until" a new term, "because." This, of course, the language does not permit.

And finally there is a rabbi who twists the word "come" and claims that it means "to set," just as the Hebrew uses the word "to come" for the setting of the sun. This fellow is given to such nonsense that I am at a loss to know whether he is trying to walk on his head or on his ears. For I fail to understand the purport of his words when he says that the scepter will not depart from Judah until Shiloh (the city) goes down (sets). Then David, the Messiah, will come. Where, to repeat what was said above, was the scepter of Judah prior to Shiloh or Saul? But they who rage against their own conscience and patent truth must needs speak such nonsense. In brief, Lyra is right when he says[60] that even if they invent these and many other similar glosses, the Chaldaean text topples all of them and convicts them of being willful liars, blasphemers, and perverters of God's word. However, I wanted to present this to us Germans[61] so that we might see what rascals the blind Jews are and how powerfully the truth of God in our midst stands with us and against them.

And now that some have noticed that such evasions and silly glosses are null and void, they admit that the Messiah came at the time of the destruction of Jerusalem; but, they say, he is in the world secretly, sitting in Rome among the beggars and doing penance for the Jews until the time for his public appearance is at hand.[62] These are not the words of Jews or of men but those of the arrogant, jeering devil, who most bitterly and venomously mocks us Christians and our Christ through the Jews, as if to say: "The Christians glory much in their Christ, but they have to submit to the yoke of the Romans; they must suffer and be beggars in the world, not only in the days of the emperors, but also in those of the pope. After all, they are impotent in my kingdom, the world, and I will surely remain their master." Yes, vile devil, just mock

---

[60] In the *Postilla* Cf. Hailperin, *Raᶜhi and the Christian Scholars*, pp. 159 f.
[61] A statement revealing something of Luther's self-understanding as he writes the treatise. He wishes to summarize and present in the vernacular certain materials otherwise available only in Latin.
[62] Cf. Tractate Sanhedrin 98a. Salo W. Baron makes reference to this tradition in his *Social and Religious History of the Jews*, Vol. XIII (cited above, p. 128, n. 14), p. 112.

and laugh your fill over this now; you will still tremble enough for it.

Thus the words of Jacob fared very much the same as did these words of Christ in our day: "This is my body which is given for you." The enthusiasts distorted each word singly and collectively, putting the last things first, rather than accept the true meaning of the text, as we have observed. It is clear in this instance too that Christians such as Lyra, Raymund, Burgensis, and others certainly went to great lengths in an effort to convert the Jews. They hounded them from one word to another, just as foxes are hunted down. But after having been hounded a long time, they still persisted in their obstinacy and now set to erring consciously, and would not depart from their rabbis. Thus we must let them go their way and ignore their malicious blasphemy and lying.

I once experienced this myself.[63] Three learned Jews came to me, hoping to discover a new Jew in me because we were beginning to read Hebrew here in Wittenberg, and remarking that matters would soon improve since we Christians were starting to read their books. When I debated with them, they gave me their glosses, as they usually do. But when I forced them back to the text, they

---

[63] Many interpreters of Luther, taking their clue from his own statement in the latter part of this paragraph, consider the incident described here to have been pivotal in Luther's development of a negative attitude toward the Jews, although as pointed out in the Introduction, many other factors must also be considered. Luther had mentioned this incident already in a sermon preached on the Twenty-fifth Sunday after Trinity in 1526 (*WA* 20, 547 ff.). Commenting on Jer. 23:6 ("This is the name by which he will be called: 'The Lord is our righteousness'"), which he interprets messianically, Luther notes that the application of the sacred name to Christ is proof of his divinity. He then adds: "I myself have discussed this with the Jews, indeed with the most learned of them, who knew the Bible so well that there wasn't a letter in it that they did not understand. I held up this text to them, and they could not think of anything to refute me. Finally they said that they believed their Talmud; this is their exegesis, and it says nothing about Christ. They had to follow this interpretation. Thus they do not stick to the text but seek to escape it. For if they held to this text alone, they would be vanquished." Cf. *WA* 20, 569 f.

The incident is also referred to in a table remark of Luther from the year 1540, wherein the names of the three Jews are given as Samaria, Schlomo, and Leo, and they are identified as "three rabbis." The account here notes that the conversation ended with both Luther and the Jews expressing the hope for the conversion of the other (*WA*, TR 4, 619 f.; Entry No. 5026). See also Mathesius, *Doctor Martin Luthers Leben* (cited above, p. 59), Sermon 14, and Lewin, *Luthers Stellung zu den Juden*, pp. 38 f.

soon fled from it, saying that they were obliged to believe their rabbis as we do the pope and the doctors, etc. I took pity on them and give them a letter of recommendation to the authorities, asking that for Christ's sake they let them freely go their way. But later, I found out that they called Christ a *tola,* that is, a hanged highwayman. Therefore I do not wish to have anything more to do with any Jew. As St. Paul says, they are consigned to wrath; the more one tries to help them the baser and more stubborn they become. Leave them to their own devices.

We Christians, however, can greatly strengthen our faith with this statement of Jacob, assuring us that Christ is now present and that he has been present for almost fifteen hundred years—but not, as the devil jeers, as a beggar in Rome; rather, as a ruling Messiah. If this were not so, then God's word and promise would be a lie. If the Jews would only let Holy Scripture be God's word, they would also have to admit that there has been a Messiah since the time of Herod (no matter where), rather than awaiting another. But before doing this, they will rather tear and pervert Scripture until it is no longer Scripture. And this is in fact their situation: They have neither Messiah nor Scripture, just as Isaiah 28 prophesied of them.

But may this suffice on the saying of Jacob. Let us take another saying which the Jews did not and cannot twist and distort in this way. In the last words of David,[64] we find him saying (II Samuel 23 [:2 f.]): "The Spirit of the Lord speaks by me, his word is upon my tongue. The God of Israel has spoken, the Rock of Israel . . . ." And a little later [in v. 5]: "Does not my house stand so with God?" Or, to translate it literally from the Hebrew: "My house is of course not thus," etc. That is to say: "My house is, after all, not worthy; this is too glorious a thing and it is too much that God does all of this for a poor man like me." "For he has made with me an everlasting covenant, ordered in all things and secure." Note well how David exults with so numerous and seemingly superfluous words that the Spirit of God has spoken through him

---

[64] A text which Luther was to examine at length in his treatise *The Last Words of David,* published later in 1543 (cf. above, p. 65, n. 1). He had already touched on it briefly in *Sabbatarians* (above, pp. 71-72).

and that God's word is upon his tongue. Thus he says: "The God of Israel has spoken, the Rock of Israel," etc. It is as if he were to say: "My dear people, give ear. Whoever can hear, let him hear. Here is God, who is speaking and saying, 'Listen,'" etc. What is it, then, that you exhort us to listen to? What is God saying through you? What does he wish to say to you? What shall we hear?

This is what you are to hear: that God made an everlasting, firm, and sure covenant with me and my house, a covenant of which my house is not worthy. Indeed, my house is nothing compared to God; and yet he did this. What is this everlasting covenant? Oh, open your ears and listen! My house and God have bound themselves together forever through an oath. This is a covenant, a promise which must exist and endure forever. For it is God's covenant and pledge, which no one shall or can break or hinder. My house shall stand eternally; it is "ordered in all things and secure." The word *aruk* ("ordered") conveys the meaning that it will not disappoint or fail one in the least. Have you heard this? And do you believe that God is truthful? Yes, without doubt. My dear people, do you also believe that he can and will keep his word?

Well and good, if God is truthful and almighty and spoke these words through David—which no Jew dares to deny—then David's house and government (which are the same thing) must have endured since the time he spoke these words, and must still endure and will endure forever—that is, eternally. Otherwise, God would be a liar. In brief, either we must have David's house or heir, who reigns from the time of David to the present and in eternity, or David died as a flagrant liar to his last day, uttering these words (as it seems) as so much idle chitchat: "God speaks, God says, God promises." It is futile to join the Jews in giving God the lie, saying that he did not keep these precious words and promises. We must, I say, have an heir of David from his time onward, in proof of the fact that his house has never stood empty— no matter where this heir may be. For his house must have been continuous and must ever remain so. Here we find God's word that this is an everlasting, firm, and sure covenant, without a flaw, but everything in it must be *aruk*, magnificently ordered, as God orders all his work. Psalm 111 [:3]: "Full of honor and majesty in his work."

Now let the Jews produce such an heir of David. For they must do so, since we read here that David's house is everlasting, a house that no one will destroy or hinder, but rather as we also read here [II Sam. 23:4], it shall be like the sun shining forth, which no cloud can hinder. If they are unable to present such an heir or house of David, then they stand fully condemned by this verse, and they show that they are surely without God, without David, without Messiah, without everything, that they are lost and eternally condemned. Of course, they cannot deny that the kingdom or house of David endured uninterruptedly until the Babylonian captivity, even throughout the Babylonian captivity, and following this to the days of Herod. It endured, I say, not by its own power and merit but by virtue of this everlasting covenant made with the house of David. For most of their kings and rulers were evil, practicing idolatry, killing the prophets, and living shamefully. For example, Rehoboam, Joram, Joash, Ahaz, Manasseh, etc., surpassed all the Gentiles or the kings of Israel in vileness. Because of them, the house and tribe of David fully deserved to be exterminated. That was what finally happened to the kingdom of Israel. However, the covenant made with David remained in effect. The books of the kings and of the prophets exultantly declare that God preserved a lamp or a light to the house of David which he would not permit to be extinguished. Thus we read in II Kings 8 [:19] and in II Chronicles 21 [:7]: "Yet the Lord would not destroy the house of David because of the covenant which he had made with David, since he had promised to give a lamp to him and to his sons forever." The same thought is expressed in II Samuel 7 [:12 f.].

By way of contrast, look at the kingdom of Israel, where the rule never remained with the same tribe or family beyond the second generation, with the exception of Jehu[65] who by reason of a special promise carried it into the fourth generation of his house. Otherwise it always passed from one tribe to another, and at times scarcely survived for one generation; moreover, it was not long

---

[65] Cf. II Kings 9 ff.

until the kingdom died out completely. But through the wondrous deeds of God the kingdom of Judah remained within the tribe of Judah and the house of David. It withstood strong opposition on the part of the Gentiles round about, from Israel itself, from uprisings within, and from gross idolatries and sins, so that it would not have been surprising if it had perished in the third generation under Rehoboam, or at least under Joram, Ahaz, and Manasseh. But it had a strong Protector who did not let it die or let its light become extinguished. The promise was given that it would remain firm, eternally firm and secure. And so it has remained and must remain down to the present and forever; for God does not and cannot lie.

The Jews drivel that the kingdom perished with the Babylonian captivity. As we said earlier, this is empty talk; for this constituted but a short punishment, definitely confined to a period of seventy years. God had pledged his word for that. Moreover, he preserved them during this time through splendid prophets. Furthermore, King Jehoiachin was exalted above all the kings in Babylon, and Daniel and his companions ruled not only over Judah and Israel but also over the Babylonian Empire.[66] Even if their seat of government was not in Jerusalem for a short span of time, they nonetheless ruled elsewhere much more gloriously than in Jerusalem. Thus we may say that the house of David did not become extinct in Babylon but shone more resplendently than in Jerusalem. They only had to vacate their homeland for a while by way of punishment. For when a king takes the field of a foreign country he cannot be regarded as an ex-king because he is not in his homeland, especially if he is attended by great victory and good fortune against many nations. Rather one should say that he is more illustrious abroad than at home.

If God kept his covenant from the time of David to that of Herod, preserving his house from extinction, he must have kept it from that time on to the present, and he will keep it eternally, so that David's house has not died and cannot die eternally. For we dare not rebuke God as half truthful and half untruthful, saying that he kept his covenant and preserved David's house faithfully

---

[66] Cf. Dan. 2:48.

from David's time to that of Herod, but that after the time of Herod he began to lie and to become deceitful, ignoring and altering his covenant. No, for as the house of David remained and shone up to Herod's time, thus it had to remain under Herod and after Herod, shining to eternity.

Now we note how nicely this saying of David harmonizes with that of the patriarch Jacob: "The scepter shall not depart from Judah, nor the *mehoqeq* from his feet until Messiah comes, and to him shall be the obedience of the peoples" [Gen. 49:10].[67] How can it be expressed more clearly or differently that David's house will shine forth until the Messiah comes? Then, through him, the house of David will shine not only over Judah and Israel but also over the Gentiles, or over other and more numerous countries. This indeed does not mean that it will become extinct, but that it will shine farther and more lustrously than before his advent. And thus, as David says, this is an eternal kingdom and an eternal covenant. Therefore it follows most cogently from this that the Messiah came when the scepter departed from Judah—unless we want to revile God by saying that he did not keep his covenant and oath. Even if the stiff-necked, stubborn Jews refuse to accept this, at least our faith has been confirmed and strengthened by it. We do not give a fig for their crazy glosses, which they have spun out of their own heads. We have the clear text.

These last words of David—to revert to them once more—are founded on God's own word, where he says to him, as he here boasts at his end: "Would you build me a house to dwell in?" (II Sam. 7 [:5]). You can read what follows there—how God continues to relate that until now he has lived in no house, but that he had chosen him [i.e., David] to be a prince over his people, to whom he would assign a fixed place and grant him rest, concluding, "I will make you a house" [cf. II Sam. 7:11]. That is to say: Neither you nor anyone else will build me a house to dwell in; I am far, far too great for that, as we read also in Isaiah 66. No, I will build you a house. For thus says the Lord, as Nathan asserts: "The Lord declares to you that the Lord will make you a house" [II Sam. 7:11]. Everyone is familiar with a house built by man—

---

[67] Cf. above, pp. 178 ff.

a very perishable structure fashioned of stone and wood. But a house built by God means the establishing of the father of a family who would ever after have heirs and descendants of his blood and lineage. Thus Moses says in Exodus 1 [:21] that God built houses for the midwives because they did not obey the king's command, but let the infants live and did not kill them. On the other hand, he breaks down and extinguishes the houses of the kings of Israel in the second generation.

Thus David has here a secure house, built by God, which is to have heirs forever. It is not a plain house; no, he says, "You shall be prince over my people Israel" [II Sam. 7:8]. Therefore it shall be called a princely, a royal house—that is, the house of Prince David or King David, in which your children shall reign forever and be princes such as you are. The books and histories of the kings prove this true, tracing it down to the time of Herod. Until that time the scepter and *saphra* are in the tribe of Judah.

Now follows the second theme, concerning Shiloh. How long shall my house thus stand and how long shall my descendants rule? He answers thus [II Sam. 7:12-16]: "When your days are fulfilled and you lie down with your fathers, I will raise up your offspring after you who shall come forth from your body (*utero*—that is, from your flesh and blood), and I will establish his kingdom. He shall build a house for my name, and I will establish the throne of his kingdom forever. I will be his father, and he shall be my son. When he commits iniquity, I will chastise him with the rod of men (as one whips children), with the stripes of the sons of men; but I will not take my steadfast love from him, as I took it from Saul, whom I put away from before you. And your house and your kingdom shall be made sure for ever before me; your throne shall be established for ever." This statement is found almost verbatim also in I Chronicles 18 [17:11-14], where you may read it.

Whoever would refer these verses to Solomon would indeed be an arbitrary interpreter. For although Solomon was not yet born at this time, indeed the adultery with his mother Bathsheba had not yet even been committed, he is nonetheless not the seed of David born after David's death, of whom the text says, "When your days are fulfilled and you lie down with your fathers, I will raise up your seed after you." For Solomon was born during David's lifetime. It would be foolish, yes, ridiculous, to say that the term "raised up" here means that Solomon should be raised up after David's death to become king or to build the house; for three other chapters (I Kings 1, I Chronicles 24 [28], and I Chronicles 29) attest that Solomon was not only instated as king during his father's lifetime, but that he also received command from his father David, as well as the entire plan of the temple, of all the rooms, its detailed equipment, and the organization of the whole kingdom. It is obvious that Solomon did not build the temple or order the kingdom or the priesthood according to his own plans but according to those of David, who prescribed everything, in fact, already arranged it during his lifetime.

There is also a great discrepancy and a difference in words between II Samuel 7 and I Chronicles 24 [28] and 29. The former states that God will build David an eternal house, the latter that Solomon shall build a house in God's name. The former passage states without any condition or qualification that it shall stand forever and be hindered by no sin. The latter passage conditions its continuance on Solomon's and his descendants' continued piety. Since he did not remain pious, he not only lost the ten tribes of Israel but was also exterminated in the seventh generation. The former is a *promissio gratiae* ["a promise of grace"], the latter a *promissio legis* ["a promise of law"]. In the former passage David thanks God that his house will stand forever, in the latter he does not thank God that Solomon's temple will stand forever. In other words, the two passages refer to different times and to different things and houses. And although God does call Solomon his son in the latter also and says that he will be his father, this promise is dependent on the condition that Solomon will remain pious. Such a condition is not found in the former passage. It is not at all rare that God calls his saints, as well as the angels, his children. But the son mentioned in II Samuel 7 [:14] is a different and special son who will retain the kingdom unconditionally and be hindered by no sin.

Also the prophets and the psalms quote II Samuel 7, which speaks of David's seed after his death, whereas they pay no attention to I Chronicles 24 [28] and 29, which speak of Solomon. In

Psalm 89 [:1-4] we read: "I will sing of thy steadfast love, O Lord, for ever; with my mouth I will proclaim thy faithfulness to all generations. For thy steadfast love was established for ever, thy faithfulness is firm as the heavens. Thou hast said, 'I have made a covenant with my chosen one, I have sworn to David my servant: "I will establish your descendants for ever, and build your throne for all generations." ' " These too are clear words. God vows and swears an oath to grant David his grace forever, and to build and preserve his house, seed, and throne eternally.

Later, in verse 19, we have an express reference to the true David. This verse contains the most beautiful prophecies of the Messiah, which cannot apply to Solomon. For he was not the sovereign of all kings on earth, nor did his rule extend over land and sea. These facts cannot be glossed over. Furthermore, the kingdom did not remain with Solomon's house. He had no absolute promise with regard to this, but only a promise conditional on his piety. But it was the house of David that had the promise, and he had more sons than Solomon. And as the history books report, the scepter of Judah at times passed from brother to brother, from cousin to cousin, but always remained in the house of David. For instance, Ahaziah left no son, and Ahaz left none, so according to the custom of Holy Scripture the nephews had to be heirs and sons.[68]

Anyone who would venture to contradict such clear and convincing statements of Scripture regarding the eternal house of David, which are borne out by the histories, showing that there were always kings or princes down to the Messiah, must be either the devil himself or whoever is his follower. For I can readily believe that the devil, or whoever it may be, would be unwilling to acknowledge a Messiah, but still he would have to acknowledge David's eternal house and throne. For he cannot deny the clear words of God in his oath vowing that his word would not be changed and that he would not lie to David, not even by reason of any sin, as the aforementioned psalm [Ps. 89] impressively and clearly states.

Now such an eternal house of David is nowhere to be found

---

[68] On Ahaziah, cf. II Kings 1:17. The reference to Ahaz is erroneous; cf. II Kings 16:20; II Chron. 28:27.

199

unless we place the scepter before the Messiah and the Messiah after the scepter, and then join the two together: namely, by asserting that the Messiah appeared when the scepter departed and that David's house was thus preserved forever.[69] In that way God is found truthful and faithful in his word, covenant, and oath. For it is obvious that the scepter of Judah completely collapsed at the time of Herod, but much more so when the Romans destroyed Jerusalem and the scepter of Judah. Now if David's house is eternal and God truthful, then the true King of Judah, the Messiah, must have come at that time. No barking, interpreting, or glossing will change this. The text is too authoritative and too clear. If the Jews refuse to admit it, we do not care.

For us it is enough that, first of all, our Christian faith finds here most substantial proof, and that such verses afford me very great joy and comfort that we have such strong testimony also in the Old Testament. Second, we are certain that even the devil and the Jews themselves cannot refute this in their hearts and that in their own consciences they are convinced. This can surely and certainly be noted by the fact that they twist this saying of Jacob concerning the scepter (as they do all of Scripture) in so many ways betraying that they are convinced and won over, and yet refuse to admit it. They are like the devil, who knows very well that God's word is the truth and yet with deliberate malice contradicts and blasphemes it. The Jews feel distinctly that these verses are solid rock and their interpretation nothing but straw or spiderweb. But with willful and malicious resolve they will not admit this; yet they insist on being and on being known as God's people, solely because they are of the blood of the patriarchs. Otherwise they have nothing of which to boast. As to what lineage alone can effect, we have spoken above.[70] It is just as if the devil were to boast that he was of angelic stock, and by reason of this was the only angel and child of God, even though he is really God's foe.

Now that we have considered these verses, let us hear what

---

[69] Cf. above, pp. 178 ff.
[70] Pp. 140 ff.

Jeremiah says.[71] His words sound very strange. For we know that he was a prophet long after the kingdom of Israel had been destroyed and exiled, when only the kingdom of Judah still existed, which itself was soon to go into captivity in Babylon, as he foretold to them and even experienced during his lifetime. Yet despite this, he dares to say in chapter 33 [:17 ff.]: " 'For thus says the Lord: David shall never lack a man to sit on the throne of the house of Israel, and the Levitical priests shall never lack a man in my presence to offer burnt offerings, to burn cereal offerings, and to make sacrifices for ever.'

"The word of the Lord came to Jeremiah: 'Thus says the Lord: If you can break my covenant with the day and my covenant with the night, so that day and night will not come at their appointed time, then also my covenant with David my servant may be broken, so that he shall not have a son to reign on his throne, and my covenant with the Levitical priests my ministers....'

"The word of the Lord came to Jeremiah: 'Have you not observed what these people are saying, "The Lord has rejected the two families which he chose"? Thus they have despised my people so that they are no longer a nation in their sight. Thus says the Lord: If I have not established my covenant with day and night and the ordinances of heaven and earth, then I will reject the descendants of Jacob and David my servant and will not choose one of his descendants to rule over the seed of Abraham, Isaac, and Jacob. For I will restore their fortunes, and will have mercy upon them.' "

What can we say to this? Whoever can interpret it, let him do so. Here we read that not only David but also the Levites will endure forever; and the same for Israel, the seed of Abraham, Isaac, and Jacob. It is emphasized that David will have a son who will sit on his throne eternally, just as surely as day and night continue forever. On the other hand, we hear that Israel will be led away into captivity, and also Judah after her, but that Israel will not be

---

[71] Luther adduces the passages from Jeremiah and Isaiah (p. 202 below) as supporting evidence for his interpretation of the "last words of David." The next major proof-text introducing a new theme will be Hag. 2:6-9 (p. 209, below). Cf. above, p. 176, n. 36.

brought home again as Judah will be. Tell me, how does all this fit together? God's word cannot lie. Just as God watches over the course of the heavens, so that day and night follow in endless succession, so too David (that is, Abraham, Isaac, and Jacob), must have a son on his throne uninterruptedly. God himself draws this comparison. It is impossible for the Jews to make sense of it; for they see with their very eyes that neither Israel nor Judah has had a government for nearly fifteen hundred years; in fact Israel has not had one for over two thousand years. Yet God must be truthful, do what we will. The kingdom of David must rule over the seed of Jacob, Isaac, and Abraham, as Jeremiah states here, or Jeremiah is not a prophet but a liar.

We shall let the Jews reconcile and interpret this as they will or can. For us this passage leaves no doubt; it affirms that David's house will endure forever, also the Levites, and Abraham's, Isaac's, and Jacob's seed under the son of David, as long as day and night— or as it is otherwise expressed, as long as sun and moon—endure. If this is true, then the Messiah must have come when David's house and rule ceased to exist. Thus David's throne assumed more splendor through the Messiah, as we read in Isaiah 9 [:6 f.]: "For to us a child is born, to us a son is given; and the government will be upon his shoulder, and his name will be called *Pele, Joets, El, Gibbor, Abi-gad, Sar shalom*.[72] Of the increase of his government and of peace there will be no end, upon the throne of David, and over his kingdom, to establish it, and to uphold it with justice and with righteousness from this time forth and for evermore." We may revert to this later,[73] but here we shall refrain from discussing how the blind Jews twist these six names of the Messiah. They accept this verse and admit—as they must admit—that it speaks of the Messiah. We quote it because Jeremiah states that David's house will rule forever: first through the scepter up to the time of the Messiah, and after that much more gloriously through the Messiah. So it must be true that David's house has not ceased up to this hour and that it will not cease to eternity. But since the scepter of Judah

---

[72] Taken by Luther as six names, which might be rendered, using the terminology of the RSV: "Wonderful, Counselor, God, Mighty One, Everlasting Father, Prince of Peace."

[73] Luther does not in fact deal with the passage again in this treatise.

departed fifteen hundred years ago, the Messiah must have come that long ago, or, as we have said above,[74] 1,468 years ago. All of this is convincingly established by Jeremiah.

However, some among us may wonder how it is possible that at the time of Jeremiah and then up to the advent of the Messiah the seed of Abraham, Isaac, and Jacob existed and remained under the tribe of Judah or the throne of David, even though only Judah remained whereas Israel was exiled. These persons must be informed that the kingdom of Israel was led into captivity and destroyed, that it never returned home and never will return home, but that Israel, or the seed of Israel, always continued to a certain extent under Judah, and that it was exiled with Judah and returned again with her. You may read about this in I Samuel, I Kings 10 [11] and 12, and II Chronicles 30 and 31. Here you will learn that the entire tribe of Benjamin—thus a good part of Israel—remained with Judah, as well as the whole tribe of Levi together with many members of the tribes of Ephraim, Manasseh, Asher, Isachar, and Zebulun who remained in the country after the destruction of the kingdom of Israel and who held to Hezekiah in Jerusalem and helped to purge the land of Israel of idols. Furthermore, many Israelites dwelt in the cities of Judah.

Since we find so many Israelites living under the rule of the son of David, Jeremiah is not lying when he says that Levites and the seed of Abraham, Isaac, and Jacob will be found under the rule of David's house. All of these, or at least a number of them, were taken to Babylon and returned from it with Judah, as Ezra enumerates and recounts.[75] Undoubtedly many more returned of those who were led away under Sennacherib, since the Assyrian or Median kingdom was brought under the Persian rule through Cyrus, so that Judah and Israel were very likely able to join and return together from Babylon to Jerusalem and the land of Canaan. For I know for certain that we find these words in Ezra 2 [:70]: "And all Israel (or all who were there from Israel) lived in their towns." And how could they live there if they had not come back? In the days of Herod and of the Messiah the land was again full

---

[74] Pp. 138 *et passim.*
[75] Ezra 2:1 ff.

of Israelites; for in the seventy weeks of Daniel,[76] that is, in four hundred and ninety years, they had assembled again. However, they did not again establish a kingdom.

Therefore the present-day Jews are very ignorant teachers and indolent pupils of Scripture when they allege that Israel has not yet returned, as though *all* of Israel would have to return. Actually not all of Judah returned either, but only a small number, as we gather from Ezra's enumeration. The majority of them remained in Babylon, as did Daniel, Nehemiah, and Mordecai themselves. Similarly, the majority of the Israelites remained in Media, though they perhaps traveled to Jerusalem for the high festivals and then returned to their homes again, as Luke writes in the Acts of the Apostles [2:5 ff.]. God never promised that the kingdom or scepter of Israel would be restored like that of Judah. But he did promise this to Judah. The latter had to recover it by virtue of God's promise that he would establish David's house and throne forever and not let it die out. For as Jeremiah declares here, God will not tolerate that anyone slander him by saying that he had rejected Judah and Israel entirely, so that they should no longer be his people and that David's throne should come to an end, as if he had forgotten his promise, when he had promised and pledged to David an eternal house. Even though they would now have to sojourn in Babylon for a little while, still, he says, it will remain an eternal house and kingdom.

I am saying this to honor and to strengthen our faith and to shame the hardened unbelief of the blinded and stubborn Jews, for whom God must ever and eternally be a liar, as though he had let David's house die out and forgotten his covenant and his oath sworn to David. For if they would admit that God is truthful, they would have to confess that the Messiah came fifteen hundred years ago, so that David's house and throne should not be desolate for so long, as they suppose, just because Jerusalem has lain in ashes and has been devoid of David's throne and house so long. For if God kept his promise from the time of David to the Babylonian captivity and from then to the days of Herod when the scepter departed, he must also have kept it subsequently and forever after,

---

[76] To be dealt with below, pp. 229 ff.

or else David's house is not an eternal but a perishable house, which has ceased together with the scepter at the time of Herod.

But as we have already said, God will not tolerate this. No, David's house will be everlasting, like "day and night and the ordinances of heaven and earth," as Jeremiah puts it [Jer. 33:25]. However, since the scepter of Judah was lost at the time of Herod, it cannot be eternal unless the son of David, the Messiah, has come, seated himself on David's throne, and become the Lord of the world. If the Jews are correct, then David's house must have been extinct for 1,568 years,[77] contrary to God's promise and oath. This it is impossible to believe. Now this is a thorough exposition of the matter, and no Jew can adduce anything to refute it. Outwardly he may pretend that he does not believe it, but his heart and his conscience are devoid of anything to contradict it.

And how could God have maintained the honor of his divine truthfulness, having promised David an eternal house and throne, if he then let it stand desolate longer than intact? Let us figure this out. In the opinion of the Jews, the time from David to Herod covers not quite a thousand years. David's house or throne stood for that length of time, inclusive of the seventy years spent in Babylon. (We would add over one hundred years to this total.) From Herod's time, or rather let us say—for this is not far from correct— from the destruction of Jerusalem, to the year 1542 there are 1,568 years, as stated above.[78] According to this computation, David's house and throne has been empty four or five hundred years longer than it was occupied. Now inquire of stone and log whether such may be called an eternal house, especially constructed by God and preserved by his sublime faithfulness and truthfulness—a house that stands for one thousand years and lies in ashes for fourteen or fifteen hundred years!

---

[77] Adding one hundred years, the approximate time between the accession of Herod the Great (placed by Luther in 31 B.C.) and the destruction of Jerusalem, to the 1,468 years since the latter event, according to Luther's chronology. Cf. above, p. 138, n. 7.

[78] The figure of 1,568 must be considered a misprint if Luther is referring to the time since the destruction of Jerusalem. It is correct, however, if he means to reckon "from Herod's time" in the sense of n. 77, above. The uncertainty as to Luther's meaning is reflected in the fact that some early printings of the treatise change the figure to 1,468, whereas others allow it to remain as above. Cf. WA 53, 472, n. 9.

Though the Jews be as hard or harder than a diamond, the lightning and thunder of such clear and manifest truth should smash, or at least soften, them. But as I said before, our faith is cheered thereby, it is strengthened, it is made sure and certain that we do have the true Messiah, who surely came and appeared at the time when Herod took away the scepter of Judah and the *saphra*,[79] so that David's house might be eternal and forever have a son upon his throne, as God said and swore to him and made a covenant with him.

Some crafty Jew might try to cast up to me my book against the Sabbatarians, in which I demonstrated that the word "eternally," *le-olam*, often means not really an eternity, but merely "a long time."[80] Thus Moses says in Exodus 21 [:6] that the master shall take the slave who wants to stay with him and bore through his ear with an awl on the door, "and he shall serve him eternally." Here the word designates a human eternity, that is, a lifetime. But I also said in the same treatise that when God uses the word "eternal," it is a truly divine eternity.[81] And he commonly adds another phrase to the effect that it shall not be otherwise, as in Psalm 110 [:4], "The Lord has sworn and will not change his mind." Similarly in Psalm 132 [:11]: "The Lord swore to David a sure oath from which he will not turn back," etc. Wherever such a "not" is added, this means surely eternal and not otherwise. Thus we read in Isaiah 9 [:7], "Of peace there will be no end." And in Daniel [7:14], "His dominion is an everlasting dominion . . . and his kingdom one that shall not be destroyed." This is eternal not before men, who do not live eternally, but before God, who lives eternally.

The promise states that David's house and throne shall be eternal before God. He says: "Before me, before me," a son shall forever sit upon your throne. In Psalm 89 [:35-37] he also adds the little word "not": "Once for all I have sworn by my holiness, I will not lie to David. His line shall endure for ever, his throne as long as the sun before me. Like the moon it shall be established for ever; it shall stand firm while the skies endure." The last words of David convey the same thought: "He has made with me an everlasting

79 Cf. above, pp. 179 ff.
80 Cf. above, pp. 81 ff.
81 Cf. above, pp. 82-83.

covenant, ordered in all things and secure." These words "ordered
and secure" mean the same as firm, sure, eternal, never-failing. The
same applies to the saying of Jacob in Genesis 49 [:10]: "The
scepter shall not depart." "Not depart" signifies eternally, until the
Messiah comes; and that surely means eternally. For all the
prophets assign to the Messiah an eternal kingdom, a kingdom
without end.

But if we assume that this refers to a human or temporal
eternity or an indefinite period of time (which is impossible), then
the meaning would necessarily be as follows: Your house shall be
eternal before me, that is, your house shall stand as long as it
stands, or for your lifetime. This would pledge and promise David
the equivalent of exactly nothing; for even in the absence of such
an oath David's house would stand "eternally," that is, as long as
it stands, or as long as he lives. But let us dismiss such nonsense
from our minds, which would occur to none but a blinded rabbi.
When Scripture glories in the fact that God did not want to destroy
Judah because of the sins committed under Rehoboam, but that a
lamp should remain to David, as God has promised him regarding
his house (II Kings 8:19), it shows that all understood the word
"eternal" in its true sense.

Someone might also cite here the instance of the Maccabees.[82]
After Antiochus the Noble had ruthlessly ravaged the people and
the country, so that the princes of the house of David became extinct, the Maccabees ruled, who were not of the house of David
but of the tribe of the priests, which meant that the scepter had
departed from Judah and that a son of David did not sit eternally
on the throne of David. Thus the eternal house of David could not
be really eternal. We reply: The Jews cannot disturb us with this
argument, and we need not answer them; for none of this is found
in Scripture, because Malachi is the last prophet and Nehemiah the
last historian, who, as we can gather from his book, lived until the
time of Alexander. Therefore both parties must rely, so far as this
question is concerned, on Jeremiah's statement that a son of David
was to occupy his throne or rule forever. For apart from Scripture,
whoever wants to concern himself with this may regard it as an

---

[82] Cf. I Macc. 1:10 ff.

open question whether the Maccabees themselves ruled or whether they served the rulers. As to the reliability of the historians, we shall have some comments later on.[83]

It seems to me, however, that the following incident recorded in Scripture[84] should not be treated lightly. At the time of Queen Athaliah, for fully six years no son of David occupied his throne; she, Athaliah the tyrant, reigned alone. She had had all the male descendants of David slain, with the single exception of Joash, an infant a quarter or a half year old, who had been secretly removed, hidden in the temple, and reared by the excellent Jehosheba, the wife of the high priest Jehoiada, daughter of King Joram and sister of King Ahaziah, whom Jehu slew. Here the eternal covenant of God made with David was in great peril indeed, resting on one young lad in hiding, who was far from occupying the throne of David. At this time his house resembled a dark lantern in which the light is extinguished, since a foreign queen, a Gentile from Sidon, was sitting and reigning on David's throne. However, she burned her backside thoroughly on that throne!

Still, all of this did not mean that the scepter had departed or that God's eternal covenant was broken. For even if the light of David was not shining brightly at this time, it was still glimmering in that child Joash, who would again shine brightly in the future and rule. He was already born as a son of David, and these six years were nothing but a *tentatio*, a temptation. God often gives the appearance that he is unmindful of his word and is failing us. This he did with Abraham when he commanded him to burn to ashes his dear son Isaac, in whom, after all, God's promise of the eternal seed was embodied. Likewise when he led the children of Israel from Egypt. In fact, he seemed to be leading them into death, with the sea before them, high cliffs on both sides, and the enemy at their back blocking their way of escape. But matters pro-

---

[83] Luther returns to the question of the Maccabees below, p. 221. Secular sources in which the story of the Maccabean revolt is recounted include the works of Josephus, Polybius, and Appian. Luther's blunt rejection here of the Apocryphal books even as historical sources contrasts with the more favorable attitude, especially toward I Maccabees, expressed in his biblical prefaces. Cf. *LW* 35, 350. On Luther's general attitude toward the "histories," or history books, see further below, pp. 217 *et passim*.

[84] Cf. II Kings 11:1 ff.

ceeded according to God's word and promises; the sea had to open, move, and make way for them. If the sea had not done this, then the cliffs would have had to split asunder and make a path for them, and they would have squeezed and squashed Pharaoh between them, just as the sea drowned the foe. For all creatures would rather have to perish a thousand thousand times than that God's word should fail and deceive, however strange things may appear. Thus Joash is king through and in God's word, and occupies the throne of David before God although he still lies in the cradle, yes, even if he lay dead and buried under the ground; for in spite of all he would have to rise, like Isaac, from the ashes.

In such a manner we might also account for that story of the Maccabees; but this is unnecessary, for it has an entirely different meaning. The Babylonian captivity might be viewed similarly; however, thanks to splendid prophets and miracles, the situation at that time was much brighter. But Joash posed a terrible temptation for the house of David, against the covenant and the oath of God, although the house and rule of David still flourished; it was only the ruler, or the head, that was suffering and that faltered in God's covenant. But this is the manner of his divine grace, that he sometimes plays and jokes with his own. He hides himself and disguises himself so that he may test us to see whether we will remain firm in faith and love toward him, just as a father sometimes does with his children.[85] Such jesting of our heavenly Father pains us immeasurably, since we do not understand it. However, this is out of place here.

We have been speaking about a statement of Jeremiah. We will now turn our attention to one of the last prophets.[86] In Haggai 2 [:6-9] we read: "For thus says the Lord of hosts: once again, in a little while, I will shake the heavens and the earth and the sea and the dry land; and I will shake all nations, so that the consolation of the Gentiles (chemdath) shall come, and I will fill this house with splendor, says the Lord of hosts. The silver is mine, and

---

[85] A classic statement of Luther's doctrine of the *Deus absconditus*. Cf. John Dillenberger, *God Hidden and Revealed: The Interpretation of Luther's Deus Absconditus and Its Significance for Religious Thought* (Philadelphia: Muhlenberg, 1953).

[86] Luther here turns to his third major proof-text. Cf. above, p. 176, n. 36.

the gold is mine, says the Lord of hosts. The splendor of this latter house [87] shall be greater than the former, says the Lord of hosts; and in this place I will give prosperity, says the Lord of hosts."

This is another of those passages which pains the Jews intensely. They test it, twist it, interpret and distort almost every word, just as they do the statement of Jacob in Genesis 49. But it does not help them. Their conscience pales before this passage; it senses that their glosses are null and void. Lyra[88] does well when he plies them hard with the phrase *adhuc modicum*, "in a little while." They cannot elude him, as we shall see. "In a little while," he says, cannot possibly mean a long period of time. Lyra is surely right here; no one can deny it, not even a Jew, try as hard as he may. In a little while, he says, the Consolation of the Gentiles will come, after this temple is built—that is, he will come when this temple is still standing. And the splendor of this latter temple will be greater than that of the former. And this will happen shortly, i.e., "in a little while."

For it is easily understood that if the consolation of the Gentiles, whom the ancients interpret as the Messiah, did not come while that temple was still standing, but is still to come (the Jews have been waiting 1,568 years[89] already since the destruction of that temple, and this cannot be termed "a little while," especially since they cannot foresee the end of this long time), then he will never come, for he neglected to come in this little, short time, and now has entered upon the great, long time, which will never result in anything. For the prophet speaks of a short, not a long time.

But they extricate themselves from this difficulty as follows. Since they cannot ignore the words "in a little while," they take up and crucify the expression "consolation of the Gentiles," in Hebrew *chemdath*, just as they did earlier with the words *shebet* and *shiloh* in the saying of Jacob.[90] They insist that this term does not refer to the Messiah, but that it designates the gold and silver of all the Gentiles. Grammatically, the word *chemdath* really means

---

[87] Thus Luther's translation; the RSV reads, "the latter splendor of this house."
[88] In his *Pulcherrimae quaestiones* cited in WA 53, 476, n. 3.
[89] This should read "1,468 years." Cf. above, p. 138, and p. 205, n. 78.
[90] Cf. above, pp. 178 ff.

desire or pleasure; thus it would mean that the Gentiles have a desire for or take pleasure and delight in something. So the text must read thus: In a short time the desire of all Gentiles will appear. And what does this mean? What do the Gentiles desire? Gold, silver, gems! You may ask why the Jews make this kind of gloss here. I will tell you. Their breath stinks with lust for the Gentiles' gold and silver; for no nation under the sun is greedier than they were, still are, and always will be, as is evident from their accursed usury. So they comfort themselves that when the Messiah comes he will take the gold and silver of the whole world and divide it among them. Therefore, wherever they can quote Scripture to satisfy their insatiable greed, they do so outrageously. One is led to believe that God and his prophets knew of nothing else to prophesy than of ways and means to satisfy the bottomless greed of the accursed Jews with the Gentiles' gold and silver.

However, the prophet has not chosen his words properly to accord with this greedy understanding. He should have said: In a little while the desire of the Jews shall come. For the Jews are the ones who desire gold and silver more avidly than any other nation on earth. In view of that, the text should more properly speak of the desire of the Jews than of the Gentiles. For although the Gentiles do desire gold and silver, nevertheless here are the Jews who desire and covet this desire of the Gentiles, who desire that it be brought to them so that they may devour it and leave nothing for the Gentiles. Why? Because they are the noble blood, the circumcised saints who have God's commandments and do not keep them, but are stiff-necked, disobedient, prophet-murderers, arrogant, usuers, and filled with every vice, as the whole of Scripture and their present conduct bear out. Such saints, of course, are properly entitled to the Gentiles' gold and silver. They honestly and honorably deserve it for such behavior—just as the devil deserves paradise and heaven.

Further, how does it happen that such very intelligent teachers and wise, holy prophets do not also apply the word "desire" (*chemdath*) to all the other desires of the Gentiles? For the Gentiles desire not only gold and silver but also pretty girls, and the women desire handsome young men. Wherever we find among the Gentiles anything other than Jews (I almost said "misers"), who will not bestow any good on their bodies,[91] they desire also beautiful houses, gardens, cattle, and property, as well as good times, clothes, food, drink, dancing, playing, and all sorts of enjoyment. Why, then, do the Jews not interpret this verse of the prophet to mean that such desires of all the Gentiles also will shortly come to Jerusalem, so that the Jews alone might fill their bellies and feast on the world's joys? For such a mode of life Muhammad promises his Saracens. In that respect he is a genuine Jew, and the Jews are genuine Saracens according to this interpretation.

The Gentiles have another desire. How could these wise, clever interpreters overlook it? I am surprised at it. The Gentiles die, and they are afflicted with much sickness, poverty, and all kinds of distress and fear. There is not one of them who does not most ardently wish that he did not have to die, that he could avoid need, misery, and sickness, or be quickly freed from them and secure against them. This desire is so pronounced that they would gladly surrender all others for its fulfillment, as experience shows daily. Why, then, do the Jews not explain that *such* desire of all the Gentiles will also come to the temple in Jerusalem in a little while? Shame on you, here, there, or wherever you may be, you damned Jews, that you dare to apply this earnest, glorious, comforting word of God so despicably to your mortal, greedy belly, which is doomed to decay, and that you are not ashamed to display your greed so openly. You are not worthy of looking at the outside of the Bible, much less of reading it. You should read only the bible that is found under the sow's tail, and eat and drink the letters that drop from there.[92] That would be a bible for such prophets, who root about like sows and tear apart like pigs the words of the divine Majesty, which should be heard with all honor, awe, and joy.

Furthermore, when the prophet says that "the splendor of this

---

[91] Luther apparently alludes to a habit of frugality rather than to any denial of bodily pleasures in principle.

[92] Luther's crude image may have been suggested by the stone relief in the parish church at Wittenberg which he describes in the treatise *Vom Schem Hamphoras*, WA 53, 600. On this page there is also printed a photograph of the sculpture to which Luther is referring. Cf. Trachtenberg, *op. cit.*, Frontispiece and index references under *Judensau*.

latter house shall be greater than the former," let us listen to the noble and filthy (I meant to say, circumcised) saints and wise prophets who want to make Jews of us Christians.[93] The greater splendor of the latter temple compared to the former consists [they say] in this: that it (that is, the temple of Haggai) stood ten years longer than the temple of Solomon, etc.[94] Alas, if they had only had a good astronomer who could have worked out the time a little more precisely. Perhaps he would have found the difference between the two to be three months, two weeks, five days, seven hours, twelve minutes, and ten half-minutes over and above the ten years. If there were a store anywhere that offered blushes for sale, I might give the Jews a few florins to go and buy a pound of them to smear over their forehead, eyes, and cheeks, if they would refuse to cover their impudent heart and tongue with them. Or do these ignorant, stupid asses suppose that they are talking to sticks and blocks like themselves?

There were many old, gray men and women, very likely also beggars and villains in Jerusalem when Solomon, a young man of twenty years, became a glorious king. Should these, for that reason, be more glorious than Solomon? Perhaps David's mule, on which Solomon became king, was older than Solomon. Should he by reason of that be greater than Solomon? But thus those will bump their heads, stumble, and fall who incessantly give God the lie and claim that they are in the right. They deserve no better fate than to compose such glosses on the Bible, such foolishness and ignominy. This they indeed do most diligently. Therefore, dear Christian, be on your guard against the Jews, who, as you discover here, are consigned by the wrath of God to the devil, who has not only robbed them of a proper understanding of Scripture, but also of ordinary human reason, shame, and sense, and only works mischief with Holy Scripture through them. Therefore they cannot be trusted and believed in any other matter either, even though a truthful word may drop from their lips occasionally. For anyone who dares to juggle the awesome word of God so frivolously and shamefully as you see it done here, and as you also noted earlier

---

[93] Cf. above, p. 137, and the treatise *Against the Sabbatarians.*
[94] Lyra, in the *Postilla* on Hag. 2:9, attributes this explanation to "certain Jews."

with regard to the words of Jacob,[95] cannot have a good spirit dwelling in him. Therefore, wherever you see a genuine Jew, you may with a good conscience cross yourself and bluntly say: "There goes a devil incarnate."[96]

These impious scoundrels know very well that their ancient predecessors applied this verse of Haggai to the Messiah, as Lyra, Burgensis, and others testify.[97] And still they wantonly depart from this and compose their own Bible out of their own mad heads, so that they hold their wretched Jews with them in their error, in violation of their conscience and to our vexation. They think that in this way they are hurting us greatly, and that God will reward them wherever for his sake (as they imagine) they have opposed us Gentiles even in open, evident truth. But what happens, as you have seen, is that they disgrace themselves and do not harm us, and further, forfeit God and his Scripture.

Thus the verse reads: "Once again, in a little while, I will shake the heavens and the earth and the sea and the dry land (these are the islands of the sea) and the *chemdath* of all Gentiles shall come"—that is, the Messiah, the Desire of all Gentiles, which we translated into German with the word *Trost* ["consolation"]. The word "desire" does not fully express this thought, since in German it reflects the inward delight and desire of the heart (active). But here the word designates the external thing (passive) which a heart longs for. It would surely not be wrong to translate it with "the joy and delight of all Gentiles." In brief, it is the Messiah, who would be the object of displeasure, disgust, and abomination for the unbelieving and hardened Jews, as Isaiah 53 prophesies. The Gentiles, on the other hand, would bid him welcome as their heart's joy, delight, and every wish and desire. For he brings them deliverance from sin, death, devil, hell, and every evil, eternally. This is, indeed, the Gentiles' desire, their heart's delight, joy, and comfort.

This agrees with the saying of Jacob in Genesis 49 [:10], "And

---

[95] Cf. above, pp. 178 ff.
[96] For the medieval background of such a statement, see Trachtenberg, *op. cit.*
[97] Lyra, in *Pulcherrimae quaestiones*, commenting on Hag. 2:9, remarks that "according to all the Jewish exegetes, the desired one is identified with the Messiah or Christ."

to Shiloh (or the Messiah) shall be the obedience of the peoples."[98] That is to say, they will receive him gladly, hear his word and become his people, without coercion, without the sword. It is as if he wished to say: The ignoble, uncircumcised Gentiles will do this, but my noble rascals, my circumcised, lost children will not do it, but will rather rave and rant against it. Isaiah 2 [:2 f.] and Micah 4 [:1 f.] also agree with this: "It shall come to pass in the latter days that the mountain of the house of the Lord shall be established as the highest of the mountains, and shall be raised above the hills; and all the nations shall flow to it (doubtless voluntarily, motivated by desire and joy) and many people shall come, and say: 'Come, let us go up to the mountain of the Lord, to the house of the God of Jacob; that he may teach us his ways and that we may walk in his path.' For out of Zion shall go forth the law, and the word of the Lord from Jerusalem."[99] Thus the prophets speak throughout of the kingdom of the Messiah established among the Gentiles.

Yes, this is it, this is the bone of contention, that is the source of the trouble, that makes the Jews so angry and foolish and spurs them to arrive at such an accursed meaning, forcing them to pervert all the statements of Scripture so shamefully: namely, they do not want, they cannot endure that we Gentiles should be their equal before God and that the Messiah should be our comfort and joy as well as theirs. I say, before they would have us Gentiles—whom they incessantly mock, curse, damn, defame, and revile—share the Messiah with them, and be called their co-heirs and brethren, they would crucify ten more Messiahs and kill God himself if this were possible, together with all angels and all creatures, even at the risk of incurring thereby the penalty of a thousand hells instead of one. Such an incomprehensibly stubborn pride dwells in the noble blood of the fathers and circumcised saints. They alone want to have the Messiah and be masters of the world. The accursed Goyim must be servants, give their desire (that is, their gold and silver) to the Jews, and let themselves be slaughtered like

---

[98] Cf. above, pp. 178 *et passim*.
[99] The passage occurs, with only minute differences, in both Isaiah and Micah; Luther quotes from Isaiah.

wretched cattle. They would rather remain lost consciously and eternally than give up this view.

From their youth they have imbibed such venomous hatred against the Goyim from their parents and their rabbis, and they still continuously drink it.[100] As Psalm 109 [:18] declares, it has penetrated flesh and blood, marrow and bone, and has become part and parcel of their nature and their life. And as little as they can change flesh and blood, marrow and bone, so little can they change such pride and envy. They must remain thus and perish, unless God performs extraordinarily great miracles. If I wished to vex and anger a Jew severely, I would say: "Listen, Jehudi, do you realize that I am a real brother of all the holy children of Israel and a co-heir in the kingdom of the true Messiah?" Without doubt, I would meet with a nasty rebuff. If he could stare at me with the eyes of a basilisk,[101] he would surely do it. And all the devils could not execute the evil he would wish me, even if God were to give them leave—of that I am certain. However, I shall refrain from doing this, and I ask also that no one else do so, for Christ's sake. For the Jews' heart and mouth would overflow with a cloudburst of cursing and blaspheming of the name of Jesus Christ and of God the Father. We must conduct ourselves well and not give them cause for this if we can avoid it, just as I must not provoke a madman if I know that he will curse and blaspheme God. Quite apart from this, the Jews hear and see enough in us for which they ever blaspheme and curse the name of Jesus in their hearts; for they really are possessed.

As we have already said, they cannot endure to hear or to see

---

[100] A common supposition in the medieval period concerning Jewish attitudes. Lyra, for example, in explaining at the conclusion of his *Pulcherrimae quaestiones* why the Jews resist conversion, comments: "From the cradle they are nourished with a hatred of Christ and of Christian practice. Thus they curse Christians all day long in the synagogue. What men know from childhood becomes second nature to them. Consequently, the Jews' rational judgment is prejudiced against any opposing truth."

James Parkes, in his *The Conflict of the Church and the Synagogue: A Study in the Origins of Antisemitism* (reprinted; New York: Atheneum, 1969), ch. 3, points out that the similar references in patristic literature to the "daily cursing of Christ in the synagogues" may well be based on the insertion of a malediction against heretics into the synagogue liturgy near the end of the first century; this would have referred to Jewish Christians.

[101] Cf. above, p. 172, n. 33.

that we accursed Goyim should glory in the Messiah as our *chemdath*, and that we are as good as they are or as they think they are. Therefore, dear Christian, be advised and do not doubt that next to the devil, you have no more bitter, venomous, and vehement foe than a real Jew who earnestly seeks to be a Jew. There may perhaps be some among them who believe what a cow or goose believes, but their lineage and circumcision infect them all. Therefore the history books often accuse them of contaminating wells, of kidnaping and piercing children, as for example at Trent, Weissensee, etc.[102] They, of course, deny this. Whether it is true or not, I do know that they do not lack the complete, full, and ready will to do such things either secretly or openly where possible. This you can assuredly expect from them, and you must govern yourself accordingly.

If they do perform some good deed, you may rest assured that they are not prompted by love, nor is it done with your benefit in mind. Since they are compelled to live among us, they do this for reasons of expediency; but their heart remains and is as I have described it. If you do not want to believe me, read Lyra, Burgensis, and other truthful and honest men. And even if they had not recorded it, you would find that Scripture tells of the two seeds, the serpent's and the woman's. It says that these are enemies, and that God and the devil are at variance with each other. Their own writings and prayer books also state this plainly enough.

A person who is unacquainted with the devil might wonder why they are so particularly hostile toward Christians. They have no reason to act this way, since we show them every kindness. They live among us, enjoy our shield and protection, they use our country and our highways, our markets and streets. Meanwhile our princes and rulers sit there and snore with mouths hanging open and permit the Jews to take, steal, and rob from their open moneybags and treasures whatever they want. That is, they let the Jews, by means of their usury, skin and fleece them and their subjects and make them beggars with their own money. For the Jews, who

---

[102] Popular medieval legend, often recorded in what here are called "history books" (*die Historien*), falsely attributed many atrocities to the Jews. See the cases recounted in *The Universal Jewish Encyclopedia*, article on "Blood Accusation," and for an extended treatment, Trachtenberg, *op. cit.*, chs. 9 and 10.

are exiles, should really have nothing, and whatever they have must surely be our property. They do not work, and they do not earn anything from us, nor do we give or present it to them, and yet they are in possession of our money and goods and are our masters in our own country and in their exile. A thief is condemned to hang for the theft of ten florins, and if he robs anyone on the highway, he forfeits his head. But when a Jew steals and robs ten tons of gold through his usury, he is more highly esteemed than God himself.

In proof of this we cite the bold boast with which they strengthen their faith and give vent to their venomous hatred of us, as they say among themselves: "Be patient and see how God is with us, and does not desert his people even in exile. We do not labor, and yet we enjoy prosperity and leisure. The accursed Goyim have to work for us, but we get their money. This makes us their masters and them our servants. Be patient, dear children of Israel, better times are in store for us, our Messiah will still come if we continue thus and acquire the *chemdath* of all the Gentiles by usury and other methods." Alas, this is what we endure for them. They are under our shield and protection, and yet, as I have said, they curse us. But we shall revert to this later.[103]

We are now speaking about the fact that they cannot tolerate having us as co-heirs in the kingdom of the Messiah, and that he is our *chemdath*, as the prophets abundantly attest. What does God say about this? He says that he will give the *chemdath* to the Gentiles, and that their obedience shall be pleasing to him, as Jacob affirms in Genesis 49, together with all the prophets. He says that he will oppose the obduracy of the Jews most strenuously, rejecting them and choosing and accepting the Gentiles, even though the latter are not of the noble blood of the fathers or circumcised saints. For thus says Hosea 2 [:23]: "And I will say to Not my people, 'You are my people'; and he shall say, 'Thou are my God.'" But to the Jew he says [in Hos. 1:9]: "Call his name Not my people (*lo-ammi*), for you are not my people and I am not your God." Moses, too, had sung this long ago in his song [Deut. 32:21]: "They have stirred me to jealousy with what is no god; they have pro-

---

[103] Cf. below, pp. 268 ff.

voked me with their vain deeds. So I will stir them to jealousy with those who are no people; I will provoke them with a foolish nation." This verse has been in force now for nearly fifteen hundred years. We foolish Gentiles, who were not God's people, are now God's people. That drives the Jews to distraction and stupidity, and over this they became Not-God's-people, who were once his people and really should still be.

But let us conclude our discussion of the saying of Haggai. We have convincing proof that the Messiah, the Gentiles' *chemdath,* appeared at the time when this temple was standing. Thus the ancients understood it, and the inane flimsy glosses of the present-day Jews also testify to this, since they do not know how to deny it except by speaking of their own shame. For he who gives a hollow, meaningless, and irrelevant answer shows that he is defeated and condemns himself. It would have been better and less shameful if he had kept quiet, rather than giving a pointless answer that disgraces him. Thus Haggai 2 [:6 f.] says, "Once again, in a little while, I will shake the heavens and the earth and the sea and the dry land; and I will shake all nations, and the desire of all the Gentiles shall come." This is how I, in the simplicity of my mind, understand these words: Since the beginning of the world there has been enmity between the seed of the serpent and that of the woman, and there has always been conflict between them—sometimes more, sometimes less.

For wherever the Seed of the woman is or appears, he causes strife and discord. This he says in the Gospel: "I have not come to bring peace on earth, but a sword and disunity" [cf. Matt. 10:34]. He takes the armor from the strong man fully armed who had peace in his palace [Luke 11:22]. The latter cannot tolerate this, and the strife is on; angels contend against the devils in the air, and man against man on earth—all on account of the woman's Seed. To be sure, there is plenty of strife, war, and unrest in the world otherwise too; but since it is not undertaken on account of this Seed, it is an insignificant thing in God's eyes, for in this conflict all the angels are involved.

Since the advent of this Seed, or of the Messiah, was close at hand, Haggai says "in a little." This means that until now the strife has been confined solely to my people Israel, that is, restricted to a small area. The devil was ever intent upon devouring them and he set all the surrounding kings upon them. For he was well aware that the promised Seed was in the people of Israel, the Seed that was to despoil him. Therefore he was always eager to harass them. And he instigated one disturbance, dissatisfaction, war, and strife after another. Well and good, now it will be but "a little while," and I shall give him strife aplenty. I will initiate a struggle, and a good one at that—not only in a narrow nook and corner among the people of Israel, but as far as heaven and earth extend, on the sea and on dry land, that is, where it is wet and where it is dry, whether on the mainland or on the islands, at the sea or on the waters, wherever human beings dwell. Or as he says, "I will shake all the Gentiles," so that all the angels will contend with all the devils in heaven or in the air, and all men on earth will quarrel over the Seed.

For I shall send the *chemdath* to all Gentiles. They will love him and adhere to him, as Genesis 49 says, "The Gentiles will gather about him," and, on the other hand, they will grow hostile to the devil, the old serpent, and defect from him. Then all will take its due course when the god and the prince of the world grows wrathful, raves and rages because he is obliged to yield his kingdom, his house, his equipment, his worship, his power, to the *chemdath* and Shiloh, the woman's Seed. Anyone can read the histories that date back to the time of Christ and learn how first the Jews and Gentiles, then the heretics, finally Muhammad, and at present the pope, have raged and still are raging "against the Lord and his Messiah" (Psalm 2 [:2]), and he will understand the words of Haggai that speak of shaking all the nations, etc. There is not a corner in the world nor a spot in the sea where the gospel has not resounded and brought the *chemdath,* as Psalm 18 [19:3-4] declares: "There is no speech, nor are there words; their voice is not heard; yet their voice goes out through all the earth, and their words to the end of the world." The devil too appeared promptly on the scene with murder by the hands of tyrants, with lies spoken by heretics, with all his devilish wiles and powers, which he still employs to impede and obstruct the course of the gospel. This is the strife in question.

220

I shall begin the story of this struggle with that great villain, Antiochus the Noble.[104] Approximately three hundred years elapsed between the time of Haggai and that of Antiochus. This is the short span of time in which peace prevailed. For the kings in Persia were very kind to them, nor did Alexander harm them, and they fared well also under his successors, up to the time of this filthy Antiochus, who ushered in the unrest and the misfortune. Through him the devil sought to exterminate the woman's Seed. He pillaged the city of Jerusalem, the temple, the country and its inhabitants, he desecrated the temple and raged as his god, the devil, impelled him. Practically all the good fortune of the Jews terminated right here. Down to the present, they have never recovered their former position, and they never will.

This will serve to supply a proper understanding of the Jews' glosses which say that the "*chemdath* of all the Gentiles," that is, gold and silver, flowed into this temple. If the earlier kings had put anything into it, then this one took it all away again. This turns their glosses upside down to read: Antiochus distributes the *chemdath* of all Jews among the Gentiles. Thus this verse of Haggai cannot be understood of the Gentiles' shirt or coat. For following these three hundred years, or this "little while," and from then on, they did not get much from the Gentiles, but rather were compelled to give them much. Soon after this, the Romans came and made a clean sweep of it, and placed Herod over them as king. What Herod gave them, they soon learned. Therefore, from the time of Antiochus on they enjoyed but a small measure of peace. Daniel's report also stops with Antiochus, as if to say: Now the end is at hand and all is over, now the Messiah is standing at the door, who will stir up ever more contention.

The detestable Antiochus not only despoiled and desecrated the temple but he also suppressed the *shebet* or sultan, the prince in the house of David, namely, the last prince, John Hyrcanus.[105] None of his descendants again ascended the throne of David or became ruler. Only the *saphra* or *mehoqeq*[106] remained till Herod.

---

[104] Cf. above, p. 207. On the chronological considerations in the following paragraphs, see Luther's *Supputatio annorum*, WA 53, 119–24.

[105] Son of Simon Maccabeus; served as king and high priest from 134 to 104 B.C.

[106] Cf. above, pp. 180 ff.

From that point on David's house looked as if its light had been extinguished, and as if there were no *shultan* or scepter in Judah. It had in fact come to an end, although there were about one hundred and fifty years left until the coming of the Messiah. Such an occurrence is not unusual; anything that is going to break will first crack or burst apart a little.[107] Whatever is going to sink will first submerge or sway a little. The scepter of Judah went through the same process toward the end: it became weak, it groaned and moaned for one hundred and fifty years until it fell apart entirely at the hands of the Romans and of Herod. During these one hundred and fifty years the princes of Judah did not rule but lived as common citizens, perhaps quite impoverished. For Mary, Christ's mother in Nazareth, states that she is a handmaid of poor and low estate [Luke 1:48].

It is also true, however, that the Maccabees fought victoriously against Antiochus. Daniel 11 [:34] refers to this as "a little help." Those who in this way ascended the throne of David and assumed the rule were priests from the tribe of Levi and Aaron. Now one could say with good reason that the royal and the priestly tribes were mixed. For in II Chronicles 22 [:11] we read that Jehoshabeath, the daughter of King Jehoram and the sister of King Ahaziah, was the wife of Jehoiada, the high priest. Thus, coming from the royal house of Solomon, she was grafted into the priestly tribe and became one trunk and tree with it. Therefore she was the ancestress of all the descendants of Jehoiada the priest, a true Sarah of the priestly family. Therefore the Maccabees may indeed be called David's blood and children, as viewed from the maternal lineage. For descent from a mother is just as valid as that from a father.[108] This is recognized also in other countries. For instance, our Emperor Charles is king in Spain by virtue of his descent from

---

107 A German proverb.

108 Rather than dismissing the question of Davidic continuity during the Maccabean period by rejecting the authority of the Apocryphal accounts, as he did above (p. 207), Luther here relies on an argument positing continuity through the maternal line. This argument had been employed by Raymund Martin (*Pugio fidei*, Part Ii, ch. 4), Nicholas of Lyra (gloss on Gen. 49), and Paul of Burgos (*Addition* to Gen. 49 and *Scrutinium*, Part I, Distinction 2, ch. 2). Still another argument used by these writers was that concerning the role of the Sanhedrin, drawn from the Davidic tribe of Judah; cf. above, p. 181, and n. 48.

his mother and not from his father; and his father Philip was duke of Burgundy not because of his father, Maximilian, but because of his mother, Mary.[109]

Thus David calls all the children of Jehoiada and of Jehoshabeath his natural children, his sons and daughters, because Jehoshabeath was descended from his son Solomon.[110] So through the Maccabees, Solomon's family regained rule and scepter through the maternal side, after it had been lost through Ahaziah on the paternal side. It remained in David's family until Herod, who did away with it and abolished both *shultan* and *saphra* or the Sanhedrin. Now finally, there lies the scepter of Judah and the *mehoqeq*, there the house of David is darkened on both the paternal and the maternal sides. Therefore the Messiah must now be at hand, the true Light of David, the true Son, who had sustained his house until that time and who would sustain it and enlighten it from that point on to all eternity. This conforms to God's promise that the scepter of Judah will remain until the Messiah appears and that the house of David will be preserved forever and will never die out. But, as we said, despite all of this God must be the Jews' liar, who has not yet sent the Messiah as he promised and vowed.

Furthermore, God says through Haggai: "I will fill this house with splendor. The silver is mine, and the gold is mine. The splendor of this latter house shall be greater than the former," etc. [Hag. 2:7 f.]. It is true that this temple displayed great splendor during the three hundred years prior to Antiochus, since the Persians and the successors of Alexander, the kings in Syria and King Philadelphus in Egypt, contributed much toward it. But despite all of this, it did not compare in magnificence with the first temple, the temple of Solomon. The text must refer to a different splendor here, or else Solomon's temple will far surpass it. For in the first temple there was also an abundance of gold and silver, and in addition the ark

---

[109] Charles of Habsburg (1500–1558), grandson of Ferdinand and Isabella, inherited the throne of Spain in 1516 through their daughter and his mother, Joanna of Castile. In 1519 he succeeded his paternal grandfather Maximilian I as emperor of the Holy Roman Empire. Charles' father, Philip the Handsome (1487–1506), succeeded to the Duchy of Burgundy through his mother, Mary of Burgundy, as Luther indicates.

[110] It is not clear to what specific utterance of David Luther might be referring.

of the covenant, the mercy-seat, the cherubim, Moses' tablets, Aaron's rod, the bread of heaven in the golden vessel, Aaron's robes, also the Urim and Thummin and the sacred oil with which the kings and priests were anointed (Burgensis on Daniel 9). When Solomon dedicated this temple, fire fell from heaven and consumed the sacrifice, and the temple was filled with what he called a cloud of divine Majesty [II Chron. 5:13, 7:1]. God himself was present in this cloud, as Solomon himself says: "The Lord has said that he would dwell in thick darkness" [II Chron. 6:1]. He had done the same thing in the wilderness as he hovered over Moses' tabernacle.

There was none of this splendor, surpassing gold and silver, in the temple of Haggai. Yet God says that it will show forth greater splendor than the first one. Let the Jews pipe up and say what constituted this greater splendor. They cannot pass over this in silence, for the text and the confession of the ancient Jews, their forefathers, both state that the *chemdath* of the Gentiles, the Messiah, came at the time when the same temple stood and glorified it highly with his presence. We Christians know that our Lord Jesus Christ, the true *chemdath*, was presented in the temple by his mother, and that he himself often taught and did miracles there. This is the true cloud—his tender humanity, in which God manifested his presence and let himself be seen and heard. The blind Jews may deride this, but our faith is strengthened by it, until they can adduce a splendor of the temple excelling this *chemdath* of all the Gentiles. That they will do when they erect the third temple, that is to say, when God is a liar, when the devil is the truth, and when they themselves again take possession of Jerusalem—not before.[111]

Josephus writes[112] that Herod razed the temple of Haggai because it was not sufficiently splendid, and rebuilt it so that it was equal or superior to the temple of Solomon in splendor. I would be glad to believe the history books; however, even if this temple had been constructed of diamonds and rubies, it would still have lacked the items mentioned from that sublime, old holy place— namely, the ark, the mercy-seat, the cherubim, etc. Furthermore,

---

[111] Cf. above, p. 80, and n. 18.
[112] *Antiquities of the Jews*, Book XV, ch. 13.

since Herod had not been commissioned by God to build it, but did so as an impious enemy of God and of his people, motivated by vanity and pride, in his own honor, his whole structure and work was not as good as the most puny little stone that Zerubbabel placed into the temple by command of God. Herod certainly did not merit much grace for tearing down and desecrating the temple which had been commanded, built, and consecrated by the word of God, and then presuming to erect a much more glorious one without God's word and command. God permitted this out of consideration for the place which he had selected for the temple, and so that the destruction of the temple might have the negative significance that the people of Israel should henceforth be without temple, word of God, and all, that it instead would be given wholly to the splendor of the world, under the guise of the service to God.

This temple was not only less splendid than Solomon's, but it was also violated in many ways more terribly than Solomon's temple, and was often completely desecrated. This happened first, against the will of the Jews, when Antiochus robbed it of all its contents, placed an idol on the altar, sacrificed pork, and made a regular pig-sty and an idolatrous desolation of the temple, instituting a horrible slaughter in Jerusalem as though he were the devil himself, as we read in I Maccabees 1 and as Daniel 11 had predicted. No lesser outrage was committed by the Romans, and especially by that filthy Emperor Caligula, who also placed his mark of abomination in the temple. Daniel 9 and 12 speak of this. Such ignominy and disgrace were not experienced by Solomon's temple at the hands of Gentiles and foreigners. This makes it difficult to see how Haggai's words were fulfilled, "I will fill this temple with glory which will exceed the glory of that temple." One might rather say that it was filled with dishonor exceeding the dishonor of that temple, that is, if one thinks of external and outward honor. Consequently, if Haggai's words are to be accounted true, he must be referring to a different kind of splendor.

Second, the Jews themselves also desecrated this temple more viciously than the other one ever was desecrated: namely, with spiritual idolatries. Lyra writes,[113] and others too, in many passages,

---

[113] Luther's reference is uncertain. This does not occur in Lyra's commentary on Haggai.

that the Jews, after their return from the Babylonian captivity, did not commit idolatry or sin by killing prophets as gravely as before. Thereby he wants to prove that their present exile must be due to a more heinous sin than idolatry, the murder of the prophets, etc.—namely, the crucifixion of the Messiah. This argument is good, valid, and cogent.[114] That they no longer killed the prophets is not to be attributed to a lack of evil intentions, but to the fact that they no longer had any prophets who reproved their idolatry, greed, and other vices. That is why they could no longer kill prophets. To be sure, the last prophet, Malachi, who began to rebuke the priests, barely escaped (if indeed he did escape).

But they did practice idolatry more outrageously at the time of this temple than at the time of the other—not the coarse, palpable, stupid variety, but the subtle, spiritual kind. Zechariah portrays this under the image of a flying scroll and of an ephah going forth (Zechariah 5 [:2, 6]). And Zechariah 11 [:12] and 12 [:10] foretell the infamy of their selling God for thirty pieces of silver and their piercing him through. More on that elsewhere;[115] is it not shame enough that the priests at the same time perverted God's Ten Commandments so flagrantly? Tell me, what idolatry compares with the abomination of changing the word of God into lies? To do that is truly to set up idols, i.e., false gods, under the cloak of God's name; and that is forbidden in the second commandment, which reads: "You shall not take the name of the Lord your God in vain."

Why, their Talmud and their rabbis record[116] that it is no sin for a Jew to kill a Gentile, but it is only a sin for him to kill a brother Israelite. Nor is it a sin for a Jew to break his oath to a Gentile. Likewise, they say that it is rendering God a service to

---

[114] Luther had made major use of this argument in *Sabbatarians*. There, however, he customarily refers simply to the Jews' nonacceptance of the Messiah, not explicitly to their "crucifixion" of him as in the present passage.

[115] Luther does not return to the theme in the present treatise.

[116] Luther cites no references, but the point made here was a commonplace in the anti-Semitic literature. Bernard Lazare (*Antisemitism: Its History and Causes*, trans. from the French [New York: International Library, 1903], pp. 262 ff.) points out that such maledictions against the Gentiles as are found in the Talmud originated, for the most part, in periods of warfare. For the role of medieval superstition in reinforcing this picture of Jewish enmity toward Christians, see Trachtenberg, *op. cit.*, especially chs. 9 and 10.

steal or rob from a Goy, as they in fact do through their usury. For since they believe that they are the noble blood and the circumcised saints and we the accursed Goyim, they cannot treat us too harshly or commit sin against us, for they are the lords of the world and we are their servants, yes, their cattle.[117]

In brief, our evangelists also tell us what their rabbis taught. In Matthew 15 [:4 ff.] we read that they abrogated the fourth commandment, which enjoins honor of father and mother; and in Matthew 23, that they were given to much shameful doctrine, not to mention what Christ says in Matthew 5 about how they preached and interpreted the Ten Commandments so deviously, how they installed money-changers, traders, and all sorts of usurers in the temple, prompting our Lord to say that they had made the house of God into a den of robbers [Matt. 21:13; Luke 19:46]. Now figure out for yourself what a great honor that is and how the temple is filled with such glory that God must call his own house a den of robbers because so many souls had been murdered through their greedy, false doctrine, that is, through double idolatry. The Jews still persist in such doctrine to the present day. They imitate their fathers and pervert God's word. They are steeped in greed, in usury, they steal and murder where they can and ever teach their children to do likewise.

Even this is not the greatest shame of this temple. The real abomination of all abominations, the shame of all shames, is this: that at the time of this temple there were several chief priests and an entire sect which were Sadducean, that is, Epicurean, who did not believe in the existence of any angel, devil, heaven, hell, or life after this life. And such fellows were expected to enter the temple, vested with the priestly office and in priestly garments, and sacrifice, pray, and offer burnt offerings for the people, preach to them, and rule them! Tell me, how much worse could Antiochus have been, with his idol and his sacrifice of pork, than were these Sad-

[117] Luther apparently felt the need of further support for the assertions made in this paragraph. In the second edition of the treatise, the following words are added at this point: "You may read further about this in Burgensis' *Additions* on Isaiah 34 and Zechariah 5. There you will learn what the rabbis really teach, and you will see that I have written much too mildly against them." Cf. WA 53, 489, footnote to line 37.

ducean pigs and sows? In view of this, what remains of Haggai's statement that this temple's glory was greater than that of Solomon's temple? Before God and reason, a real pig-sty might be called a royal hall when compared with this temple, because of such great, horrible, and monstrous sows.

How much more honorably do the pagan philosophers, as well as the poets, write and teach not only about God's rule and about the life to come but also about temporal virtues. They teach that man by nature is obliged to serve his fellow man, to keep faith also with his enemies, and to be loyal and helpful especially in time of need.[118] Thus Cicero and his kind teach. Indeed, I believe that three of Aesop's fables, half of Cato, and several comedies of Terence contain more wisdom and more instruction about good works than can be found in the books of all the Talmudists and rabbis and more than may ever occur to the hearts of all the Jews.

Someone may think that I am saying too much. I am not saying too much, but too little; for I see their writings. They curse us Goyim.[119] In their synagogues and in their prayers they wish us every misfortune. They rob us of our money and goods through their usury, and they play on us every wicked trick they can. And the worst of it is that they still claim to have done right and well, that is, to have done God a service. And they teach the doing of such things. No pagan ever acted thus; in fact, no one acts thus except the devil himself, or whomever he possesses, as he has possessed the Jews.

Burgensis, who was one of their very learned rabbis, and who through the grace of God became a Christian[120]—a very rare happening—is much agitated by the fact that they curse us Christians so vilely in their synagogues (as Lyra also writes), and he deduces from this that they cannot be God's people.[121] For if they were, they would emulate the example of the Jews in the Babylonian captivity. To them Jeremiah wrote, "Seek the welfare of the city

[118] On Luther's doctrine of natural law, cf. above, pp. 90-95, 110-111 et passim (see index). The present paragraph presents one of his strongest statements on the value of classical literature: its wisdom extends even to theological themes (their writing and teaching *"von Gottes regiment und vom kuenfftigen leben"*).
[119] Cf. above, n. 116.
[120] Cf. above, p. 68, n. 5 and p. 176, n. 37.
[121] Specific statements to this effect in Lyra and Burgensis have not been located.

where I have sent you into exile, and pray to the Lord on its behalf, for in its welfare you will find your welfare" [Jer. 29:7]. But
our bastards and pseudo-Jews think they must curse us, hate us,
and inflict every possible harm upon us, although they have no
cause for it. Therefore they surely are no longer God's people.
But we shall say more about this later.[122]

To return to the subject of Haggai's temple, it is certain that
no house was ever disgraced more than this holy house of God was
by such vile sows as the Sadducees and Pharisees. Yet Christ calls
it God's house, because the four pillars are his.[123] Therefore, to off-
set this disgrace a greater and different splendor must have inhered in it than that of silver and gold. If not, Haggai will fare ill
with his prophecy that the splendor of this temple will surpass that
of Solomon's temple. Amid such colossal shame no splendor can be
found here other than that of the *chemdath*, who will appear in a
short time and surpass such shame with his splendor. The Jews can
produce no other splendor; their mouth is stopped.

I must break off here and leave the last part of Haggai to
others, the section in which he prophesies that the Lord, as he says,
"will give peace in this place" [cf. Hag. 2:9b]. Can it be possible
that this applies to the time from Antiochus up to the present during which the Jews have experienced every misfortune and are
still in exile? For there shall be peace in this place, says the Lord.
The place is still there; the temple and peace have vanished. No
doubt the Jews will be able to interpret this. The history books
inform me that there was but little peace prior to Antiochus for
about three hundred years, and subsequent to that time none at
all down to the present hour, except for the peace that reigned at
the time of the Maccabees. As I have already said, I shall leave this
to others.

Finally we must lend ear to the great prophet Daniel.[124]

---

[122] Cf. below, p. 291.
[123] There is no New Testament source for this curious statement.
[124] Luther takes up here the fourth and final proof-text dealt with in the middle section of the treatise. In Lyra's *Pulcherrimae quaestiones*, too, the treatment of Dan. 9:24 follows upon that of Hag. 2:6–9. Luther had already dealt
with the Daniel passage at considerable length in his treatise of 1523, *That
Jesus Christ Was Born a Jew*; cf. LW 45, 221 ff.

A special angel with a proper name—Gabriel—talks with him. The like of this is not found elsewhere in the Old Testament. The fact that the angel is mentioned by name marks it as something extraordinary. This is what he tells Daniel: "Seventy weeks of years are decreed concerning your people and your holy city, to finish the transgression, to put an end to sin, and to atone for iniquity, to bring in everlasting righteousness, to seal both vision and prophet, and to anoint a most holy place" [Dan. 9:24].

We cannot now discuss this rich text, which actually is one of the foremost in all of Scripture. And, as is only natural, everybody has reflected on it; for it not only fixes the time of Christ's advent but also foretells what he will do—namely, take away sin, bring righteousness, and do this by means of his death. It establishes Christ as the Priest who bears the sin of the whole world. This, I say, we must now set aside and deal only with the question of the time, as we determined to do—whether such a Messiah or Priest has already come or is still to come. [This we do] for the strengthening of our faith, against all devils and men.

In the first place, there is complete agreement on this:[125] that the seventy weeks are not weeks of days but of years; that one week comprises seven years, which produces a sum total of four hundred and ninety years. That is the first point. Second, it is also agreed that these seventy weeks had ended when Jerusalem was destroyed by the Romans. There is no difference of opinion on these two points, although many are in the dark when it comes to the matter of knowing the precise time of which these seventy weeks began and when they terminated. It is not necessary for us to settle this question here, since it is generally assumed that they were fulfilled about the time of the destruction of Jerusalem. This will suffice us for the present.

If this is true—as it must be true, since after the destruction of Jerusalem none of the seventy weeks was left, then the Messiah must have come before the destruction of Jerusalem, while something of those seventy weeks still remained: namely, the last week, as the text later clearly and convincingly attests. After the seven

---

[125] Luther refers here to a venerable tradition shared by both Jewish and Christian commentators.

and sixty-two weeks[126] (that is, after sixty-nine weeks), namely, in the last or seventieth week, Christ will be killed—in such a way, however, that he will become alive again. For the angel says that "he shall make a strong covenant with many in the last week" [Dan. 9:27].[127] This he cannot do while dead; he must be alive. "To make a covenant" can have no other meaning than to fulfill God's promise given to the fathers, namely, to disseminate the blessing promised in Abraham's seed to all the Gentiles. As the angel states earlier [v. 24], the visions and prophecies shall be sealed or fulfilled. This requires a live Messiah, who, however, has previously been killed. But the Jews will have none of this. Therefore we shall let it rest at that and hold to our opinion that the Messiah must have appeared during these seventy weeks; this the Jews cannot refute.

For in their books as well as in certain histories[128] we learn that not just a few Jews but all of Jewry at that time assumed that the Messiah must have come or must be present at that very moment. This is what we want to hear! When Herod was forcibly made king of Judah and Israel by the Romans, the Jews surely realized that the scepter would thus depart from them. They resisted this move vigorously, and in the thirty years of their resistance many thousand Jews were slain and much blood was shed, until they finally surrendered in exhaustion. In the meantime the Jews looked about for the Messiah. Thus a hue and cry arose that the Messiah had been born—as, in truth, he had been. For our Lord Christ was born in the thirtieth year of Herod's reign. But Herod forcibly suppressed this report, slaying all the young children in the region of Bethlehem, so that our Lord had to be taken for refuge to Egypt. Herod even killed his own son because he was born of a Jewish mother. He was worried that through this son the scepter might revert to the Jews and that he might gain the Jews' loyalty, since, as Philo records,[129] the rumor of the birth of Christ had been spread abroad.

As our evangelists relate, more than thirty years later John

---

[126] Cf. Dan. 9:10, which alludes to two periods of these respective durations.
[127] The RSV reads "for a week" instead of Luther's "in the last week."
[128] Probably referring to the works of Josephus.
[129] In *Breviarium de Temporibus,* a pseudo-Philonic work; cf. WA 53, 19 ff.

the Baptist comes out of the wilderness and proclaims that the Lord had not only been born but also was already among them and would reign shortly after him. Suddenly thereafter Christ himself appears, preaches, and performs great miracles, so that the Jews hoped that now, after the loss of the scepter, Shiloh had come. But the chief priests, the rulers, and their followers took offense at the person, since he did not appear as a mighty king but wandered about as a poor beggar. They had made up their mind that the Messiah would unite the Jews and not only wrest the scepter from the foreign king but also subdue the Romans and all the world under himself with the sword, installing them as mighty princes over all the Gentiles. When they were disappointed in these expectations, the noble blood and circumcised saints were vexed, as people who had the promise of the kingdom and could not attain it through this beggar. Therefore they despised him and did not accept him.

But when they disdained John and his [Christ's] message and miracles, reviling them as the deeds of Beelzebub, he spoiled and ruined matters entirely. He rebuked and chided them severely—something he should not, of course, have done—for being greedy, evil, and disobedient children, false teachers, seducers of the people, etc.; in brief, a brood of serpents and children of the devil. On the other hand, he was friendly to sinners and tax collectors, to Gentiles and to Romans, giving the impression that he was the foe of the people of Israel and the friend of Gentiles and villains. Now the fat was really in the fire; they grew wrathful, bitter, and hateful, and ranted against him; finally they contrived the plot to kill him. And that is what they did; they crucified him as ignominiously as possible. They gave free rein to their anger, so that even the Gentile Pilate noticed this and testified that they were condemning and killing him out of hatred and envy, innocently and without cause.

When they had executed this false Messiah (that is the conception they wanted to convey of him), they still did not abandon the delusion that the Messiah had to be at hand or nearby. They constantly murmured against the Romans because of the scepter. Soon, too, the rumor circulated that Jesus, whom they had killed, had again arisen and that he was now really being proclaimed openly and freely as the Messiah. The people in the city of Jerusalem were adhering to him, as well as the Gentiles in Antioch and everywhere in the country. Now they really had their hands full. They had to oppose this dead Messiah and his followers, lest he be accepted as resurrected and as the Messiah. They also had to oppose the Romans, lest their hoped-for Messiah be forever bereft of the scepter. At one place a slaughter of the Christians was initiated, at another an uprising against the Romans. To these tactics they devoted themselves for approximately forty years, until the Romans finally were constrained to lay waste country and city. This delusion regarding their false Christ and their persecution of the true Christ cost them eleven times one hundred thousand men, as Josephus reports,[130] together with the most horrible devastation of country and city, as well as the forfeiture of scepter, temple, priesthood, and all that they possessed.

This deep and cruel humiliation, which is terrible to read and to hear about, surely should have made them pliable and humble. Alas, they became seven times more stubborn, viler, and prouder than before. This was due in part to the fact that in their dispersion they had to witness how the Christians daily grew and increased with their Messiah. The saying of Moses found in Deuteronomy 32 [:21] was now completely fulfilled in them: "They have stirred me to jealousy with what is no god; so I will stir them to jealousy with those who are no people." Likewise, as Hosea says: "I will say to Not my people, 'You are my people,' but you are not my people and I am not your God" (Hosea 2 [:23, 1:9]. They stubbornly insisted on having their own Messiah in whom the Gentiles should not claim a share, and they persisted in trying to exterminate this Messiah in whom both Jews and Gentiles gloried. Everywhere throughout the Roman Empire they intervened and wherever they could ferret out a Christian in any corner they dragged him out before the judges and accused him (they themselves could not pass sentence on him, since they had neither legal authority nor power) until they had him killed. Thus they shed very much

---

[130] *The Jewish War*, Book VII, ch. 17.

Christian blood and made innumerable martyrs, also outside the Roman Empire, in Persia and wherever they could.

Still they clung to the delusion that the Messiah must have appeared, since the seventy weeks of Daniel had expired and the temple of Haggai had been destroyed. However, they disliked the person of Jesus of Nazareth, and therefore they went ahead and elevated one of their own number to be the Messiah. This came about as follows: They had a rabbi, or Talmudist, named Akiba,[131] a very learned man, esteemed by them more highly than all other rabbis, a venerable, honorable, gray-haired man. He taught the verses of Haggai and of Daniel, also of Jacob in Genesis 49, with ardor, saying that there had to be a Messiah among the people of God since the time fixed by Scripture was at hand. Then he chose one, surnamed Kokhba,[132] which means "a star." According to Burgensis his right name was Heutoliba. He is well known in all the history books, where he is called Ben Koziba or Bar Koziban.[133] This man had to be their Messiah; and he gladly complied. All the people and the rabbis rallied about him and armed themselves thoroughly with the intention of doing away with both Christians and Romans. Now they had the Messiah fashioned to their liking and their mind, who was proclaimed by the aforementioned passages of Scripture.

This unrest began approximately thirty years after the destruction of Jerusalem, under the reign of the emperor Trajan.[134]

[131] Akiba ben Joseph (ca. 50–ca. 132), a figure of great stature in the rabbinic tradition, who lent his support to the messianic claims of Bar Kokhba, leader of the final Jewish revolt against Rome (A.D. 132–135). Lyra refers to him in this connection (Gloss on Hag. 2:6-9), as does Paul of Burgos (Scrutinium, Part I, Distinction 3, ch. 3).

[132] "Kochab," in the transliteration used by Luther; the name is also rendered "Kokba," etc. The messianic interpretation of the term "star" is derived from the verses from Num. 24 cited immediately below. For a further discussion of the events dealt with by Luther here, see The Jewish Encyclopedia (New York: Funk and Wagnalls Co., 1906–1907), articles "Akiba ben Joseph" and "Bar Kokba."

[133] In the Hebrew and Aramaic forms, respectively. According to The Jewish Encyclopedia, these appellations are found exclusively in the Jewish literature, "Bar Kokhba" in the Christian literature.

[134] Luther appears to combine earlier disturbances with the rebellion led by Bar Kokhba. The latter took place during the reign of Hadrian (A.D. 117–138) rather than that of Trajan (98–117). On the peculiarities of his chronology at this point, see WA 53, 128, footnote e. A general discussion of Luther's historical sources and methods is provided by Ernst Schaefer, Luther als Kirchenhistoriker: Ein Beitrag zur Geschichte der Wissenschaft (Gütersloh, 1897).

Rabbi Akiba was Kokhba's prophet and spirit who inflamed and incited him and vehemently urged him on, applying all the verses of Scripture that deal with the Messiah to him before all the people and proclaiming: "You are the Messiah!" He applied to him especially the saying of Balaam recorded in Numbers 24 [:17-19], by reason of his surname Kokhba ("star"). For in that passage Balaam says in a vision: "A star shall come forth out of Jacob, and a scepter shall rise out of Israel; it shall crush the forehead of Moab, and break down all the sons of Sheth. Edom shall be dispossessed, Seir also, his enemies, shall be dispossessed, while Israel does valiantly. By Jacob shall dominion be exercised, and the survivors of cities be destroyed!"

That was a proper sermon for thoroughly misleading such a foolish, angry, restive mob—which is exactly what happened. To insure the success of this venture and guard against its going awry, that exalted and precious Rabbi Akiba, the old fool and simpleton, made himself Kokhba's guardsman or armor-bearer, his *armiger*, as the history books have it; if I am not translating the term correctly, let some one else improve on it.[135] The person is meant who is positioned beside the king or prince and whose chief duty it is to defend him on the battlefield or in combat, either on horse or on foot. To be sure, something more is implied here, since he is also a prophet—a Münzer[136] (to use contemporary terms). So this is where the scepter of Judah and the Messiah now resided; they are sure of it. They carried on like this for some thirty years. Kokhba always had himself addressed as King Messiah, and butchered throngs of Christians who refused to deny our Messiah Jesus Christ.[137] His captains also harassed the Romans where they could. Especially in Egypt they at one time defeated the Roman

---

[135] Modern lexicons confirm Luther's interpretation.

[136] Thomas Münzer (*ca.* 1488–1525), revolutionary spiritualist and, for Luther, the prototype of "fanaticism" (*Schwärmerei*). Cf. George Huntston Williams, *The Radical Reformation* (Philadelphia: Westminster, 1962), pp. 44–78, and Eric W. Gritsch, *Reformer Without a Church: The Life and Thought of Thomas Muentzer, 1488?–1525* (Philadelphia: Fortress, 1967).

[137] Justin Martyr (*ca.* 100–*ca.* 165) already charges that "In the recent Jewish war, Bar Kocheba, the leader of the Jewish uprising, ordered that only the Christians should be subjected to dreadful torments, unless they renounced and blasphemed Jesus Christ" (*First Apology*, ch. 31). Reports of widespread massacres, however, appear to be due to later exaggeration. Cf. Graetz, *History of the Jews* (cited above, p. 129, n. 17), II, 409 ff.

captain during the reign of Trajan.[138] Now their heart, brain, and belly began to swell with conceit. God, they inferred, had to be for them and with them. They occupied a town near Jerusalem, called Bittir; in the Bible it is known as Beth-horon [Josh. 10:10].

At this point they were convinced that their Messiah, King Kokhba, was the lord of the world and had vanquished the Christians and the Romans and had carried the day. But Emperor Hadrian sent his army against them, laid siege to Bittir, conquered it, and slew Messiah and prophet, star and darkness, lord and armor-bearer. Their own books lament that there were twice eighty thousand men at Bittir who blew the trumpets, who were captains over vast hosts of men, and that forty times one hundred thousand men were slain, not including those slain at Alexandria. The latter are said to have numbered twelve times one hundred thousand. However, it seems to me that they are exaggerating enormously. I interpret this to mean that the two times eighty thousand trumpeters represent that many valiant and able-bodied men equipped for battle, each of whom would have been able to lead large bodies of soldiers in battle. Otherwise this sounds too devilishly mendacious.

After this formidable defeat they themselves called Kokhba, their lost Messiah, "Kozba,"[139] which rhymes with it and has a similar ring. For thus write their Talmudists: You must not read "Kokhba," but "Kozba." Therefore all history books now refer to him as Koziban. "Kozba" means "false." His attempt had miscarried, and he had proved a false and not a true Messiah. Just as we Germans might say by way of rhyme: You are not a *Deutscher* but a *Täuscher* ["not a German but a deceiver"]; not a *Welscher* but a *Fälscher* ["not a foreigner of Romance origin but a falsifier"]. Of a usurer I may say: You are not a *Bürger*, but a *Würger* ["not a citizen but a slayer"]. Such rhyming is customary in all languages. Our Eusebius reports this story in his *Ecclesiastical History*, Book 4, chapter 6. Here he uses the name Barcochabas, saying that this

---

[138] Cf. above, n. 134.
[139] From the Hebrew root meaning "to lie." This appellation, however, may in fact have been derived from the name of his native city; cf. *The Jewish Encyclopedia*, article "Bar Kokba."

was an extremely cruel battle in which the Jews "were driven so far from their country that their impious eyes were no longer able to see their fatherland even if they ascended the highest mountains."

Such horrible stories are sufficient witness that all of Jewry understood that this had to be the time of the Messiah, since the seventy weeks had elapsed, Haggai's temple had been destroyed, and the scepter had been wrested from Judah, as the statements of Jacob in Genesis 49, of Haggai 2, and of Daniel 9 clearly indicated and announced. God be praised that we Christians are certain and confident of our belief that the true Messiah, Jesus Christ, did come at that time. To prove this, we have not only his miraculous deeds, which the Jews themselves cannot deny, but also the gruesome downfall and misfortune, because of the name of the Messiah, of his enemies who wanted to exterminate him together with all his adherents. How could they otherwise have brought such misery upon their heads if they had not been convinced that the time of the Messiah was at hand? And I think this does surely constitute coming to grief and running their heads (now for the second time) against "the stone of offence and the rock of stumbling," to quote Isaiah 8 [:14]. So many hundreds of thousands attempted to devour Jesus of Nazareth, but over this they themselves "stumbled and fell and were broken, snared, and taken," as Isaiah says [8:15].

Since two such terrible and awesome attempts had most miserably failed, the first at Jerusalem under Vespasian, the other at Bittir under Hadrian, they surely should have come to their senses, have become pliable and humble, and concluded: God help us! How does this happen? The time of the Messiah's advent has, in accord with the prophets' words and promises, come and gone, and we are beaten so terribly and cruelly over it! What if our ideas regarding the Messiah—that he should be a secular Kokhba—have deceived us, and he came in a different manner and form? Is it possible that the Messiah is Jesus of Nazareth, to whom so many Jews and Gentiles adhere, who daily perform so many wondrous signs? Alas, they became seven times more stubborn and baser than before. Their conception of a worldly Messiah must be right and cannot fail; there must be a mistake about the designated time. The prophets must be lying and fail rather than they. They will have nothing of this Jesus, even if they must pervert all of Scripture, have no god, and never get a Messiah. That's the way they want it.

Since they were beaten into defenseless impotence by the Romans, from that time on they have turned against Scripture, and have boldly tried to take it from us and to pervert it with strange and different interpretations. They have digressed from the understanding of all their forefathers and prophets, and furthermore from their own reason. Because of this they have lost so many hundreds of thousands of men, land, and city, and have fallen prey to every misery. They have done nothing these fourteen hundred years but take any verse which we Christians apply to our Messiah and violate it, tear it to bits, crucify it, and twist it in order to give it a different nose and mask. They deal with it as their fathers dealt with our Lord Christ on Good Friday, making God appear as the liar but themselves as the truthful ones, as you heard before. They assign practically ten different interpretations to Jacob's saying in Genesis 49.[140] Likewise they know how to twist the nose of Haggai's statement. Here you have two good illustrations which show you how masterfully the Jews exegete the Scriptures, in such a way that they do not arrive at any definite meaning.

They have also distorted in this way the passage from Daniel. I cannot enumerate all their shameful glosses, but shall submit just one—the one which Lyra and Burgensis[141] consider to be the most famous and widespread among the Jews, from which they dare not depart on pain of losing their souls. It reads as follows. Gabriel says to Daniel: "Seventy weeks of years are decreed concerning your people and your holy city, to finish the transgression, to put an end to sin, and to atone for iniquity, to bring in everlasting righteousness, to seal both vision and prophet, and to anoint a most holy place, . . ." [Dan. 9:24]. This is the text. Now their beautiful commentary follows:

"It will still be seventy weeks before Jerusalem will be de-

---

[140] Cf. above, pp. 178 ff.
[141] Cf. Lyra and Paul of Burgos in the *Postilla* to Dan. 9:24, and Paul of Burgos in *Scrutinium*, Part I, Distinction 3, ch. 3. The interpretation cited is found in Rashi's Commentary on the prophets.

stroyed and the Jews are led into exile by the Romans. This will happen so that they may be induced by this exile to depart from their sins, that they may be punished for them, pay for them, render satisfaction, atone for them, and thus become pious eternally and merit the fulfillment of the messianic promises, the reconstruction of the holy temple," etc.

Here you perceive, in the first place, that the Jews' immeasurable holiness presumes that God will fulfill his promise regarding the Messiah not because of his sheer grace and mercy but because of their merit and repentance and their extraordinary piety. And how could or should God, that poor fellow, do otherwise? For when he promised the Messiah to Jacob, David, and Haggai out of sheer grace, he neither thought nor knew that such great saints—whose merits would exact the Messiah from his—would appear after seventy weeks and after the destruction of Jerusalem, that he would have to grant the Messiah not out of grace but would be obliged to send him by reason of their great purity and holiness, when, where, and in the way that they desired. Such is the imposing story of the Jews, who repented after the seventy weeks and became so pious.

You can easily infer that they did not repent, nor were they pious before and during the seventy weeks. As a result the priests in Jerusalem all starved to death because there was no penance, no sin or guilt offerings (which the priests needed for sustenance). All this was postponed and saved for the penance and holiness which were to begin after the seventy weeks. Where there is no repentance, or anything to repent for, there is no sin. But where then, we wonder, did the sin come from for which they have to repent after the seventy weeks, since they had atoned daily through so many sacrifices of the priests, ordained by Moses for this purpose, for all previous sin? Why do they have to begin to do penance now after the seventy weeks, when temple, office, sacrifice for sins no longer exist?

But the following even surpasses this. Gabriel says, according to their gloss, that the Jews will repent and become pious after the seventy weeks, so that the Messiah will come on account of their merit. Well and good, here we have it! If Gabriel is speaking the truth and not lying, then the Jews have now repented, they have become pious, they have merited the Messiah ever since the passing of those seventy weeks. For he says that all of this will be done by the Jews subsequent to the seventy weeks. What follows now? They confess, indeed they wail, that the Messiah has not come since the end of those seventy weeks, that he has not come to date, approximately 1,468 years later; nor do they know when he will come. So they will also have to confess that they have not done penance for any sin nor become pious during these 1,468 years following the seventy weeks, nor merited the Messiah. It follows that the angel Gabriel must be lying when he promises in God's behalf that the Jews will repent, be pious, and merit the Messiah after the seventy weeks.

In Leviticus 26 [:40 ff.] and in Deuteronomy 4 [:29 ff.] and 30 [:1 ff.], Moses, too, proves very clearly that they have never sincerely done penance for sin since the seventy weeks. In many beautiful words he promises that God will return them to their fatherland, even if they are dispersed to the end of the heavens, etc., if they turn to God with all their heart and confess their sin. Moses utters these words as the spokesman of God, whom one must not accuse of lying. Since the Jews have not been returned to their country to date, it is proved that they have never repented for sin with all their heart since the seventy weeks. So it must be falsehood when they incorrectly interpret Gabriel as speaking about their repentance.

We also know that God is so gracious by nature that he forgives man his sin in every hour in which man sincerely repents and is sorry for it, as David says in Psalm 32 [:5]: "I said, I will confess my transgressions to the Lord: then thou didst forgive the guilt of my sin." We also read that when the prophet Nathan rebuked David for his sin and the latter thereupon declared, "I have sinned against the Lord," he was immediately absolved by Nathan, who replied, "The Lord has put away your sin" [II Sam. 12:13]. Even if God in many instances does not remove the punishment as promptly as he did with David, he nonetheless assures man of the remission of his sin. And if neither prophet nor priest were available, an angel would have to appear instead and announce, "Your sins are forgiven you," so that a sinner in his sorrow and punishment might not lose heart and despair. We observe also how during the Babylonian captivity God graciously and paternally consoles the people who confess their sins, enabling them to bear the punishment. Nor can the punishment endure forever; it must have its definite time, measure, and end wherever genuine contrition and repentance are found.

But there is no remission of sin for these Jews, no prophet to console them with the assurance of such forgiveness, no definite time limit for their punishment, but only interminable wrath and disfavor, devoid of any mercy. So it is not only an unmitigated lie but also an impossibility to understand Gabriel's promises in terms of their repentance, much less of their merit and righteousness.

But why should we waste so many words and so much time! The land of Canaan was hardly as big as a beggar's alms or as a crust of bread in comparison with the empire of the whole world. Yet they did not merit even this land through their repentance, or righteousness. Thus Moses declares in Deuteronomy 9 [:4 f.] that they were not granted the possession of the land because of their righteousness, but it was given to them, a stiff-necked and disobedient people, that is, very sinful and unworthy people, solely by reason of God's gracious promise, although Hosea [Hos. 11:1 ff.] and Balaam (Numbers 24 [:5 ff.]) praise them for being at their peak of piety at that time. They still had Moses, Aaron, the divine worship, prophets, God himself with his miracles, bread from heaven, water from the rock, clouds by day, pillars of fire by night, indestructible shoes and garments, etc. And these dreary dregs, this stinking scum, this dried-up froth, this moldy leaven and boggy morass of Jewry should merit, on the strength of their repentance and righteousness, the empires of the whole world—that is, the Messiah and the fulfillment of the prophecies—though they possess none of the aforementioned items and are nothing but rotten, stinking, rejected dregs of their fathers' lineage!

In brief, Moses and all true Israelites understood these verses regarding the Messiah [as signifying that all this would be given them] out of sheer grace and mercy and not because of penitence and merit. This we gathered from the cited verses of Jacob, David, and Haggai. Likewise Daniel does not ask, desire, or think that such a glorious promise of the seventy weeks should be revealed to him, but it is granted him out of grace, far, far beyond his asking.

From this you can learn what fine repentance the Jews practiced, and still practice, after those seventy weeks. They began it with lies and blasphemies, in which they continued and still persist. Whoever wishes may imitate the Jews' example of repentance and say: "God and his angels are liars, they speak about things that are not." Then you will merit grace as they merit the Messiah.

If they were not so stone-blind, their own vile external life would indeed convince them of the true nature of their penitence. For it abounds with witchcraft, conjuring signs, figures, and the tetragrammaton of the name, that is, with idolatry, envy, and conceit.[142] Moreover, they are nothing but thieves and robbers who daily eat no morsel and wear no thread of clothing which they have not stolen and pilfered from us by means of their accursed usury. Thus they live from day to day, together with wife and child, by theft and robbery, as arch-thieves and robbers, in the most impenitent security. For a usurer is an arch-thief and a robber who should rightly be hanged on the gallows seven times higher than other thieves.[143] Indeed, God should prophesy about such beautiful penitence and merit from heaven through his holy angel and become a flagrant, blasphemous liar for the sake of the noble blood and circumcised saints who boast of being hallowed by God's commandments, although they trample all of them under foot and do not keep one of them.

The passage in Daniel continues: "Know therefore and understand that from the time when the order goes forth to restore and build Jerusalem to the coming of the Messiah, the prince, there shall be seven weeks and sixty-two weeks. It shall be built again with streets and walls, but in a troubled time. And after the sixty-two weeks, the Messiah shall be killed, and shall have nothing" [Dan. 9:25 f.].[144]

---

[142] Allegations deriving from medieval superstition concerning the Jews. Cf. above, pp. 217 ff., and n. 102, and for further details, Trachtenberg, *op. cit.*
[143] Cf. above, p. 169, n. 31.
[144] Rendered from Luther's German, and in accordance with his interpretation of the sentence structure as explained below. This division was already found in the Septuagint and was followed by Jerome, as well as by the English trans-

Oh, how ridiculous it seems to these circumcised saints that we accursed Goyim have interpreted and understand this saying thus, especially since we did not consult their rabbis, Talmudists, and Kokhbaites, whom they regard as more authoritative than all of Scripture. For they do a far better job of it. This is what they say: "Know therefore and understand from the going forth of the word to restore and rebuild Jerusalem"—this means, Ponder and understand it well that the word has gone forth that Jerusalem is to be restored. That is one point. Further, "To the coming of the Messiah, the prince"—this means, until the time of King Cyrus— "there shall be seven weeks." That is another point. Further, "For sixty-two weeks it shall be built again with walls and streets, but in a troubled time." That is another point. "And after sixty-two weeks the Messiah (that means King Agrippa) will be killed and will not be"—this means, will be no king, etc.[145]

It is indeed tiresome to discuss such confused lies and such tomfoolery. But I have to give our people occasion for pondering the devilish wantonness which the rabbis perpetrate with this splendid saying. So here you see how they separate the text where it should be read connectedly, and join it where it should be separated. This is the way in which it should be connected:

"Know therefore and understand that from the going forth of the word about how Jerusalem is to be restored and rebuilt to the coming of the Messiah, there shall be seven weeks and sixty-two weeks." These words, I say, are to be joined together to form one complete text. Then follows: "It shall be built again with walls and streets, but in a troubled time." This sentence, separate though it is, they connect with the foregoing words about the sixty-two weeks,

---

lators of the Authorized Version. The RSV in contrast, returns to an interpretation corresponding to that of the Jewish source cited by Luther: "Know therefore and understand that from the going forth of the word to restore and build Jerusalem to the coming of the Messiah, a prince, there shall be seven weeks. Then for sixty-two weeks it shall be built again with streets and walls, but in a troubled time. . . ."

[145] Paul of Burgos, in his *Addition* to Lyra's gloss on Dan. 9:24 ff., cites Rashi's interpretation of v. 25: "Know and understand concerning the Jerusalem to be restored and rebuilt: . . . the time will be given from the day of destruction until Cyrus comes . . . Agrippa, King of Judah, who reigned at the time of the destruction, will be killed." Most of the other features of Jewish interpretation cited by Luther below can be confirmed in Rashi's Commentary on Daniel; cf. the citations in WA 53, 503–509 (footnotes).

so as to convey the meaning that the building of the walls and the streets will occupy sixty-two weeks.

That is truly a knavish trick. It reminds me of the rascal of whom I once heard as a young monk. He hacked the Lord's Prayer to pieces and re-arranged it to read thus: Our Father, hallowed be in heaven; thy name come; thy kingdom be done; thy will as in heaven, so also on earth. Or as that ignorant priest read the lesson in the Vigils from I Corinthians 15: *Ubi est mors stimulus, tuus stimulus autem mortis, peccatum est virtus vero,*[146] etc.

That is the way the Jews tear apart the text wherever they can, solely for the purpose of spoiling the words of Scripture for us Christians, although it serves no purpose for them either. For it teaches them nothing, it does not comfort them, it gives them nothing; it results in nothing but meaningless words. It is the same as if the angel had said nothing at all. But they would rather surrender such comforting, joyous words and suffer the loss than to have them benefit us. Similarly, Bodenstein[147] maliciously tore the words of the sacrament apart lest they prove useful to us. However, this will not help the rabbis, those night herons and screech owls. With the help of God we will bring their howling and lying to light. Let us take up the several parts in order.

First I want to ask the Hebraists[148] whether the word *intellige* ["know"] is construed with the word *de* ["from"] in any other place in Scripture. I have not found any, and this seems to me quite arbitrary. If it is to mean *de* as in the phrase *de subjecta materia,* the Hebrew uses the preposition *al,* just as the Latins use the word *super* ("*Multa super Priamo,*" etc.[149]). I know very well, however,

---

[146] "Where is death a sting? Indeed your sting of death, sin, is truly virtue"— a nonsense rendering derived from re-grouping the words of the text.

[147] Luther's antagonist in the eucharistic controversy, Andreas Bodenstein von Karlstadt; cf. above, p. 116, n. 16.

[148] "Hebraists" here no doubt refers to those who, in the exegetical controversies of the Reformation period, insisted on the primacy of the Hebrew text and tended to grant a *prima facie* validity to Jewish interpretations, especially on matters of grammar.

The differences between Luther's interpretation and that which he attributes to the Jews can be brought out in English as follows: according to the former, the phrase should read (as it does in the RSV), "Know *that from* the going forth of the word . . . "; according to the latter, it should be, "Know *about* the going forth of the word. . . ."

[149] A phrase from Virgil's *Aeneid,* Book I, line 750 ("[Asking] many a thing of Priam").

that the Jews cannot prove that such a construction obtains here. The biblical examples agree that it stands as an absolute, independently. But to ascribe something to God maliciously of which one is uncertain, and which one cannot prove, is tantamount to tempting him and giving him the lie.

Now let us see how they tear the text apart. "Know therefore and understand, from the going forth of the word, that Jerusalem will again be built." This, they claim, does not speak of the beginning of the seventy weeks but of the word that has gone forth. Then follows: "To the coming of the Messiah, the prince, there shall be seven weeks." Now it is in agreement with the customary usage of all languages that the word *donec,* "until" [or "to"], presupposes a beginning. However, the Jews assign it none; they refuse to have the text read "from the beginning of the word to the coming of Messiah." I must draw an analogy.

If some one on St. Gall Square here in Wittenberg were to tell you: "You have heard a sermon based on God's word, declaring that the church is holy. Ponder this and mark it well." All right, you look at him expectantly to hear what else he has to say; for he does have more to say. Then he abruptly blurts out: "There are still seven weeks till Michaelmas." Or, "It is a distance of three miles to Halle." Here you would look at him and say, What sense is there in that? Are you crazy? Are the seven weeks to begin now on the market-place? Or are the three miles to begin in Wittenberg? "No," he would reply, "you must understand this to mean from the Day of St. Lawrence to Michaelmas, and from Bitterfeld to Halle." At this point you would be tempted to rejoin: "Go plant a kiss of peace on a sow's rump! Where did you learn to jabber so foolishly? And what do the seven weeks have to do with your statement that I should note well the sermon that I heard at Wittenberg?"

The rabbis treat the angel Gabriel's words in the same way. They make his speech read thus: "There are seven weeks until the Messiah." Suppose now Daniel replies, "My dear Gabriel, what do you mean? Are the seven weeks to begin now that you are speaking with me?" "No," he says, "you must understand this to mean that they begin with the destruction of Jerusalem." Thank you, indeed, you noble, circumcised rabbis, for teaching the angel

Gabriel to speak, as though he were unable to tell of the beginning of the seven weeks, which is all-important, as well as of the middle and the end of them. No, Daniel is to assume it. This is just nonsense. Shame on you, you vile rabbis, to attribute this foolish talk of yours to the angel of God! With this you disgrace yourselves and convict yourselves of being malicious liars and blasphemers of God's words. But this is just the grammatical side of the matter. Now let us study the theological aspect.

These holy, circumcised ravens[150] say that the seventy weeks begin with the first destruction of Jerusalem and end with its second destruction. What better method could they have pursued for arriving at this conclusion than to close their eyes and ears, ignore Scripture and the history books, and let their imagination run freely, saying: "This is the way it seems right to us, and we insist upon it. Therefore it follows that God and his angel must agree with us. How could we be wrong? We are the ravens who are able to teach God and the angels."

Oh, what a base, vexatious, blasphemous people, that can merit the Messiah with such penitence! But let us listen to their wisdom. The seventy weeks begin with the destruction of Jerusalem by the king of Babylon; from that event until the coming of the Messiah, the prince (that is, King Cyrus), are seven weeks. Now tell me: Where is this written? Nowhere. Who has said it? Markolf the mockingbird. Who else might say or write it?

In the beginning of this ninth chapter stands Daniel's clear and plain statement that the revelation regarding the seventy weeks had come to him in the first year of the reign of Darius the Mede, who had conquered the Babylonian kingdom, which event had been preceded by the first destruction of Jerusalem seventy years earlier. For Daniel clearly states that seventy years of the devastation had been fulfilled, in accordance with Jeremiah 29 [:10]. This we also read in II Chronicles, the last chapter [36:22]. And yet these two clear passages of Scripture, Daniel 9 and II Chronicles 36, must be accounted as lies by the rabbis. They insist that they are right and that the seventy weeks must have begun seventy years before they were revealed to Daniel. Isn't that great? Now

---

[150] A play on the similarity of the word *Raben* ("ravens") to *Rabinen* (rabbis).

go and believe the rabbis, those ignorant, untutored asses, who look neither at the Scriptures nor at the history books and who spew forth from their vicious mouth whatever they choose against God and angels.

For they herewith stand openly convicted of their lies and their erring arbitrariness. Since the seventy weeks which were revealed in the first year of the reign of Darius the Mede cannot begin seventy years previously with the destruction of Jerusalem, all their lies founded on this are simultaneously refuted, and this verse of Daniel regarding the seventy weeks must remain for us undefiled and unadulterated—no thanks to them. Eternal disgrace will be their reward for this impertinent and patent lie. With this lie another one also collapses; namely, their claim that the words about the Messiah, the prince, refer to King Cyrus, who supposedly appeared seven weeks after the destruction, although in fact he came ten weeks (that is, seventy years) after the destruction. This is recorded in II Chronicles 36, Daniel 9, and Ezra 1.

Even if we would assume—which is impossible—that the seventy weeks began with the destruction of Jerusalem, we could still not justify this stupid lie. And with this the third lie collapses. For they say that Cyrus came fifty-two years after the destruction—the equivalent of seven weeks and three years, or seven and a half weeks. Thus they tear three years, or half a week, from the sixty-two weeks and add them to the first seven weeks. It is as though the angel were such a consummate fool or child that he could not count up to seven, and says seven when he should say seven and a half. Why do they do this? So that we might perceive how they indulge in lies for the purpose of tearing apart and turning upside down God's word for us. Therefore they insist that Cyrus came seven and a half weeks (which they call seven weeks) after the destruction, whereas (as was said) he really came ten weeks, i.e., seventy years, later.

Nor does the angel tolerate that these weeks be mangled and mutilated, subtracting three years from one and leaving it only four years, and adding to the one that has seven years three more, making it ten years or one and a half weeks. For he says that the seventy weeks are to be taken exactly; they are counted and reckoned precisely.

Much less does he tolerate the fourth lie—that Cyrus is here called the Messiah—even if the other lies were to be upheld, to the effect that Cyrus had appeared after seven weeks, that is, after fifty-two years. For here we find the unmistakable and simple words of the angel: "Seventy weeks of years are decreed concerning *your* people and *your* holy city" [Dan. 9:24]. He means to say: In other chapters I spoke of strange people and kings; but in this verse concerning the seventy weeks I am speaking of your people, of your city, and of your Messiah. And whoever refers this to a different people and to different kings is a wanton, incorrigible liar.

The fourth lie is followed by the fifth, in which they divorce the seven weeks from the sixty-two. But these belong together, and there is no reason to separate them, especially since the lie regarding King Cyrus miscarried. It was for this reason that they severed the seven from the sixty-two weeks so that they could give him seven, that is, seven and a half. In biblical Hebrew it is customary to count the years thus: first to give the one, then the other number of years, but with both placed together. We find many illustrations for this in Genesis 5 and 11, where reference is made to the deceased fathers. For instance: "When Seth had lived five years and a hundred years, he became the father of Enosh. Seth lived after the birth of Enosh seven years and eight hundred years" [Gen. 5:6 f.]. Similarly Genesis 11 [:17]: "Eber lived after the birth of Peleg thirty years and four hundred years." And Genesis 25 [:7]: "Abraham lived one hundred years, seventy years, and five years." From these illustrations one can easily see how arbitrary it is to separate the seven years from the sixty-two years in this verse.

The Latin and German languages prevent such a disruption nicely, since they do not repeat the little word "year" so often, but read the number connectedly, saying: "Abraham lived one hundred seventy-five years." In that way these words also are to be taken: "From the going forth of the word to the coming of the Messiah, the prince, there are seven weeks and sixty-two weeks." These two numbers belong together and compose one number, to the coming of the Messiah. The angel has a reason for designating the entire sum of years as seven weeks and sixty-two weeks. He might have spoken of nine weeks and sixty weeks, or found many different ways to name such a sum, such as five weeks and sixty-four weeks, or six weeks and sixty-three weeks, etc. He must have the seven weeks for the construction of the walls and streets of Jerusalem; and he must have the sixty-two, up to the last week, which is all-important, for in it the Messiah will die, fulfill the covenant, etc.

Then comes the sixth lie which says that the walls and streets of Jerusalem were rebuilt for sixty-two weeks (minus three years). That would be up to the last week, after which—as they lie for the seventh time—Jerusalem was again destroyed. For with the last week the seventy weeks are ended. According to this, Jerusalem had not stood again for longer than one week, which means seven years. Go ahead, Jew, lie boldly and unashamedly! Nehemiah stands against you with his book and testifies that he built the walls, set the gates, and arranged the city, and that he himself gloriously consecrated it. Thus the temple was already completed in the sixth year of the reign of Darius (Ezra 7 [6:16]). Alexander the Great found the city of Jerusalem already long completed. After him that villain Antiochus found the city even further restored and the temple full of wealth, and he plundered them horribly.

The eighth rude lie follows when they interpret the words of the angel, "And after sixty-two weeks the Messiah will be killed, and shall have nothing," as if the Messiah refers to King Agrippa, who was killed and had nothing after his death; no king succeeded him. Why would it not be just as true to say that Emperor Nero was the Messiah? He was killed at that time and left no heirs. I believe that they would designate Markolf or Thersites[151] as the Messiah rather than accept the true Messiah. How can God, who loves the truth and who is the truth himself, tolerate such shameful, open lies if these are intolerable even to a person who is given to lies or is untruthful or is at least not so strict a lover of the truth? And this eighth lie is a multiple one—in the first place, because they assign different meanings to the word "Messiah" within such a brief passage: there he has to be Cyrus after the seven weeks, here Agrippa after the sixty-two weeks. Just as though the angel

---

[151] A Greek warrior at Troy, depicted in the *Iliad* as ugly, impudent, and thoroughly disliked by all.

were a fool who would point to a different Messiah with every other word!

As we heard earlier, the angel is not referring to a foreign people and city, but says, "I am speaking of your people and of your city." Therefore we must conceive of the Messiah in this verse not as two different beings, but as one—namely, the Messiah of this people and of this city, the Shiloh of Judah who came after the scepter departed from Judah, the Son of David, the *chemdath* of Haggai. This verse indeed refers to him, excluding all others. For Agrippa was not king in Jerusalem, much less the Messiah, before the last week (that is, after seven and sixty-two weeks). The Romans had graciously granted him a little country beyond the Jordan. The Roman procurators such as Felix, Festus, Albinus, etc., ruled the land of Judea. Nor was Agrippa killed after the sixty-two weeks. In brief, all that they say is a lie.

Since they now confess, and have to confess, that a Messiah was killed after the sixty-two weeks, that is, in the first year of the last week, and since this cannot have been Agrippa (as they would like to have it, in confirmation of their lie), nor anyone else, I am curious to learn where they might find one. It must be someone who lived before the expiration of the seventy weeks and who was killed after sixty-two weeks. Furthermore, as Gabriel says, he must have come from among their people, undoubtedly from the royal tribe of Judah. Now it is certain that since Herod's time they had had no king who was a member of their people or race. But, on the other hand, it is just as certain that Gabriel must be believed, with his statement regarding a Messiah of their nation. How is this difficulty to be solved?

And there is more. They themselves confess that they had no Messiah, that is, no anointed king ("Messiah" means "the anointed one"), between the first and the last destruction of Jerusalem, for the sacred anointing oil, of which Moses writes in Exodus 30 [:22 ff.], with which kings and priests were anointed, no longer existed after the first destruction. Consequently, Zedekiah was the last anointed king; his descendants were princes, not kings, down to the time of Herod, when the scepter departed and Shiloh, the true Messiah, was to appear.

We want to purge out their lies completely. With reference to Daniel's saying, "And he shall make a strong covenant with many for one week" [Dan. 9:27], that is, the last week, they perpetrate the ninth lie, saying that the Romans agreed to a peace or a truce for this last week (or seven years) with the Jews; but since the Jews grew rebellious the Romans returned in three years and destroyed Jerusalem. Now how does this bear out Gabriel, who says that the peace or truce (as they interpret the word "covenant") is to last seven years? If it did not endure longer than three years, then Gabriel, who speaks of seven years or the last week, must be lying. Thus the mendacious hearts of these incorrigible liars falsely impugn the truthfulness of the angel Gabriel. Alas, what truce? What peace? Read Josephus and the history books and you will learn that the Romans slew many thousands of Jews a long time before, and that there was no peace up to the time when they were constrained to destroy Jerusalem and the country.[152]

The tenth and final lie concerns the assertion that the destruction of Jerusalem will last until the end of the strife. They interpret this as meaning: until the strife of their Messiah, who will kill Gog and Magog and conquer the whole world. This is a vicious, miserable lie which is dead before it is born. Let those who maintain that the Messiah appeared before the expiration of the seventy weeks be informed that such a lie was discredited as long as fifteen hundred years ago. Thus the Jews do not retain a single word of Gabriel's statement intact; they pervert all his words into lies, with the exception of the angel's prophecy regarding the destruction of Jerusalem. But no one need thank them for believing that and admitting the truth of it now. While they still inhabited Jerusalem, they believed this prophecy still less than they believe now in our Messiah, although it was foretold plainly enough, here in Daniel 9 as well as in Zechariah 14. If they were still dwelling in Jerusalem today, they would invent a hundred thousand lies before they would believe it, just as their ancestors did prior to the first destruction. The latter were not persuaded by any prophet that the holy city of God would be laid waste. They harried them, they raved like mad dogs until they stood face to face with the fulfill-

---

[152] Cf. Josephus, *The Jewish War.*

251

ment of the prophecy. This has always been a stiff-necked, unbelieving, proud, base, incorrigible people, and so it ever remains.

From all of this we gather that Daniel with his seventy weeks takes our position against the Jews' lies and folly, a position as reliable and firm as an iron wall and an immovable rock, affirming that the true Messiah must have come before the termination of the seventy weeks; that he was killed and made alive again; that he fulfilled God's covenant (for why should Daniel here be speaking of the Gentiles' covenant, which, moreover, did not even exist at the time?) in the last week; that he thereby took leave of the city and the people at the end of the seventy weeks; that the city was razed by the Romans shortly after; that the people were destroyed, with their government and all they had—all of this in accordance with the angel's words: "Seventy weeks of years are decreed or reckoned concerning your people and your holy city" [Dan. 9:24].[153] But enough!

No doubt it is necessary for the Jews to lie and to misinterpret in order to maintain their error over against such a clear and powerful text. Their previous lies broke down under their own weight. But even if they were to lie for a hundred thousand years and call all the devils in to aid them, they would still come to nought. For it is impossible to name a Messiah at the time of the seventy weeks,

---

[153] When viewed in terms of the history of exegesis, the Daniel text does not appear to be so unambiguous as Luther here indicates. Already St. Jerome (died *ca.* A.D. 419) had written concerning the interpretation of the "seventy weeks": "I realize that this question has been argued over in various ways by men of greatest learning, and that each of them has expressed his views according to the capacity of his own genius. And so, because it is unsafe to pass judgment upon the opinions of the great teachers of the Church and to set one above another, I shall simply repeat the view of each, and leave it to the reader's judgment as to whose explanation ought to be followed" (*Jerome's Commentary on Daniel,* trans. by Gleason L. Archer, Jr. [Grand Rapids, Mich.: Baker Book House, 1958], p. 95).

For a survey of the diverse interpretations up to the time of Luther, see Franz Sales Fraidl, *Die Exegese der Siebzig Wochen Daniels in der alten und mittleren Zeit* (Graz, 1883). The viewpoint of modern scholarship is, of course, decisively affected by the supposition that the book of Daniel is a pseudonymous work written during the Maccabean period. See "Note on the Interpretation of the Seventy Weeks" in James A. Montgomery, *A Critical and Exegetical Commentary on the Book of Daniel* (International Critical Commentary; New York: Scribner's, 1927), pp. 390–401, or for a popular treatment, E. W. Heaton, *The Book of Daniel: Introduction and Commentary* (Torch Bible Commentaries; London, 1956).

as Gabriel's revelation would necessitate, other than our Lord Jesus Christ. We are certain, sure, and cheerful about this, as we snap our fingers at all the gates of hell and defy them, together with all the gates of the world and everything that wants to be or might be exalted, smart, and wise against us. I, a plain insignificant saint in Christ, venture to oppose all of them singlehandedly and to defend this viewpoint easily, comfortably, and gladly. However, it is impossible to convert the devil and his own, nor are we commanded to attempt this.[154] It suffices to uncover their lies and to reveal the truth. Whoever is not actuated to believe the truth for the sake of his own soul will surely not believe it for my sake.

We will limit ourselves for the time being to these four texts— those of Jacob, David, Haggai, and Daniel—wherein we see what a fine job the Jews have done these fifteen hundred years with Scripture, and what a fine job they still do. For their treatment of these texts parallels their treatment of all others, especially those that are in favor of us and our Messiah. These, of course, must be accounted as lies, whereas they themselves cannot err or be mistaken. However, they have not acquired a perfect mastery of the art of lying; they lie so clumsily and ineptly that anyone who is just a little observant can easily detect it.

But for us Christians they stand as a terrifying example of God's wrath. As St. Paul declares in Romans 11, we must fear God and honor his word as long as the time of grace remains, so that we do not meet with a similar or worse fate. We have seen this happen in the case of the papacy and of Muhammad. The example of the Jews demonstrates clearly how easily the devil can mislead people, after they once have digressed from the proper understanding of Scripture, into such blindness and darkness that it can be readily grasped and perceived simply by natural reason, yes, even by irrational beasts. And yet they who daily teach and hear God's word do not recognize this darkness but regard it as the true light. O Lord God, have mercy on us!

If I had to refute all the other articles of the Jewish faith, I should be obliged to write against them as much and for as long

---

[154] A recurrence of the note of pessimism concerning the possibility of converting the Jews that Luther had struck in the first paragraphs of the treatise, as well as already in his *Sabbatarians*.

a time as they have used for inventing their lies—that is, longer than two thousand years. I stated earlier that they corrupt their circumcision with human ordinances and ruin their heritage with their arrogance. In the same manner they also desecrate their Sabbath and all their festivals. In brief, all their life and all their deeds, whether they eat, drink, sleep, wake, stand, walk, dress, undress, fast, bathe, pray, or praise, are so sullied with rabbinical, foul ordinances and unbelief, that Moses can no longer be recognized among them. This corresponds to the situation of the papacy in our day, in which Christ and his word can hardly be recognized because of the great vermin of human ordinances. However, let this suffice for the time being on their lies against doctrine or faith.[155]

In conclusion we want to examine their lies against persons, which, after all, do not make the doctrine either worse or better, whether the persons are pious or base. Specifically, we want to look at their lies about the person of our Lord, as well as those about his dear mother and about ourselves and all Christians. These lies are such as the devil resorts to when he cannot assail the doctrine. Then he turns against the person—lying, maligning, cursing, and ranting against him. That is what the papists' Beelzebub[156] did to me. When he was unable to refute my gospel, he wrote that I was possessed of the devil, that I was a changeling, that my dear mother was a whore and a bathhouse attendant.[157] Of course, no sooner had he written this than my gospel was destroyed and the papists carried the day! Similarly, John the Baptist and Christ himself were charged with having a devil [Matt. 11:18; John 8:20] and were called Samaritans—and shortly thereafter John's and Christ's doctrine was shown to be false, and that of the Pharisees true. The same thing happened to all the prophets. Recently also, when the stealthy, murdering arsonist of Wolfen-

---

[155] Having concluded the lengthy middle section of the treatise dealing with the nature and timing of the messianic fulfillment, Luther now moves on to other matters of controversy between Jews and Christians, grouped under the heading "lies against persons."
[156] Probably a reference to Luther's arch-antagonist John Eck.
[157] Cf. Ottmar Hegemann, *Luther im katholischen Urteil* (Munich, 1905), pp. 18 f.

büttel[158]—who, next to the archbishop of Mainz, is the holy
Roman Church's one relic and jewel—shamefully slandered and
defamed the persons of the elector of Saxony and the landgrave of
Hesse, both were instantly doomed; but he, the holy man, king
over all kings, was crowned with a diadem and gold so heavy that
he could not bear it and had to flee.

Therefore, whenever you wish to win in an evil cause, do as
they do and as the glib babblers do in court when the silver- or
gold-fever seizes them. Scold and lie boldly about the person, and
your cause will win out. It is like the mother who instructed her
child: "Dear son, if you cannot win otherwise, start a brawl."
These are lies in which the liar does not fabricate or err in the chief
question at issue (as happens also in religious disputes), but nevertheless is well aware that he is lying and wants to lie against the
person. He does not dream of proving his point, either by appearances or by truth, and is unable to do so.

That is how the Jews, too, are acting in this instance. They
blatantly inveigh and lie against and curse the person, against
their own conscience. In that way they have long since won their
case, so that God had to listen to them. Already for fifteen hundred years they have been sitting in Jerusalem, in a golden city, as
we can clearly see. They are the lords of the world, and all the
Gentiles flock to them with their *chemdath*, their coats, pants, and
shoes, and permit themselves to be slain by the noble princes and
lords of Israel, giving them land and people and all that they have,
while the Jews curse, spit on, and malign the Goyim.

And you can well imagine that if they would not lie so outrageously, curse, defame, blaspheme, and revile the persons, God
would not have heard them, and their cause would have been lost
long ago; they would not be lords in Jerusalem today but live dispersed over the world, without seeing Jerusalem, and making their
living among the accursed Goyim by means of lying, cheating,
stealing, robbing, usury, and all sorts of other vices. So effective
is it to curse the person if the cause in question is evil and there-

---

[158] Henry of Brunswick-Wolfenbüttel (cf. above, p. 18, n. 46). Earlier in
1542, Henry had been driven from his lands by the forces of John Frederick
of Saxony and Philip of Hesse.

fore doomed! Consequently, if you have a poor cause to defend, do not overlook this example of the Jews. They are the noble princes of Israel who are capable of everything. When their cause is lost, they still can curse the Goyim thoroughly.

In the first place, they defame our Lord Jesus Christ, calling him a sorcerer and tool of the devil.[159] This they do because they cannot deny his miracles. Thus they imitate their forefathers, who said, "He casts out demons by Beelzebub, the prince of demons" [Luke 11:15]. They invent many lies about the name of God, the tetragrammaton, saying that our Lord was able to define this name (which they call *Schem Hamphoras*),[160] and whoever is able to do that, they say, is also able to perform all sorts of miracles. However, they cannot cite a single instance of any men who worked a miracle worth a gnat by means of this *Schem Hamphoras*. It is evident that as consummate liars they fabricate this about our Lord. For if such a rule of *Schem Hamphoras* were true, someone else would have employed it before or afterward. Otherwise, how could one know that such power inhered in the *Schem Hamphoras*? But this is too big a subject; after this booklet is finished, I plan to issue a special essay and relate what Porchetus writes on this subject.[161] It serves them right that, rejecting the truth of God, they have to believe instead such abominable, stupid, inane lies, and that instead of the beautiful face of the divine word, they have to look into the devil's black, dark, lying behind, and worship his stench.

In addition they rob Jesus of the significance of his name, which in Hebrew means "savior" or "helper." The name Helfrich or Hilfrich was common among the old Saxons; this is the equivalent of the name Jesus. Today we might use the name Hulfrich—that is, one who can and will help. But the Jews, in their malice, call him

---

[159] Most of these and the following charges are contained in the works of Margaritha and Porchetus which Luther had consulted (cf. Introduction), and beyond this, were part of the common medieval tradition. In many cases, the charges and countercharges are traceable to the earliest polemics between Jews and Christians in the first and second centuries.

[160] I.e., "the Ineffable Name." A more adequate transliteration of the Hebrew would be *Shem ha-memphorash*. Luther dealt further with this subject in his treatise published in March, 1543, *Vom Schem Hamphoras und vom Geschlecht Christi* (WA 53, 579–648).

[161] Cf. n. 160.

Jesu, which in Hebrew is neither a name nor a word but three letters, like ciphers or numeral letters. It is as if, for example, I were to take the three numeral letters C, L, and V as ciphers and form the word Clu. That is 155. In this manner they use the name Jesu, signifying 316. This number then is to denote another word, in which *Hebel Vorik*[162] is found. For further information on their devilish practices with such numbers and words, you may read Anthony Margaritha.

When a Christian hears them utter the word "Jesu," as will happen occasionally when they are obliged to speak to us, he assumes that they are using the name Jesus. But in reality they have the numeral letters Jesu in mind, that is, the numeral 316 in the blasphemous word *Vorik*. And when they utter the word "Jesu" in their prayer, they spit on the ground three times in honor of our Lord and of all Christians, moved by their great love and devotion. But when they are conversing with one another they say, *Deleatur nomen eius,* which means in plain words, "May God exterminate his name," or "May all the devils take him."[163]

They treat us Christians similarly in receiving us when we go to them. They pervert the words *Seid Gott willkommen* [literally, "Be welcome to God"] and say, *Sched wil kem!* which means: "Come, devil," or "There comes a devil." Since we are not conversant with the Hebrew, they can vent their wrath on us secretly. While we suppose that they are speaking kindly to us, they are calling down hellfire and every misfortune on our heads. Such splendid guests we poor, pious Christians are harboring in our country in the persons of the Jews—we who mean well with them, who would gladly serve their physical and spiritual welfare, and who suffer so many coarse wrongs from them.

Then they also call Jesus a whore's son, saying that his mother Mary was a whore, who conceived him in adultery with a blacksmith.[164] I have to speak in this coarse manner, although I do so with great reluctance, to combat the vile devil. Now they know

---

[162] Interpreted by Margaritha in *Der gantz Jüdisch glaub* to mean "folly and vanity" (*thorheyt und eytelkeyt*); cf. citation in WA 53, 513 f., n. 12.
[163] The material in this and the following two paragraphs is taken directly from Margaritha.
[164] Margaritha says, "with a carpenter or a blacksmith."

very well that these lies are inspired by sheer hatred and spite, solely for the purpose of bitterly poisoning the minds of their poor youth and the simple Jews against the person of our Lord, lest they adhere to his doctrine (which they cannot refute). Still they claim to be the holy people to whom God must grant the Messiah by reason of their righteousness! In the eighth commandment, God forbade us to speak falsehoods against our neighbor, to lie, to deceive, to revile, to defile. This prohibition also includes one's enemies. For when Zedekiah did not keep faith with the king of Babylon, he was severely rebuked for his lie by Jeremiah and Ezekiel and was also led into wretched captivity because of it [Jer. 21: 1 ff.; Ezek. 12:1 ff.].

However, our noble princes of the world and circumcised saints, against this commandment of God, invented this beautiful doctrine: namely, that they may freely lie, blaspheme, curse, defame, murder, rob, and commit every vice, however, whenever, and on whom they wish. Let God keep his own commandment: the noble blood and circumcised people will violate it as they desire and please. Despite this, they insist that they are doing right and good and meriting the Messiah and heaven thereby. They challenge God and all the angels to refute this, not to speak of the devil and the accursed Goyim who find fault with it; for here is the noble blood which cannot sin and which is not subject to God's commands.

What harm has the poor maiden Mary done to them? How can they prove that she was a whore? She did no more than bear a son, whose name is Jesus. Is it such a great crime for a young wife to bear a child? Or are all who bear children to be accounted whores? What, then, is to be said about their own wives and about themselves? Are they, too, all whores and children of whores? You accursed Goyim, that is a different story! Do you not know that the Jews are Abraham's noble blood, circumcised, and kings in heaven and on earth? Whatever they say is right. If there were a virgin among the accursed Goyim as pure and holy as the angel Gabriel, and the least of these noble princes were to say that she is an archwhore and viler than the devil, it would necessarily have to be so. The fact that a noble mouth of the lineage of Abraham said this would be sufficient proof. Who dares contradict him? Conversely, any arch-whore of the noble blood of the Jews, though she were as ugly as the devil himself, would still be purer than any angel if the noble lords were pleased to say this. For the noble, circumcised lords have the authority to lie, to defame, revile, blaspheme, and curse the accursed Goyim as they wish. On the other hand, they are privileged to bless, honor, praise, and exalt themselves, even if God disagrees with them. Do you suppose that a Jew is such a bad fellow? God in heaven and all the angels have to laugh and dance when they hear a Jew pass wind, so that you accursed Goyim may know what excellent fellows the Jews are. For how could they be so bold as to call Mary a whore, with whom they can find no fault, if they were not vested with the power to trample God and his commandment under foot?

Well and good, you and I, as accursed Goyim, wish to submit a simple illustration by means of which we, as benighted heathen, might comprehend this lofty wisdom of the noble, holy Jews a little. Let us suppose that I had a cousin or another close blood relative of whom I knew no evil, and in whom I had never detected any evil; and other people, against whom I bore a grudge, praised and extolled her, regarded her as an excellent, pious, virtuous, laudable woman, and said: This dunce is not worthy of having such a fine, honorable woman as his cousin; a she-dog or a she-wolf would be more fit for him. Then I, upon hearing such eulogies of my cousin spoken, would begin to say, against my own conscience: They are all lying, she is an arch-whore. And now I would, though lacking any proof, demand that everyone believe me, despite the fact that I was well aware of my cousin's innocence, while I, a consummate liar, was cursing all who refused to believe my lie—which I knew in my heart to be just that.

Tell me, how would you regard me? Would you not feel impelled to say that I was not a human being but a monster, a repulsive fiend, not worthy of gazing at sun, leaves, grass, or any creature? Indeed, you would consider me to be possessed by devils. I should rather treat my cousin's disgrace, if I knew of any, as though it were my own, and cover it up if it threatened to become public, just as all other people do. But although no one, including myself, knows anything but honorable things about her, I dare to step to the fore and defame my cousin as a scoundrel, with false slander, oblivious to the fact that this shame reflects on me.

That is the type of human beings—if I should or could call them that—which these noble, circumcised saints are. We Goyim, with whom they are hostile and angry, confess that Mary is not ours but rather the Jews' cousin and blood relative, descended from Abraham. When we praise and laud her highly, they proceed to defame her viciously. If there were a genuine drop of Israelite blood in such miserable Jews, do you not suppose that they would say: "What are we to do? Can she help it that her son provoked our ire? Why should we slander her? After all, she is our flesh and blood. It has undoubtedly happened before that a bad son issued from a pious mother." No, such human and responsible thoughts will not occur to these holy people; they must entertain nothing but devilish, base, lying thoughts, so that they may in that way do penance and merit the Messiah soon—as they have, of course, merited him now for fifteen hundred years.

They further lie and slander him and his mother by saying that she conceived him at an unnatural time. About this they are most malicious and malignant and malevolent. In Leviticus 20 [:18] Moses declares that a man must not approach a woman nor a woman a man during the female's menstrual uncleanness. This is forbidden on pain of loss of life and limb; for whatever is conceived at such a time results in imperfect and infirm fruit, that is, in insane children, mental deficients, demon's offspring, change-lings, and the like—people who have unbalanced minds all their lives. In this way the Jews would defame us Christians, by saying that we honor as the Messiah a person who was mentally deficient from birth, or some sort of demon. These most intelligent, circumcised, highly enlightened saints regard us as such stupid and accursed Goyim. Truly, these are the devil's own thoughts and words!

Do you ask what prompts them to write this, or what is the cause of it? You stupid, accursed Goy, why should you ask that? Does it not satisfy you to know that this is said by the noble, circumcised saints? Are you so slow to learn that such a holy people is exempt from all the decrees of God and cannot sin? They may lie, blaspheme, defame, and murder whom they will, even God himself and all his prophets. All of this must be accounted as nothing but a fine service rendered to God. Did I not tell you earlier that a Jew is such a noble, precious jewel that God and all the angels dance when he farts? And if he were to go on to do something coarser than that, they would nevertheless expect it to be regarded as a golden Talmud. Whatever issues from such a holy man, from above or from below, must surely be considered by the accursed Goyim to be pure holiness.

For if a Jew were not so precious and noble, how would it be possible for him to despise all Christians with their Messiah and his mother so thoroughly, to vilify them with such malicious and poisonous lies? If these fine, pure, smart saints would only concede us the qualities of geese or ducks, since they refuse to let us pass for human beings! For the stupidity which they ascribe to us I could not assign to any sow, which, as we know, covers itself with mire from head to foot and does not eat anything much cleaner. Alas, it cannot be anything but the terrible wrath of God which permits anyone to sink into such abysmal, devilish, hellish, insane baseness, envy, and arrogance. If I were to avenge myself on the devil himself I should be unable to wish him such evil and misfortune as God's wrath inflicts on the Jews, compelling them to lie and to blaspheme so monstrously, in violation of their own conscience. Anyway, they have their reward for constantly giving God the lie.

In his Bible, Sebastian Münster[165] relates that a malicious rabbi does not call the dear mother of Christ *Maria* but *haria*—i.e., *sterquilinium*, a dung heap. And who knows what other villainy they may indulge in among themselves, unknown to us? One can readily perceive how the devil constrains them to the basest lies and blasphemies he can contrive. Thus they also begrudge the dear mother Mary, the daughter of David, her right name, although she

---

[165] Sebastian Münster (1489–1552), eminent Hebraist and professor at the University of Basel, in 1535 published an edition of the Hebrew Bible accompanied by his own translation. The source of the comment mentioned here by Luther is uncertain.

has not done them any harm. If they do that, why should they not also begrudge her, her life, her goods, and her honor? And if they wish and inflict all kinds of disgrace and evil on their own flesh and blood, which is innocent and about which they know nothing evil, what, do you suppose, might they wish us accursed Goyim?

Yet they presume to step before God with such a heart and mouth; they utter, worship, and invoke his holy name, entreating him to return them to Jerusalem, to send them the Messiah, to kill all the Gentiles, and to present them with all the goods of the world. The only reason that God does not visit them with thunder and lightning, that he does not deluge them suddenly with fire as he did Sodom and Gomorrah, is this: This punishment would not be commensurate with such malice. Therefore he strikes them with spiritual thunder and lightning, as Moses writes in Deuteronomy 28 [:18] among other places: "The Lord will smite you with madness and blindness and confusion of mind." Those are, indeed, the true strokes of lightning and thunder: madness, blindness, confusion of mind.

Although these terrible, slanderous, blasphemous lies are directed particularly against the person of our Lord and his dear mother, they are also intended for our own persons. They want to offer us the greatest affront and insult for honoring a Messiah whom they curse and malign so terribly that they do not consider him worthy of being named by them or any human being, much less of being revered. Thus we must pay for believing in him, for praising, honoring, and serving him.

I should like to ask, however: What harm has the poor man Jesus done to these holy people? If he was a false teacher, as they allege, he was punished for it; for this he recived his due, for this he suffered with a shameful death on the cross, for this he paid and rendered satisfaction. No accursed heathen in all the world will persecute and malign forever and ever a poor dead man who suffered his punishment for his misdeeds. How, then, does it happen that these most holy, blessed Jews outdo the accursed heathen? To begin with, they declare that Jerusalem was not destroyed nor were they led into captivity for their sin of crucifying Jesus. For they claim to have done the right thing when they meted out justice to the seducer and thus merited their Messiah. Is it the fault of the dead man, who has now met his judgment, that we Goyim are so stupid and foolish as to honor him as our Messiah? Why do they not settle the issue with us, convince us of our folly and demonstrate their lofty, heavenly wisdom? We have never fled from them; we are still standing our ground and defying their holy wisdom. Let us see what they are able to do. For it is most unseemly for such great saints to crawl into a corner and to curse and scold in hiding.

Now as I began to ask earlier: What harm has the poor Jesus done to the most holy children of Israel that they cannot stop cursing him after his death, with which he paid his debt? Is it perhaps that he aspires to be the Messiah, which they cannot tolerate? Oh no, for he is dead. They themselves crucified him, and a dead person cannot be the Messiah. Perhaps he is an obstacle to their return into their homeland? No, that is not the reason either; for how can a dead man prevent that? What, then, is the reason? I will tell you. As I said before, it is the lightning and thunder of Moses to which I referred before: "The Lord will smite you with madness and blindness and confusion of mind." It is the eternal fire of which the prophets speak: "My wrath will go forth like fire, and burn with none to quench it" [Jer. 4:4]. John the Baptist proclaimed the same message to them after Herod had removed their scepter, saying [Luke 3:17]: "His winnowing fork is in his hand, and he will clear his threshing-floor and gather his wheat into his granary, but his chaff he will burn with unquenchable fire." Indeed, such fire of divine wrath we behold descending on the Jews. We see it burning, ablaze and aflame, a fire more horrible than that of Sodom and Gomorrah.

Now such devilish lies and blasphemy are aimed at the person of Christ and of his dear mother; but our person and that of all Christians are also involved. They are also thinking of us. Because Christ and Mary are dead and because we Christians are such vile people to honor these despicable, dead persons, they also assign us our special share of slander. In the first place, they lament before God that we are holding them captive in exile, and they implore him ardently to deliver his holy people and dear children from our power and the imprisonment in which we hold them. They dub us Edom and Haman, with which names they would insult us grievously before God, and hurt us deeply. However, it would carry us too far afield to enlarge on this. They know very well that they are lying here. If it were possible, I would not be ashamed to claim Edom as my forefather. He was the natural son of the saintly Rebekah, the grandson of the dear Sarah; Abraham was his grandfather and Isaac his real father. Moses himself commands them to regard Edom as their brother (Deut. 23 [:7]). They indeed obey Moses as true Jews!

Further, they presume to instruct God and prescribe the manner in which he is to redeem them. For the Jews, these very learned saints, look upon God as a poor cobbler equipped with only a left last for making shoes. This is to say that he is to kill and exterminate all of us Goyim through their Messiah, so that they can lay their hands on the land, the goods, and the government of the whole world. And now a storm breaks over us with curses, defamation, and derision that cannot be expressed with words. They wish that sword and war, distress and every misfortune may overtake us accursed Goyim. They vent their curses on us openly every Saturday in their synagogues and daily in their homes. They teach, urge, and train their children from infancy to remain the bitter, virulent, and wrathful enemies of the Christians.

This gives you a clear picture of their conception of the fifth commandment and their observation of it. They have been bloodthirsty bloodhounds and murderers of all Christendom for more than fourteen hundred years in their intentions, and would undoubtedly prefer to be such with their deeds. Thus they have been accused[166] of poisoning water and wells, of kidnaping children, of piercing them through with an awl, of hacking them in pieces, and in that way secretly cooling their wrath with the blood of Christians, for all of which they have often been condemned to death

---

[166] The element of caution in Luther's phraseology here perhaps indicates some awareness on his part of the unsupported character of such accusations. In 1510, for example, thirty-eight Jews had been executed in Berlin on a charge of descrecation of the host. In 1539, however, in the context of a debate on policy toward the Jews at the assembly of Protestant estates at Frankfurt, Philip Melanchthon presented convincing evidence that they had been innocent (cf. Stern, *Josel of Rosheim*, pp. 37 f., 170). The use of torture to extract "confessions" to such crimes was common.

by fire. And still God refused to lend an ear to the holy penitence of such great saints and dearest children. The unjust God lets such holy people curse (I wanted to say "pray") so vehemently in vain against our Messiah and all Christians. He does not care to see or have anything to do either with them or with their pious conduct, which is so thickly, thickly, heavily, heavily coated with the blood of the Messiah and his Christians. For these Jews are much holier than were those in the Babylonian captivity, who did not curse, who did not secretly shed the blood of children, nor poison the water, but who rather as Jeremiah had instructed them [Jer. 29:7] prayed for their captors, the Babylonians. The reason is that they were not as holy as the present-day Jews, nor did they have such smart rabbis as the present-day Jews have; for Jeremiah, Daniel, and Ezekiel were big fools to teach this. They would, I suppose, be torn to shreds by the teeth of today's Jews.

Now behold what a fine, thick, fat lie they pronounce when they say that they are held captive by us. Jerusalem was destroyed over fourteen hundred years ago, and at that time we Christians were harassed and persecuted by the Jews throughout the world for about three hundred years, as we said earlier.[167] We might well complain that during that time they held us Christians captive and killed us, which is the plain truth. Furthermore, we do not know to the present day which devil brought them into our country. We surely did not bring them from Jerusalem.

In addition, no one is holding them here now. The country and the roads are open for them to proceed to their land whenever they wish. If they did so, we would be glad to present gifts to them on the occasion; it would be good riddance. For they are a heavy burden, a plague, a pestilence, a sheer misfortune for our country. Proof for this is found in the fact that they have often been expelled forcibly from a country, far from being held captive in it. Thus they were banished from France (which they call *Tsorfath*, from Obadiah [20]), which was an especially fine nest.[168] Very re-

---

[167] Cf. above, pp. 233-234.

[168] The Jewish community had flourished in medieval France; the exegete Rashi was among its most eminent representatives. However, after some Parisian Jews had been convicted of re-converting a baptized Jew, King Charles VI took the occasion to expel all Jews from his domain in 1394.

cently they were banished by our dear Emperor Charles from Spain,[169] the very best nest of all (which they called *Sefarad,* also on the basis of Obadiah). This year they were expelled from the entire Bohemian crownland, where they had one of the best nests, in Prague.[170] Likewise, during my lifetime they have been driven from Regensburg, Magdeburg, and other places.[171]

If you cannot tolerate a person in a country or home, does that constitute holding him in captivity? In fact, they hold us Christians captive in our own country. They let us work in the sweat of our brow to earn money and property while they sit behind the stove, idle away the time, fart, and roast pears.[172] They stuff themselves, guzzle, and live in luxury and ease from our hard-earned goods. With their accursed usury they hold us and our property captive. Moreover, they mock and deride us because we work and let them play the role of lazy squires at our expense and in our land. Thus they are our masters and we are their servants, with our property, our sweat, and our labor. And by way of reward and thanks they curse our Lord and us! Should the devil not laugh and dance if he can enjoy such a fine paradise at the expense of us Christians? He devours what is ours through his saints, the Jews, and repays us by insulting us, in addition to mocking and cursing both God and man.

They could not have enjoyed such good times in Jerusalem under David and Solomon with their own possessions as they now do with ours, which they daily steal and rob. And yet they wail that we have taken them captive. Indeed, we have captured them and hold them in captivity just as I hold captive my gallstone, my bloody tumor, and all the other ailments and misfortunes which I have to nurse and take care of with money and goods and all that I have. Alas, I wish that they were in Jerusalem with the Jews and whomever else they would like to have there.

---

[169] Luther mistakenly attributes to Charles the expulsion ordered by Ferdinand and Isabella in 1492.

[170] After charges of treasonable intrigue with the Turks, the Jews were expelled from Prague during the years 1541–1543.

[171] From Regensburg (Ratisbon) in 1519; from Magdeburg in 1492. On the general situation reflected in these expulsions, see the Introduction together with the works by Maurer and Lowenthal cited therein.

[172] "Roast pears"—a proverbial expression for laziness.

Since it has now been established that we do not hold them captive, how does it happen that we deserve the enmity of such noble and great saints? We do not call their women whores as they do Mary, Jesus' mother. We do not call them children of whores as they do our Lord Jesus. We do not say that they were conceived at the time of cleansing and were thus born as idiots, as they say of our Lord. We do not say that their women are *haria,* as they do with regard to our dear Mary. We do not curse them but wish them well, physically and spiritually. We lodge them, we let them eat and drink with us. We do not kidnap their children and pierce them through; we do not poison their wells; we do not thirst for their blood. How, then, do we incur such terrible anger, envy, and hatred on the part of such great and holy children of God?

There is no other explanation for this than the one cited earlier from Moses—namely, that God has struck them with "madness and blindness and confusion of mind." So we are even at fault in not avenging all this innocent blood of our Lord and of the Christians which they shed for three hundred years after the destruction of Jerusalem, and the blood of the children they have shed since then (which still shines forth from their eyes and their skin). We are at fault in not slaying them. Rather we allow them to live freely in our midst despite all their murdering, cursing, blaspheming, lying, and defaming; we protect and shield their synagogues, houses, life, and property. In this way we make them lazy and secure and encourage them to fleece us boldly of our money and goods, as well as to mock and deride us, with a view to finally overcoming us, killing us all for such a great sin, and robbing us of all our property (as they daily pray and hope). Now tell me whether they do not have every reason to be the enemies of us accursed Goyim, to curse us and to strive for our final, complete, and eternal ruin!

From all of this we Christians see—for the Jews cannot see it— what terrible wrath of God these people have incurred and still incur without ceasing, what a fire is gleaming and glowing there, and what they achieve who curse and detest Christ and his Christians. O dear Christians, let us take this horrible example to heart, as St. Paul says in Romans 11, and fear God lest we also finally fall victim to such wrath, and even worse! Rather, as we said also earlier, let us honor his divine word and not neglect the time of grace, as Muhammad and the pope have already neglected it, becoming not much better than the Jews.

What shall we Christians do with this rejected and condemned people, the Jews? Since they live among us, we dare not tolerate their conduct, now that we are aware of their lying and reviling and blaspheming. If we do, we become sharers in their lies, cursing, and blasphemy. Thus we cannot extinguish the unquenchable fire of divine wrath, of which the prophets speak, nor can we convert the Jews. With prayer and the fear of God we must practice a sharp mercy to see whether we might save at least a few from the glowing flames. We dare not avenge ourselves. Vengeance a thousand times worse than we could wish them already has them by the throat. I shall give you my sincere advice:[173]

First, to set fire to their synagogues or schools and to bury and cover with dirt whatever will not burn, so that no man will ever again see a stone or cinder of them. This is to be done in honor of our Lord and of Christendom, so that God might see that we are Christians, and do not condone or knowingly tolerate such public lying, cursing, and blaspheming of his Son and of his Christians. For whatever we tolerated in the past unknowingly—and I myself was unaware of it—will be pardoned by God. But if we, now that we are informed, were to protect and shield such a house for the Jews, existing right before our very nose, in which they lie about, blaspheme, curse, vilify, and defame Christ and us (as was heard

---

[173] Most of Luther's proposals are paralleled in the other anti-Jewish literature of the period, but the specific formulation which follows may be attributed to him. Fortunately, as has been noted above (p. 135), most of the authorities proved unwilling to carry out his recommendations, whether out of horror at their inhumanity or out of self-interest (since Jews played an important role in the economy).

It is impossible to publish Luther's treatise today, however, without noting how similar to his proposals were the actions of the National Socialist regime in Germany in the 1930's and 1940's. On the night of November 9–10, 1938, the so-called Kristallnacht, for example, 119 synagogues in all parts of Germany, together with many Jewish homes and shops, were burned to the ground (cf. William H. Shirer, The Rise and Fall of the Third Reich: A History of Nazi Germany [New York: Simon and Schuster, 1960], pp. 430 ff.). In subsequently undertaking the physical annihilation of the Jews, however, the Nazis surpassed even Luther's severity.

above), it would be the same as if we were doing all this and even worse ourselves, as we very well know.

In Deuteronomy 13 [:12 ff.] Moses writes that any city that is given to idolatry shall be totally destroyed by fire, and nothing of it shall be preserved. If he were alive today, he would be the first to set fire to the synagogues and houses of the Jews. For in Deuteronomy 4 [:2] and 12 [:32] he commanded very explicitly that nothing is to be added to or subtracted from his law. And Samuel says in I Samuel 15 [:23] that disobedience to God is idolatry. Now the Jews' doctrine at present is nothing but the additions of the rabbis and the idolatry of disobedience, so that Moses has become entirely unknown among them (as we said before), just as the Bible became unknown under the papacy in our day. So also, for Moses' sake, their schools cannot be tolerated; they defame him just as much as they do us. It is not necessary that they have their own free churches for such idolatry.

Second, I advise that their houses also be razed and destroyed. For they pursue in them the same aims as in their synagogues. Instead they might be lodged under a roof or in a barn, like the gypsies. This will bring home to them the fact that they are not masters in our country, as they boast, but that they are living in exile and in captivity, as they incessantly wail and lament about us before God.

Third, I advise that all their prayer books and Talmudic writings, in which such idolatry, lies, cursing, and blasphemy are taught, be taken from them.

Fourth, I advise that their rabbis be forbidden to teach henceforth on pain of loss of life and limb. For they have justly forfeited the right to such an office by holding the poor Jews captive with the saying of Moses (Deuteronomy 17 [:10 ff.]) in which he commands them to obey their teachers on penalty of death, although Moses clearly adds: "what they teach you in accord with the law of the Lord." Those villains ignore that. They wantonly employ the poor people's obedience contrary to the law of the Lord and infuse them with this poison, cursing, and blasphemy. In the same way the pope also held us captive with the declaration in Matthew 16 [:18], "You are Peter," etc., inducing us to believe all the lies and deceptions that issued from his devilish mind. He did not teach in accord with the word of God, and therefore he forfeited the right to teach.

Fifth, I advise that safe-conduct on the highways be abolished completely for the Jews. For they have no business in the country-side, since they are not lords, officials, tradesmen, or the like. Let them stay at home. I have heard it said that a rich Jew is now traveling across the country with twelve horses—his ambition is to become a Kokhba—devouring princes, lords, lands, and people with his usury, so that the great lords view it with jealous eyes. If you great lords and princes will not forbid such usurers the highway legally, some day a troop may gather against them,[174] having learned from this booklet the true nature of the Jews and how one should deal with them and not protect their activities. For you, too, must not and cannot protect them unless you wish to become participants in all their abominations in the sight of God. Consider carefully what good could come from this, and prevent it.

Sixth, I advise that usury be prohibited to them, and that all cash and treasure of silver and gold be taken from them and put aside for safekeeping. The reason for such a measure is that, as said above, they have no other means of earning a livelihood than usury, and by it they have stolen and robbed from us all they possess. Such money should now be used in no other way than the following: Whenever a Jew is sincerely converted, he should be handed one hundred, two hundred, or three hundred florins, as personal circumstances may suggest. With this he could set himself up in some occupation for the support of his poor wife and children, and the maintenance of the old or feeble. For such evil gains are cursed if they are not put to use with God's blessing in a good and worthy cause.

But when they boast that Moses allowed or commanded them to exact usury from strangers, citing Deuteronomy 23 [:20]—apart

---

[174] Apparently Luther anticipates that the political authorities will find his proposals too severe. He envisions and perhaps even sanctions action against the Jews by a *Reuterei*, probably meaning a band of robber barons. Prof. Jacob R. Marcus, in citing this passage, identifies Luther's "rich Jew" with "the wealthy Michael," court-Jew of Joachim II of Brandenburg. Cf. Jacob R. Marcus, *The Jew in the Medieval World: A Source Book* (Cincinnati, Ohio: Sinai Press, 1938), p. 168.

from this they cannot adduce as much as a letter in their support—we must tell them that there are two classes of Jews or Israelites. The first comprises those whom Moses, in compliance with God's command, led from Egypt into the land of Canaan. To them he issued his law, which they were to keep in that country and not beyond it, and then only until the advent of the Messiah. The other Jews are those of the emperor and not of Moses. These date back to the time of Pilate, the procurator of the land of Judah. For when the latter asked them before the judgment seat, "Then what shall I do with Jesus who is called Christ?" they all said, "Crucify him, crucify him!" He said to them, "Shall I crucify your King?" They shouted in reply, "We have no king but Caesar!" [Matt. 27:22; John 19:15]. God had not commanded of them such submission to the emperor;[175] they gave it voluntarily.

But when the emperor demanded the obedience due him, they resisted and rebelled against him. Now they no longer wanted to be his subjects. Then he came and visited his subjects, gathered them in Jerusalem, and then scattered them throughout his entire empire, so that they were forced to obey him. From these the present remnant of Jews descended, of whom Moses knows nothing, nor they of him; for they do not deserve a single passage or verse of Moses. If they wish to apply Moses' law again, they must first return to the land of Canaan, become Moses' Jews, and keep his laws. There they may practice usury as much as strangers will endure from them. But since they are dwelling in and disobeying Moses in foreign countries under the emperor, they are bound to keep the emperor's laws and refrain from the practice of usury until they become obedient to Moses. For Moses' law has never passed a single step beyond the land of Canaan or beyond the people of Israel. Moses was not sent to the Egyptians, the Babylonians, or any other nation with his law, but only to the people whom he led from Egypt into the land of Canaan, as he himself testifies frequently in Deuteronomy. They were expected to keep his commandments in the land which they would conquer beyond the Jordan.

---

[175] The same German word (*Kaiser*) underlies the English words "Caesar" and "emperor" in this passage.

Moreover, since priesthood, worship, government—with which the greater part, indeed, almost all, of those laws of Moses deal— have been at an end for over fourteen hundred years already, it is certain that Moses' law also came to an end and lost its authority. Therefore the imperial laws must be applied to these imperial Jews. Their wish to be Mosaic Jews must not be indulged. In fact, no Jew has been that for over fourteen hundred years.

Seventh, I recommend putting a flail, an ax, a hoe, a spade, a distaff, or a spindle into the hands of young, strong Jews and Jewesses and letting them earn their bread in the sweat of their brow, as was imposed on the children of Adam (Gen. 3 [:19]). For it is not fitting that they should let us accursed Goyim toil in the sweat of our faces while they, the holy people, idle away their time behind the stove, feasting and farting, and on top of all, boasting blasphemously of their lordship over the Christians by means of our sweat. No, one should toss out these lazy rogues by the seat of their pants.

But if we are afraid that they might harm us or our wives, children, servants, cattle, etc., if they had to serve and work for us —for it is reasonable to assume that such noble lords of the world and venomous, bitter worms are not accustomed to working and would be very reluctant to humble themselves so deeply before the accursed Goyim—then let us emulate the common sense of other nations such as France, Spain, Bohemia, etc., compute with them how much their usury has extorted from us, divide this amicably,[176] but then eject them forever from the country.[177] For, as we have heard, God's anger with them is so intense that gentle mercy will only tend to make them worse and worse, while sharp mercy will reform them but little. Therefore, in any case, away with them!

I hear it said that the Jews donate large sums of money and thus prove beneficial to governments. Yes, but where does this money come from? Not from their own possessions but from that of the lords and subjects whom they plunder and rob by means of usury. Thus the lords are taking from their subjects what they receive from the Jews, i.e., the subjects are obliged to pay addi-

---

[176] I.e., confiscate a portion of the Jews' wealth before expelling them.
[177] Expulsion of the Jews had already occurred in England, France, Spain, and some German principalities. Luther urges those other rulers who may be susceptible to his influence to follow suit.

tional taxes and let themselves be ground into the dust for the Jews, so that they may remain in the country, lie boldly and freely, blaspheme, curse, and steal. Shouldn't the impious Jews laugh up their sleeves because we let them make such fools of us and because we spend our money to enable them to remain in the country and to practice every malice? Over and above that we let them get rich on our sweat and blood, while we remain poor and they suck the marrow from our bones. If it is right for a servant to give his master or for a guest to give his host ten florins annually and, in return, to steal one thousand florins from him, then the servant or the guest will very quickly and easily get rich and the master or the host will soon become a beggar.

And even if the Jews could give the government such sums of money from their own property, which is not possible, and thereby buy protection from us, and the privilege publicly and freely to slander, blaspheme, villify, and curse our Lord Jesus Christ so shamefully in their synagogues, and in addition to wish us every misfortune, namely, that we might all be stabbed to death and perish with our Haman, emperor, princes, lords, wife, and children—this would really be selling Christ our Lord, the whole of Christendom together with the whole empire, and ourselves, with wife and children, cheaply and shamefully. What a great saint the traitor Judas would be in comparison with us! Indeed, if each Jew, as many as there are of them, could give one hundred thousand florins annually, we should nevertheless not yield them for this the right so freely to malign, curse, defame, impoverish by usury a single Christian. That would still be far too cheap a price. How much more intolerable is it that we permit the Jews to purchase with our money such license to slander and curse the whole Christ and all of us and, furthermore, reward them for this with riches and make them our lords, while they ridicule us and gloat in their malice. That would prove a delightful spectacle for the devil and his angels, over which they could secretly grin like a sow grins at her litter, but which would indeed merit God's great wrath.

In brief, dear princes and lords, those of you who have Jews under your rule—if my counsel does not please you,[178] find better advice, so that you and we all can be rid of the unbearable,

---

[178] Cf. above, n. 174.

devilish burden of the Jews, lest we become guilty sharers before God in the lies, the blasphemy, the defamation, and the curses which the mad Jews indulge in so freely and wantonly against the person of our Lord Jesus Christ, his dear mother, all Christians, all authority, and ourselves. Do not grant them protection, safe-conduct, or communion with us. Do not aid and abet them in acquiring your money or your subjects' money and property by means of usury. We have enough sin of our own without this, dating back to the papacy, and we add to it daily with our ingratitude and our contempt of God's word and all his grace; so it is not necessary to burden ourselves also with these alien, shameful vices of the Jews and, over and above it all, to pay them for it with money and property. Let us consider that we are now daily struggling with the Turks, which surely calls for a lessening of our sins and a reformation of our life. With this faithful counsel and warning I wish to cleanse and exonerate my conscience.

And you, my dear gentlemen and friends who are pastors and preachers,[179] I wish to remind very faithfully of your official duty, so that you too may warn your parishioners concerning their eternal harm, as you know how to do—namely, that they be on their guard against the Jews and avoid them so far as possible. They should not curse them or harm their persons, however. For the Jews have cursed and harmed themselves more than enough by cursing the Man Jesus of Nazareth, Mary's son, which they unfortunately have been doing for over fourteen hundred years. Let the government deal with them in this respect, as I have suggested. But whether the government acts or not, let everyone at least be guided by his own conscience and form for himself a definition or image of a Jew.

When you lay eyes on or think of a Jew you must say to yourself: Alas, that mouth which I there behold has cursed and execrated and maligned every Saturday my dear Lord Jesus Christ, who has redeemed me with his precious blood; in addition, it prayed and pleaded before God that I, my wife and children, and all Christians might be stabbed to death and perish miserably. And he himself would gladly do this if he were able, in order to appropriate our goods. Perhaps he has spat on the ground many times

---

[179] Luther turns here from the civil to the ecclesiastical authorities.

this very day over the name of Jesus, as is their custom, so that the spittle still clings to his mouth and beard, if he had a chance to spit. If I were to eat, drink, or talk with such a devilish mouth, I would eat or drink myself full of devils by the dish or cupful, just as I surely make myself a cohort of all the devils that dwell in the Jews and that deride the precious blood of Christ. May God preserve me from this!

We cannot help it that they do not share our belief. It is impossible to force anyone to believe. However, we must avoid confirming them in their wanton lying, slandering, cursing, and defaming. Nor dare we make ourselves partners in their devilish ranting and raving by shielding and protecting them, by giving them food, drink, and shelter, or by other neighborly acts, especially since they boast so proudly and despicably when we do help and serve them that God has ordained them as lords and us as servants. For instance, when a Christian kindles their fire for them on a Sabbath, or cooks for them in an inn whatever they want, they curse and defame and revile us for it, supposing this to be something praiseworthy, and yet they live on our wealth, which they have stolen from us. Such a desperate, thoroughly evil, poisonous, and devilish lot are these Jews, who for these fourteen hundred years have been and still are our plague, our pestilence, and our misfortune.

Especially you pastors who have Jews living in your midst, persist in reminding your lords and rulers to be mindful of their office and of their obligation before God to force the Jews to work, to forbid usury, and to check their blasphemy and cursing. For if they punish thievery, robbery, murder, blasphemy, and other vices among us Christians, why should the devilish Jews be scot-free to commit their crimes among us and against us? We suffer more from them than the Italians do from the Spaniards,[180] who plunder the host's kitchen, cellar, chest, and purse, and, in addition, curse him and threaten him with death. Thus the Jews, our guests, also treat us; for we are their hosts. They rob and fleece us and hang about our necks, these lazy weaklings and indolent bellies; they swill and

---

[180] In 1527, Charles V, reigning also as Charles I of Spain, had invaded Italy, leaving behind as he advanced upon Rome a train of destruction and pillage that became proverbial.

feast, enjoy good times in our homes, and by way of reward they curse our Lord Christ, our churches, our princes, and all of us, threatening us and unceasingly wishing us death and every evil. Just ponder this: How does it happen that we poor Christians nourish and enrich such an idle and lazy people, such a useless, evil, pernicious people, such blasphemous enemies of God, receiving nothing in return but their curses and defamation and every misfortune they may inflict on us or wish us? Indeed, we are as blind and unfeeling clods in this respect as are the Jews in their unbelief, to suffer such great tyranny from these vicious weaklings, and not perceive and sense that they are our lords, yes, our mad tyrants, and that we are their captives and subjects. Meanwhile they wail that they are our captives, and at the same time mock us —as though we had to take this from them!

But if the authorities are reluctant to use force and restrain the Jews' devilish wantonness, the latter should, as we said, be expelled from the country and be told to return to their land and their possessions in Jerusalem, where they may lie, curse, blaspheme, defame, murder, steal, rob, practice usury, mock, and indulge in all those infamous abominations which they practice among us, and leave us our government, our country, our life, and our property, much more leave our Lord the Messiah, our faith, and our church undefiled and uncontaminated with their devilish tyranny and malice. Any privileges[181] that they may plead shall not help them; for no one can grant privileges for practicing such abominations. These cancel and abrogate all privileges.

If you pastors and preachers have followed my example and have faithfully issued such warnings, but neither prince nor subject will do anything about it, let us follow the advice of Christ (Matthew 10 [:14]) and shake the dust from our shoes, and say, "We are innocent of your blood." For I observe and have often experienced how indulgent the perverted world is when it should be strict, and, conversely, how harsh it is when it should be merciful. Such was the case with King Ahab, as we find recorded in I Kings 20. That is the way the prince of this world reigns. I sup-

[181] I.e., legal precedents or agreements, grants of travel and trading rights, etc., made by civic or imperial authorities.

pose that the princes will now wish to show mercy to the Jews, the bloodthirsty foes of our Christian and human name, in order to earn heaven thereby. But that the Jews enmesh us, harass us, torment and distress us poor Christians in every way with the abovementioned devilish and detestable deeds, this they want us to tolerate, and this is a good Christian deed—especially if there is any money involved (which they have filched and stolen from us).

What are we poor preachers to do meanwhile? In the first place, we will believe that our Lord Jesus Christ is truthful when he declares of the Jews who did not accept but crucified him, "You are a brood of vipers and children of the devil" [cf. Matt. 12:34]. This is a judgment in which his forerunner John the Baptist concurred, although these people were his kin. Now our authorities and all such merciful saints as wish the Jews well will at least have to let us believe our Lord Jesus Christ, who, I am sure, has a more intimate knowledge of all hearts than do those compassionate saints. He knows that these Jews are a brood of vipers and children of the devil, that is, people who will accord us the same benefits as does their father, the devil—and by now we Christians should have learned from Scripture as well as experience just how much he wishes us well.

I have read and heard many stories about the Jews which agree with this judgment of Christ, namely, how they have poisoned wells, made assassinations, kidnaped children, as related before.[182] I have heard that one Jew sent another Jew, and this by means of a Christian, a pot of blood, together with a barrel of wine, in which when drunk empty, a dead Jew was found. There are many other similar stories. For their kidnaping of children they have often been burned at the stake or banished (as we already heard). I am well aware that they deny all of this. However, it all coincides with the judgment of Christ which declares that they are venomous, bitter, vindictive, tricky serpents, assassins, and children of the devil, who sting and work harm stealthily wherever they cannot do it openly. For this reason I should like to see them where there are no Christians. The Turks and other heathen do not tolerate what we Christians endure from these venomous serpents and

---

[182] Cf. above, pp. 217, 242.

THE CHRISTIAN IN SOCIETY

young devils.[183] Nor do the Jews treat any others as they do us Christians. That is what I had in mind when I said earlier[184] that, next to the devil, a Christian has no more bitter and galling foe than a Jew. There is no other to whom we accord as many benefactions and from whom we suffer as much as we do from these base children of the devil, this brood of vipers.

Now let me commend these Jews sincerely to whoever feels the desire to shelter and feed them, to honor them, to be fleeced, robbed, plundered, defamed, vilified, and cursed by them, and to suffer every evil at their hands—these venomous serpents and devil's children, who are the most vehement enemies of Christ our Lord and of us all. And if that is not enough, let him stuff them into his mouth, or crawl into their behind and worship this holy object. Then let him boast of his mercy, then let him boast that he has strengthened the devil and his brood for further blaspheming our dear Lord and the precious blood with which we Christians are redeemed. Then he will be a perfect Christian, filled with works of mercy—for which Christ will reward him on the day of judgment, together with the Jews—in the eternal fire of hell!

That is speaking coarsely about the coarse cursing of the Jews. Others write much about this, and the Jews know very well that it is cursing, since they curse and blaspheme consciously. Let us also speak more subtly and, as Christians, more spiritually about this. Thus our Lord Jesus Christ says in Matthew 10 [:40], "He who receives me receives him who sent me." And in Luke 10 [:16], "He who rejects you rejects me. And he who rejects me rejects him who sent me." And in John 15 [:23], "He who hates me hates my father also." In John 5 [:23], "That all may honor the Son, even as they honor the Father. He who does not honor the Son does not honor the Father who sent him," etc.

These are, God be praised, clear and plain words, declaring that all that is done to the honor or to the dishonor of the Son is surely also done to the honor or to the dishonor of God the Father

---

[183] A misleading statement, inasmuch as during the medieval period Jews customarily enjoyed greater freedom under Islam than under Christianity. Cf. on this point H. Coudenhove-Kalergi, *Anti-Semitism throughout the Ages* (London, 1935), pp. 166 ff.

[184] Cf. above, p. 217.

himself. We Christians cannot have or countenance any doubt of this. Whoever denies, defames, and curses Jesus of Nazareth, the Virgin Mary's Son, also denies, defames, and curses God the Father himself, who created heaven and earth. But that is what the Jews do, etc.

And if you say that the Jews do not believe or know this since they do not accept the New Testament, I reply that the Jews may know or believe this or that; we Christians, however, know that they publicly blaspheme and curse God the Father when they blaspheme and curse this Jesus. Tell me, what are we going to answer God if he takes us to account now or on the day of judgment, saying: "Listen, you are a Christian. You are aware of the fact that the Jews openly blasphemed and cursed my Son and Me, you gave them opportunity for it, you protected and shielded them so that they could engage in this without hindrance or punishment in your country, city, and house." Tell me: What will we answer to this?

Of course, we accord anyone the right not to believe *omissive et privatim* ["by neglect and privately"];[185] this we leave to everyone's conscience. But to parade such unbelief so freely in churches and before our very noses, eyes, and ears, to boast of it, to sing it, teach it, and defend it, to revile and curse the true faith, and in this way lure others to them and hinder our people—that is a far, far different story. And this is not changed by the fact that the Jews do not believe the New Testament, that they are unacquainted with it, and that they pay it no heed. The fact remains that *we* are acquainted with it and that we cannot acquiesce in having the Jews revile and curse it in our hearing. To witness this and keep silent is tantamount to doing it ourselves. Thus the accursed Jews encumber us with their diabolical, blasphemous, and horrible sins in our own country.

It will not do for them to say at this point: "We Jews care nothing about the New Testament or about the belief of the Christians." Let them express such sentiments in their own country or secretly. In our country and in our hearing they must suppress these words, or we will have to resort to other measures. These in-

---

[185] A legal phrase. Toleration extended only to the inward man, not to the public expression of unbelief.

corrigible rascals know very well that the New Testament deals with our Lord Jesus Christ, God's Son, while they claim to be unacquainted with its contents. My friend, it is not a question of what you know or what you wish to know, but of what you ought to know, what you are obliged to know. As it happens, not only the Jew but all the world is obliged to know that the New Testament is God the Father's book about his Son Jesus Christ. Whoever does not accept and honor that book does not accept and honor God the Father himself. For we read, "He who rejects me rejects my Father." And if the Jews do not want to know this, then, as I said, we Christians do know it.

Thus if we ourselves do not wish to stand condemned by their sins, we cannot tolerate that the Jews publicly blaspheme and revile God the Father before our very ears by blaspheming and reviling Jesus our Lord, for as he says, "He who hates me hates my Father also." Similarly we cannot tolerate their stating openly and in our hearing that they have no regard for the New Testament but look upon it as a pack of lies. This is tantamount to saying that they care nothing for God the Father and regard him as a liar, for this is God the Father's book, it is the word about his Son Jesus Christ. It will not avail them but rather prejudice their case if they plead ignorance or rejection of the book. For it is incumbent on all to know God's book. He did not reveal it to have it ignored or rejected; he wants it to be known, and he excuses no one from this.

It is as if a king were to instate his only son in his place and command the country to regard him as its sovereign (although he would also be entitled to this by right of natural inheritance), and the country as a whole readily accepted him. A few, however, band together in opposition, alleging that they know nothing about this, despite the fact that the king had in confirmation of his will issued seal and letters and other testimony. They still insist that they do not want to know this or respect it. The king would be obliged to take these people by the nape of the neck and throw them into a dungeon and entrust them to Master Hans,[186] who would teach them to say, "We are willing to acknowledge it." The alternative

---

[186] I.e., the executioner.

would be to keep them incarcerated forever, lest they contaminate with their refractory attitude others who do want to learn it.

This is what God, too, has done. He instated his Son Jesus Christ in Jerusalem in his place and commanded that he be paid homage, according to Psalm 2 [:11–12]: "Kiss the Son, lest he be angry, and you perish in the way."[187] Some of the Jews would not hear of this. God bore witness by the various tongues of the apostles and by all sorts of miraculous signs, and cited the statements of the prophets in testimony. However, they did then what they still do now; they were obstinate, and absolutely refused to give ear to it. Then came Master Hans—the Romans—who destroyed Jerusalem, took the villains by the nape of the neck and cast them into the dungeon of exile, which they still inhabit and in which they will remain forever, or until they say, "We are willing to acknowledge it."

God surely did not do this secretly or in some nook or corner, so that the Jews would have an excuse for disregarding the New Testament without sin. As we noted above, he gave them a reliable sign through the patriarch Jacob, namely, that they could confidently expect the Messiah when the scepter had departed from Judah. Or, when the seventy weeks of Daniel had expired; or, a short time after the construction of Haggai's temple but before its destruction. He also informed them through Isaiah that when they would hear a voice in the wilderness (as happened when the scepter had departed), that is, when they heard the voice of a preacher and prophet proclaiming, "Repent, the Lord is at hand, and is himself coming," then they should be certain that the Messiah had come [cf. Isa. 40:3 ff.].

Shortly thereafter the Messiah himself appeared on the scene, taught, baptized, and performed innumerable great miracles, not secretly but throughout the entire country, prompting many to exclaim, "This is the Messiah" [John 7:41]. Also [John 7:31]: "When the Messiah appears, will he do more signs than this man has done?" And they themselves said, "What are we to do? For this

---

[187] Luther has conflated vv. 11 and 12. The Hebrew original is difficult to interpret; Luther's rendering, "Kiss the Son," follows one tradition. The RSV gives the following translation for these verses: "Serve the Lord with fear, with trembling kiss his feet, lest he be angry, and you perish in the way."

man performs many signs. If we let him go on thus, every one will believe in him" [John 11:47]. When he was on the cross, they said, "He saved others; he cannot save himself" [Matt. 27:42]. Should God concede that these circumcised saints are ignorant of all this, when they already stand convicted by the four statements cited (Jacob's, Haggai's, Daniel's, and David's), all of which show that the Messiah must have come at that time? Several of their rabbis also declared that he was in the world and was begging in Rome, etc.[188]

Furthermore, he saw to it that they were warned not to be offended at his person, for in Zechariah 9 [:9 f.] he announced that he would come to Jerusalem "riding on an ass," wretched and poor, but as a propitious King who would teach peace, who would "cut off" the chariots, steeds, and bows (that is, not rule in a worldly manner, as the mad Kokhbaites, these bloodthirsty Jews, rave), and that this poor yet peaceful, propitious King's dominion should extend to the ends of the world. That is, indeed, a very clear statement, setting forth that the Messiah should reign in all the world without a sword, with pure peace, as a King bringing salvation. I am extremely surprised that the devil can be so powerful as to delude a person, to say nothing of an entire nation which boasts of being God's people, into believing something at variance with this clear text.

He faithfully forewarned them, furthermore, not to be offended when they see that such a great miracle-worker and poor King, who had ridden in on an ass, would let himself be killed and crucified. For he had had it proclaimed in advance (Daniel 9 [:26] and Isaiah 53 [:2 ff. and 52:14 f.]) that "his Servant, who will startle the kings, will be smitten and afflicted"; but all of this will occur because "God laid on him the sins of us all and wounded him for our transgressions, but he was to make himself an offering for sin, intercede for the transgressors, and by his knowledge make many to be accounted righteous." Such the text clearly states.

But the sun has never seen or heard anything more disgraceful than the abuse of this passage by these blasphemous Jews. They apply it to themselves in their exile. At the present we lack the time

---

[188] Cf. above, p. 190, and n. 62.

to deal with this. Alas, should they be the ones who were smitten because of our sin, who bore our transgressions, who made us righteous, and who intercede for us, etc.? There was never a viler people than they, who with their lying, blaspheming, cursing, maligning, their idolatry, their robbery, usury, and all vices accuse us Christians and all mankind more before God and the world than any others. By no means do they pray for us sinners as the text says; they curse us most vehemently, as we proved earlier from Lyra and Burgensis.[189] Their great slothfulness and malice prompt these blasphemous scoundrels to mock Scripture, God, and all the world with their impudent glosses. This they do in accord with their merit and true worth.

After the crucifixion of the King, God first presented the proper signs that this Jesus was the Messiah. Poor, timid, unlearned, unconsecrated fishermen, who did not even have a perfect mastery of their own language, stepped forth and preached in the tongues of the whole world. All the world, heaven and earth, is still filled with wonder at this. They interpreted the writings of the prophets with power and correct understanding; in addition they performed such signs and wonders, that their message was accepted throughout the world by Jews and Gentiles. Innumerable people, both young and old, accepted it with such sincerity that they willingly suffered gruesome martyrdom because of it. This message has now endured these fifteen hundred years down to our day, and it will endure to the end of time.

If such signs did not move the Jews of that time, what can we expect of these degenerate Jews who haughtily disdain to know anything about this story? Indeed, God, who revealed these things so gloriously to all the world, will see to it that they hear us Christians preach and see us keep this message, which we did not invent but heard from Jerusalem fourteen hundred years ago.[190] No enemies, no heathen, and especially no Jews have been able to suppress it, no matter how strongly they opposed it. It would be impossible for such a thing to maintain itself if it were not of God.

---

[189] Cf. above, p. 228.

[190] Apparently a misprint or a mistake in Luther's manuscript; the figure should be fifteen hundred.

The Jews themselves in their fifteen-hundred-year exile[191] must confess that this message has been preached in all the world before their very ears, that it was assailed by much heresy and yet survived. Therefore God cannot be accused of having done all this secretly or in hiding, or of never having brought it to the attention of the Jews or of any other people. For they have all persecuted it vehemently and vigorously these fifteen hundred years. And yet the blasphemous Jews oppose it so impudently and sneeringly, as though it had just recently been invented by a drunkard who deserves no credence. They feel free to revile and damn it with impunity, and we Christians have to offer them room and place, house and home in the bargain, we have to protect and defend them all so that they can confidently and freely revile and condemn such a word of God. And by way of reward we let them take our money and property through their usury.

No, you vile father of such blasphemous Jews, you hellish devil, these are the facts: God has preached long enough to your children, the Jews, publicly and with miraculous signs throughout the world. He has done so for almost fifteen hundred years now, and still preaches. They were and still are obliged to obey him; but they were hardened and ever resisted, blasphemed, and cursed. Therefore we Christians, in turn, are obliged not to tolerate their wanton and conscious blasphemy. As we heard above, "He who hates the Son also hates the Father" [John 15:23]. For if we permit them to do this where we are sovereign, and protect them to enable them to do so, then we are eternally damned together with them because of their sins and blasphemies, even if we in our persons are as holy as the prophets, apostles, or angels. *Quia faciens et consentiens pari poena* ["Doing and consenting deserve equal punishment"]. Whether doer, adviser, accomplice, consenter, or concealer —one is as pious as the other. It does not help us (and the Jews still less) that the Jews refuse to acknowledge this. As has already been said, we Christians know it, and the Jews ought to know it, having heard it together with us for almost fifteen hundred years, having beheld all sorts of miracles and having heard how this doctrine has

---

[191] Here, perhaps, Luther meant to write "fourteen hundred"; he reckons the precise number of years as 1,468 (cf. above, *passim*).

survived, by nothing but divine strength, against all devils and the whole world.

This is certain, borne out by such an enduring and impressive testimony in all the world, that "He who does not honor the Son does not honor the Father," and that he who does not have the Son cannot have the Father. The Jews ever blaspheme and curse God the Father, the Creator of us all, just by blaspheming and cursing his Son, Jesus of Nazareth, Mary's Son, whom God has proclaimed as his Son for fifteen hundred years in all the world by preaching and miraculous signs against the might and the trickery of all devils and men; and he will proclaim him as such until the end of the world. They dub him *Hebel Vorik*, that is, not merely a liar and deceiver, but lying and deception itself,[192] viler even than the devil. We Christians must not tolerate that they practice this in their public synagogues, in their books, and in their behavior, openly under our noses, and within our hearing, in our own country, houses, and regimes. If we do, we together with the Jews and on their account will lose God the Father and his dear Son, who purchased us at such cost with his holy blood, and we will be eternally lost, which God forbid!

Accordingly, it must and dare not be considered a trifling matter but a most serious one to seek counsel against this and to save our souls from the Jews, that is, from the devil and from eternal death. My advice, as I said earlier, is:[193]

First, that their synagogues be burned down, and that all who are able toss in sulphur and pitch; it would be good if someone could also throw in some hellfire. That would demonstrate to God our serious resolve and be evidence to all the world that it was in ignorance that we tolerated such houses, in which the Jews have reviled God, our dear Creator and Father, and his Son most shamefully up till now, but that we have now given them their due reward.

---

[192] Cf. above, p. 257, and n. 162.

[193] Addressing himself now to the ecclesiastical leadership, Luther repeats several of his earlier recommendations (above, pp. 268 ff.). He omits, however, those which have no explicitly religious reference (destruction of houses, denial of safe-conduct, prohibition of usury, and assignment to manual labor), and adds a new point—the fourth in the present list—concerning use of the name of God.

Second, that all their books—their prayer books, their Talmudic writings, also the entire Bible[194]—be taken from them, not leaving them one leaf, and that these be preserved for those who may be converted. For they use all of these books to blaspheme the Son of God, that is, God the Father himself, Creator of heaven and earth, as was said above; and they will never use them differently.

Third, that they be forbidden on pain of death to praise God, to give thanks, to pray, and to teach publicly among us and in our country.[195] They may do this in their own country or wherever they can without our being obliged to hear it or know it. The reason for this prohibition is that their praise, thanks, prayer, and doctrine are sheer blasphemy, cursing, and idolatry, because their heart and mouth call God the Father *Hebel Vorik* as they call his Son, our Lord Jesus, this. For as they name and honor the Son, thus they also name and honor the Father. It does not help them to use many fine words and to make much ado about the name of God. For we read, "You shall not take the name of the Lord your God in vain" [Exod. 20:7]. Just as little did it avail their ancestors at the time of the kings of Israel that they bore God's name, yet called him Baal.

Fourth, that they be forbidden to utter the name of God within our hearing. For we cannot with a good conscience listen to this or tolerate it, because their blasphemous and accursed mouth and heart call God's Son *Hebel Vorik*, and thus also call his Father that. He cannot and will not interpret this otherwise, just as we Christians too cannot interpret it otherwise, we who believe that however the Son is named and honored thus also the Father is named and honored. Therefore we must not consider the mouth of the Jews as worthy of uttering the name of God within our hearing. He who hears this name from a Jew must inform the authorities, or else throw sow dung at him when he sees him and chase him away. And may no one be merciful and kind in this regard, for

---

[194] Exceeding in severity the former recommendation, which did not speak of seizing the Bible itself.

[195] Likewise exceeding in severity the fourth point in the former list, which spoke only of the prohibition of teaching, not of worship (though the destruction of the synagogues was no doubt intended to put an end to all such activities).

286

God's honor and the salvation of us all, including that of the Jews, are at stake!

And if they, or someone else in their behalf, were to suggest that they do not intend any such great evil, or that they are not aware that with such blaspheming and cursing they are blaspheming and cursing God the Father—alleging that though they blaspheme Jesus and us Christians, they nonetheless praise and honor God most highly and beautifully—we answer as we have done before: that if the Jews do not want to admit this or try to put a better face on it, we Christians at least are bound to admit it. The Jews' ignorance is not to be excused, since God has had this proclaimed for almost fifteen hundred years. They are obliged to know it, and God demands this knowledge of them. For if anyone who hears God's words for fifteen hundred years still constantly remarks, "I do not want to acknowledge this," his ignorance will provide a very poor excuse. He thereby really incurs a sevenfold guilt.

To be sure, they did not know at that time that it was God's word; but now they have been informed of it these fifteen hundred years. They have witnessed great signs. Yet they have raged against this, and because of it lived in such exile for fifteen hundred years. All right, let them even now hear and believe it, and all will be simple. If they refuse, it is certain that they will never acknowledge it but are bent on cursing it forever, as their forebears have done for these fifteen hundred years. So we Christians, who do acknowledge it, cannot tolerate or take upon our conscience their willful, everlasting ignorance and blasphemy in our midst. Let them wander back to their country, be ignorant and blaspheme there as long as they can, and not burden us with their wicked sins.

But what will happen even if we do burn down the Jews' synagogues and forbid them publicly to praise God, to pray, to teach, to utter God's name? They will still keep doing it in secret. If we know that they are doing this in secret, it is the same as if they were doing it publicly. For our knowledge of their secret doings and our toleration of them implies that they are not secret after all, and thus our conscience is encumbered with it before God. So let us beware. In my opinion the problem must be resolved thus:

287

If we wish to wash our hands of the Jews' blasphemy and not share in their guilt, we have to part company with them. They must be driven from our country. Let them think of their fatherland; then they need no longer wail and lie before God against us that we are holding them captive, nor need we then any longer complain that they are burdening us with their blasphemy and their usury. This is the most natural and the best course of action, which will safeguard the interest of both parties.

But since they are loath to quit the country, they will boldly deny everything and will also offer the government money enough for permission to remain here. Woe to those who accept such money, and accursed be that money, which they have stolen from us so damnably through usury. They deny just as brazenly as they lie. And wherever they can secretly curse, poison, or harm us Christians they do so without any qualms of conscience. If they are caught in the act or charged with something, they are bold enough to deny it impudently, even to the point of death,[196] since they do not regard us worthy of being told the truth. In fact, these holy children of God consider any harm they can wish or inflict on us as a great service to God. Indeed, if they had the power to do to us what we are able to do to them, not one of us would live for an hour. But since they lack the power to do this publicly, they remain our daily murderers and bloodthirsty foes in their hearts. Their prayers and curses furnish evidence of that, as do the many stories which relate their torturing of children and all sorts of crimes for which they have often been burned at the stake or banished.

Therefore I firmly believe that they say and practice far worse things secretly than the histories and others record about them, meanwhile relying on their denials and on their money. But even if they could deny all else, they cannot deny that they curse us Christians openly—not because of our evil life, but because we regard Jesus as the Messiah, and because they view themselves as our captives, although they know very well that the latter is a lie, and that they are really the ones who hold us captive in our own country by means of their usury, and that everyone would gladly

---

[196] Probably a reference to the effort to extract confessions by the use of torture. Cf. above, p. 264, n. 166.

be rid of them. Because they curse us, they also curse our Lord; and if they curse our Lord, they also curse God the Father, the Creator of heaven and earth. Thus their lying cannot avail them. Their cursing alone convicts them, so that we are indeed compelled to believe all the evil things written about them. Undoubtedly they do more and viler things than those which we know and discover. For Christ does not lie or deceive us when he adjudges them to be serpents and children of the devil, that is, his and all his followers' murderers and enemies, wherever they find it possible.

If I had power over the Jews, as our princes and cities have, I would deal severely with their lying mouth. They have one lie with which they work great harm among their children and their common folk and with which they slander our faith so shamefully: namely, they accuse us and slander us among their people, declaring that we Christians worship more than one God. Here they vaunt and pride themselves without measure. They beguile their people with the claim that they are the only people, in contrast to all the Gentiles, who worship no more than one God. Oh, how cocksure they are about this!

Even though they are aware that they are doing us an injustice and are lying on this point as malicious and wicked scoundrels, even though they have heard for fifteen hundred years, and still hear, that all of us Christians disavow this, they still stuff their ears shut like serpents and deliberately refuse to hear us, but rather insist that their venomous lies about us must be accepted by their people as the truth. This they do even though they read in our writings that we agree with Moses' words in Deuteronomy 6 [:4]: "Hear, O Israel, the Lord our God is one God," and that we confess, publicly and privately, with our hearts, tongues and writings, our life and our death, that there is but one God, of whom Moses writes here and whom the Jews themselves call upon. I say, even if they know this and have heard and read it about us for almost fifteen hundred years, it is of no avail; their lies must still stand, and we Christians have to tolerate their slander that we worship many gods.

Consequently, if I had power over them, I would assemble their scholars and their leaders and order them, on pain of losing

289

their tongues down to the root, to convince us Christians within eight days of the truth of their assertions and to prove this blasphemous lie against us, to the effect that we worship more than the one true God. If they succeeded, we would all on the self-same day become Jews and be circumcised. If they failed, they should stand ready to receive the punishment they deserve for such shameful, malicious, pernicious, and venomous lies. For, thanks be to God, we are after all not such ducks, clods, or stones as these most intelligent rabbis, these senseless fools, think us, that we do not know that one God and many gods cannot truly be believed in simultaneously.

Neither Jew nor devil will in any way be able to prove that our belief that the one eternal Godhead is composed of three persons implies that we believe in more than one God.[197] If the Jews maintain that they cannot understand how three persons can be one God, why then must their blasphemous, accursed, lying mouth deny, condemn, and curse what it does not understand? Such a mouth should be punished for two reasons; in the first place, because it confesses that it does not understand this; in the second place, because it nevertheless blasphemes something which it does not understand. Why do they not first ask? Indeed, why have they heard it for fifteen hundred years and yet refused to learn or understand it? Therefore such lack of understanding cannot help or excuse them, nor us Christians if we tolerate this any longer from them. As already said, we must force them to prove their lies about us or suffer the consequences. For he who slanders and maligns us as being idolatrous in this respect, slanders and maligns Christ, that is, God himself, as an idol. For it is from him that we learned and received this as his eternal word and truth, confirmed mightily by signs and confessed and taught now for nearly fifteen hundred years.

No person has yet been born, or will ever be born, who can grasp or comprehend how foliage can sprout from wood or a tree,

---

[197] This subject was to receive major attention in Luther's treatise published later in 1543, *The Last Words of David.* It played a prominent role in the anti-Jewish treatises of both Lyra and Paul of Burgos; the latter devotes seventeen chapters in *Scrutinium* (Part I, Distinction 9) to the doctrine of the Trinity, refuting the accusation of polytheism.

or how grass can grow forth from stone or earth, or how any creature can be begotten. Yet these filthy, blind, hardened liars presume to fathom and to know what is happening outside and beyond the creature in God's hidden, incomprehensible, inscrutable, and eternal essence. Though we ourselves can grasp only with difficulty and with weak faith what has been revealed to us about this in veiled words, they give vent to such terrible blasphemy over it as to call our faith idolatrous, which is to reproach and defame God himself as an idol. We are convinced of our faith and doctrine; and they, too, ought to understand it, having heard for fifteen hundred years that it is by God and from God through Jesus Christ.

If these vulgar people had expressed themselves more mildly and said, "The Christians worship one God and not many gods, and we are lying and doing the Christians an injustice when we allege that they are worshiping more than one God, though they do believe that there are three persons in the Godhead; we cannot understand this but are willing to let the Christians follow their convictions," etc.—that would have been sensible. But now they proceed, impelled by the devil, to fall into this like filthy sows fall into the trough, defaming and reviling what they refuse to acknowledge and to understand. Without further ado they declare: We Jews do not understand this and do not want to understand it; therefore it follows that it is wrong and idolatrous.

These are the people to whom God has never been God but a liar in the person of all the prophets and apostles, no matter how much God had these preach to them. The result is that they cannot be God's people, no matter how much they teach, clamor, and pray. They do not hear God; so he, in turn, does not hear them, as Psalm 18 [:26] says: "With the crooked thou dost show thyself perverse." The wrath of God has overtaken them. I am loath to think of this, and it has not been a pleasant task for me to write this book, being obliged to resort now to anger, now to satire, in order to avert my eyes from the terrible picture which they present. It has pained me to mention their horrible blasphemy concerning our Lord and his dear mother, which we Christians are grieved to hear. I can well understand what St. Paul means in Romans 10 [9:2] when he says that he is saddened as he considers them. I think that every

Christian experiences this when he reflects seriously, not on the temporal misfortunes and exile which the Jews bemoan, but on the fact that they are condemned to blaspheme, curse, and vilify God himself and all that is God's, for their eternal damnation, and that they refuse to hear and acknowledge this but regard all of their doings as zeal for God. O God, heavenly Father, relent and let your wrath over them be sufficient and come to an end, for the sake of your dear Son! Amen.

I wish and I ask that our rulers who have Jewish subjects exercise a sharp mercy toward these wretched people, as suggested above, to see whether this might not help (though it is doubtful). They must act like a good physician who, when gangrene has set in, proceeds without mercy to cut, saw, and burn flesh, veins, bone, and marrow. Such a procedure must also be followed in this instance. Burn down their synagogues, forbid all that I enumerated earlier, force them to work, and deal harshly with them, as Moses did in the wilderness, slaying three thousand lest the whole people perish. They surely do not know what they are doing; moreover, as people possessed, they do not wish to know it, hear it, or learn it. Therefore it would be wrong to be merciful and confirm them in their conduct. If this does not help we must drive them out like mad dogs, so that we do not become partakers of their abominable blasphemy and all their other vices and thus merit God's wrath and be damned with them. I have done my duty. Now let everyone see to his. I am exonerated.[198]

Finally I wish to say this for myself: If God were to give me no other Messiah than such as the Jews wish and hope for, I would much, much rather be a sow than a human being. I will cite you a good reason for this. The Jews ask no more of their Messiah than that he be a Kokhba and worldly king who will slay us Christians

---

[198] In this and the preceding paragraph, Luther has remarked on the pain of writing the treatise; has offered a brief and pointed prayer for the Jews; and has summarized his recommendations to the authorities. All give the impression that this was intended as the conclusion of the treatise. A brief section follows, however, dealing with the contrast between Jewish and Christian notions of Messiahship, and referring once more, in conclusion, to the four major proof-texts discussed in the main body of the work. Several motifs in this concluding section, e.g., those of the peaceful character of Christ's kingdom and its universal extent, are found also in the conclusion of Lyra's *Pulcherrimae quaestiones*.

and share out the world among the Jews and make them lords, and who finally will die like other kings, and his children after him. For thus declares a rabbi: You must not suppose that it will be different at the time of the Messiah than it has been since the creation of the world,[199] etc.; that is, there will be days and nights, years and months, summer and winter, seedtime and harvest, begetting and dying, eating and drinking, sleeping, growing, digesting, eliminating—all will take its course as it does now, only the Jews will be the masters and will possess all the world's gold, goods, joys, and delights, while we Christians will be their servants. This coincides entirely with the thoughts and teachings of Muhammad. He kills us Christians as the Jews would like to do, occupies the land, and takes over our property, our joys and pleasures. If he were a Jew and not an Ishmaelite, the Jews would have accepted him as the Messiah long ago, or they would have made him the Kokhba.

Even if I had all of that, or if I could become the ruler of Turkey or the Messiah for whom the Jews hope, I would still prefer being a sow. For what would all of this benefit me if I could not be secure in its possession for a single hour? Death, that horrible burden and plague of all mankind, would still threaten me. I would not be safe from him; I would have to fear him every moment. I would still have to quake and tremble before hell and the wrath of God. And I would know no end of all this, but would have to expect it forever. The tyrant Dionysius illustrated this well when he placed a person who praised his good fortune at the head of a richly laden table. Over his head he suspended an unsheathed sword attached to a silk thread, and below him he put a red-hot fire, saying: Eat and be merry, etc. That is the sort of joy such a Messiah would dispense. And I know that anyone who has ever tasted of death's terror or burden would rather be a sow than bear this forever and ever.

For a sow lies down on her featherbed, on the street, or on a dung-heap; she rests securely, snores gently, sleeps sweetly, fears neither king nor Lord, neither death nor hell, neither the devil nor God's wrath, and lives entirely without care so long as she has her

---

[199] Luther gives no source, but cf. the citations given by A. Cohen, *Everyman's Talmud* (London, 1932), p. 356. Cohen, however, notes that this is a minority opinion in the Talmud.

bran. And if the emperor of Turkey were to draw near with all his might and his wrath, she in her pride would not move a bristle for his sake. If someone were to rouse her, she, I suppose, would grunt and say, if she could talk: You fool, why are you raving? You are not one-tenth as well off as I am. Not for an hour do you live as securely, as peacefully and tranquilly as I do constantly, nor would you even if you were ten times as great or rich. In brief, no thought of death occurs to her, for her life is secure and serene.

And if the butcher performs his job with her, she probably imagines that a stone or piece of wood is pinching her. She never thinks of death, and in a moment she is dead. Neither before, during, or in death did she feel death. She feels nothing but life, nothing but everlasting life! No king, not even the Jews' Messiah, will be able to emulate her, nor will any person, however great, rich, holy, or mighty he might be. She never ate of the apple which taught us wretched men in Paradise the difference between good and evil.

What good would the Jews' Messiah do me if he were unable to help a poor man like me in face of this great and horrible lack and grief and make my life one-tenth as pleasant as that of a sow? I would say: Dear Lord God, keep your Messiah, or give him to whoever will have him. Instead, make me a sow. For it is better to be a live sow than a man who is eternally dying. Yea, as Christ says: "It would have been better for that man if he had not been born" [Matt. 26:24].

However, if I had a Messiah who could remedy this grief, so that I would no longer have to fear death but would be always and eternally sure of life, and able to play a trick on the devil and death and no longer have to tremble before the wrath of God, then my heart would leap for joy and be intoxicated with sheer delight; then would a fire of love for God be enkindled, and my praise and thanks would never cease. Even if he would not, in addition, give me gold, silver, and other riches, all the world would nonetheless be a genuine paradise for me, though I lived in a dungeon.

That is the kind of Messiah we Christians have, and we thank God, the Father of all mercy, with the full, overflowing joy of our hearts, gladly and readily forgetting all the sorrow and harm which the devil wrought for us in Paradise. For our loss has been richly compensated for, and all has been restored to us through this Messiah. Filled with such joy, the apostles sang and rejoiced in dungeons and amid all misfortunes as did even young girls, such as Agatha, Lucia, etc. The wretched Jews, on the other hand, who rejected this Messiah, have languished and perished since that time in anguish of heart, in trouble, trembling, wrath, impatience, malice, blasphemy, and cursing, as we read in Isaiah 65 [:14 f.]: "Behold, my servants shall sing for gladness of heart, but you shall cry out for pain of heart, and shall wail for anguish of spirit. You shall leave your name to my chosen for a curse, and the Lord God will slay you; but his servants he will call by a different name." And in the same chapter we read [vv. 1 f.]: "I was ready to be sought by those who did not ask for me; I was ready to be found by those who did not seek me. I said, 'Here am I, here am I,' to a nation that did not call on my name (that is, who were not my people). I spread out my hands all the day to a rebellious people."

We, indeed, have such a Messiah, who says to us (John 11 [:25]): "I am the resurrection and the life; he who believes in me, though he die, yet shall he live, and whoever lives and believes in me shall never die." And John 8 [:51]: "Truly, truly, I say to you, if any one keeps my word, he will never see death." The Jews and the Turks care nothing for such a Messiah. And why should they? They must have a Messiah from the fool's paradise, who will satisfy their stinking belly, and who will die together with them like a cow or dog.

Nor do they need him in the face of death, for they themselves are holy enough with their penitence and piety to step before God and attain this and everything. Only the Christians are such fools and timid cowards who stand in such awe of God, who regard their sin and his wrath so highly that they do not venture to appear before the eyes of his divine Majesty without a mediator or Messiah to represent them and to sacrifice himself for them. The Jews, however, are holy and valiant heroes and knights who dare to approach God themselves without mediator or Messiah, and ask for and receive all they desire. Obviously the angels and God himself must rejoice whenever a Jew condescends to pray; then the angels must take this prayer and place it as a crown on God's divine head. We have witnessed this for fifteen hundred years. So highly does God esteem the noble blood and circumcised saints because they can call his son *Hebel Vorik*!

Furthermore, not only do we foolish, craven Christians and accursed Goyim regard our Messiah as so indispensable for delivering us from death through himself and without our holiness, but we wretched people are also afflicted with such great and terrible blindness as to believe that he needs no sword or worldly power to accomplish this. For we cannot comprehend how God's wrath, sin, death, and hell can be banished with the sword, since we observe that from the beginning of the world to the present day death has not cared a fig for the sword; it has overcome all emperors, kings, and whoever wields a sword as easily as it overcomes the weakest infant in the cradle.

In this respect, the great seducers Isaiah, Jeremiah, and all the other prophets do us great harm. They beguile us mad Goyim with their false doctrine, saying that the kingdom of the Messiah will not bear the sword. Oh, that the holy rabbis and the chivalrous, bold heroes of the Jews would come to our rescue here and extricate us from these abominable errors! For when Isaiah 2 [:2 f.] prophesies concerning the Messiah that the Gentiles shall come to the house and mountain of the Lord and let themselves be taught (for undoubtedly they do not expect to be murdered with the sword; in this case they would surely not approach but would stay away), he says [v. 4]: "He (the Messiah) shall judge between the nations, and shall decide for many peoples; and they shall beat their swords into plowshares, and their spears into pruning hooks; nation shall not lift up sword against nation, neither shall they learn war any more."

Similar sorcery is also practiced upon us poor Goyim in Isaiah 11 [:9]: "They shall not hurt or destroy in all my holy mountain; for the earth shall be full of the knowledge of the Lord." We poor blind Goyim cannot conceive of this "knowledge of the Lord" as a sword, but as the instruction by which one learns to know God; our understanding agrees with Isaiah 2, cited above, which also speaks of the knowledge which the Gentiles shall pursue. For knowledge does not come by the sword, but by teaching and hearing, as we stupid Goyim assume. Likewise Isaiah 53 [:11]: "By his knowledge shall the righteous one, my servant, make many to be accounted righteous"; that is, by teaching them and by their hearing him and believing in him. What else might "his knowledge" mean? In brief, the knowledge of the Messiah must come by preaching.

The proof of this is before your eyes, namely, that the apostles used no spear or sword but solely their tongues. And their example has been followed in all the world now for fifteen hundred years by all the bishops, pastors, and preachers, and is still being followed. Just see whether the pastor wields sword or spear when he enters the church, preaches, baptizes, administers the sacrament, when he retains and remits sin, restrains evildoers, comforts the godly, and teaches, helps, and nurtures everyone's soul. Does he not do all of this exclusively with the tongue or with words? And the congregation, likewise, brings no sword or spear to such a ministry, but only its ears.

And consider the miracles. The Roman Empire and the whole world abounded with idols to which the Gentiles adhered; the devil was mighty and defended himself vigorously. All swords were against it, and yet the tongue alone purged the entire world of all these idols without a sword. It also exorcised innumerable devils, raised the dead, healed all types of diseases, and snowed and rained down sheer miracles. Thereafter it swept away all heresy and error, as it still does daily before our eyes. And further—this is the greatest miracle—it forgives and blots out all sin, creates happy, peaceful, patient hearts, devours death, locks the doors of hell and opens the gate of heaven, and gives eternal life. Who can enumerate all the blessings effected by God's word? In brief, it makes all who hear and believe it children of God and heirs of the kingdom of heaven. Do you not call this a kingdom, power, might, dominion, glory? Yes, most certainly, this is a comforting kingdom and the true *chemdath* of all Gentiles. And should I, in company with the Jews, desire or accept bloodthirsty Kokhba in place of such a kingdom? As I said, in such circumstances I would rather be a sow than a man.

All the writings of the prophets agree fully with this interpretation, that the nations, both Jews and Gentiles, flocked to Shiloh after the scepter had been wrested from Judah (as Jacob says in Genesis 49); likewise, that the seventy weeks of Daniel are fulfilled; that the temple of Haggai is destroyed, but the house and throne of David have remained until the present time and will endure forever. On the other hand, according to the mischievous denial, lying, and cursing of the Jews, whom God has rejected, this is not the meaning [of these passages], much less has it been fulfilled.

To speak first of the saying of Jacob in Genesis 49, we heard before what idle and senseless foolishness the Jews have invented regarding it, yet without hitting upon any definite meaning. But if we confess our Lord Jesus and let him be the "Shiloh" or Messiah, all agrees, coincides, rhymes, and harmonizes beautifully and delightfully. For he appeared promptly on the scene at the time of Herod, after the scepter had departed from Judah. He initiated his rule of peace without a sword, as Isaiah and Zechariah had prophesied, and all the nations gathered about him—both Jews and Gentiles—so that on one day in Jerusalem three thousand souls became believers, and many members of the priesthood and of the princes of the people also flocked to him, as Luke records in Acts 3 and 4.

For more than one hundred years after Jesus' resurrection, that is, from the eighteenth year of the reign of Emperor Tiberius until the eighteenth year of the reign of Emperor Hadrian, who inflicted the second and last bloodbath of the Jews, who defeated Kokhba and drove the Jews utterly and completely from their country, there were always bishops in Jerusalem from the tribe of the children of Israel, all of whom our Eusebius mentions by name (*Eccl. Hist.*, Bk. 4, ch. 5).[200] He begins with St. James the apostle and enumerates about fifteen of them, all of whom preached the gospel with great diligence, performed miracles and lived a holy life, converting many thousands of Jews and children of Israel to their promised Messiah who had now appeared, Jesus of Nazareth; apart from these there were the Jews living in the Diaspora who were converted together with the Gentiles by St. Paul, other

---

[200] Luther's note.

apostles, and their disciples. This was accomplished despite the fact that the other faction, the blind, impenitent Jews—the fathers of the present-day Jews—raved, raged, and ranted against it without letup and without ceasing, and shed much blood of members of their own race both within their own country and abroad among the Gentiles, as was related earlier also of Kokhba.

After Hadrian had expelled the Jews from their country, however, it was necessary to choose the bishops in Jerusalem from the Gentiles who had become Christians, for the Jews were no longer found or tolerated in the country because of Kokhba and his rebellious followers, who gave the Romans no rest. Yet the other, pious, converted Jews who lived dispersed among the Gentiles converted many of the children of Israel, as we gather from the Epistles of St. Paul and from the histories. But these always and everywhere suffered persecution at the hands of the Kokhbaites, so that the pious children of Israel had no worse enemies than their own people. This is true today in the instance of converted Jews.

The Gentiles all over the world now also gathered about these pious, converted children of Israel. This they did in great numbers and with such zeal that they gave up not only their idols and their own wisdom but also forsook wife and child, friends, goods and honor, life and limb for the sake of it. They suffered everything that the devil and all the other Gentiles, as well as the mad Jews, could contrive. For all of that, they did not seek a Kokhba, nor the Gentiles' gold, silver, possessions, dominion, land, or people; they sought eternal life, a life other than this temporal one. They were poor and wretched voluntarily, and yet were happy and content. They were not embittered or vindictive, but kind and merciful. They prayed for their enemies, and, in addition, performed many and great miracles. That has lasted uninterruptedly from that time on down to the present day, and it will endure to the end of the world.

It is a great, extraordinary, and wonderful thing that the Gentiles in all the world accepted, without sword or coercion, with no temporal benefits accruing to them, gladly and freely, a poor Man of the Jews as the true Messiah, one whom his own people had crucified, condemned, cursed, and persecuted without end.

They did and suffered so much for his sake, and forsook all idolatry, just so that they might live with him eternally. This has been going on now for fifteen hundred years. No worship of a false god ever endured so long, nor did all the world suffer so much because of it or cling so firmly to it. And I suppose one of the strongest proofs is found in the fact that no other god ever withstood such hard opposition as the Messiah, against whom alone all other gods and peoples have raged and against whom they all acted in concert, no matter how varied they were or how they otherwise disagreed.

Whoever is not moved by this miraculous spectacle quite deserves to remain blind or to become an accursed Jew. We Christians perceive that these events are in agreement with the statement of Jacob found in Genesis 49: "To the Shiloh or Messiah (after the scepter has dropped from the hands of Judah) shall be the obedience of the peoples." We have the fulfillment of this before our eyes: The peoples, that is, not only the Jews but also the Gentiles, are in perfect accord in their obedience to this Shiloh; they have become one people, that is, Christians. One cannot mention or think of anyone to whom this verse of Jacob applies and refers so fittingly as to our dear Lord Jesus. It would have had to be someone who appeared just after the loss of the scepter, or else the Holy Spirit lied through the mouth of the holy patriarch Jacob, and God forgot his promise. May the devil say that, or anyone who wishes to be an accursed Jew!

Likewise the verse regarding the everlasting house and throne of David fits no other than this our Messiah, Jesus of Nazareth [II Sam. 23:5]. For subsequent to the rule of the kings from the tribe of Judah and since the days of Herod, we cannot think of any son of David who might have sat on his throne or still occupies it today "to preserve his throne eternally." Yet that is what had to take place and still must take place, since God promised it with an oath. But when this Son of David arose from the dead, many, many thousands of children of Israel rallied about him, both in Jerusalem and throughout the world, accepting him as their King and Messiah, as the true Seed of Abraham and of their lineage. These were and still are the house, the kingdom, the throne of David. For they are

300

the descendants of the children of Israel and the seed of Abraham, over whom David was king.

That they have now died and lie buried does not matter; they are nonetheless his kingdom and his people before him. They are dead to us and to the world, but to him they are alive and not dead. It is natural that the blind Jews are unaware of this; for he who is blind sees nothing at all. We Christians, however, know that he says in John 8 [:56] and in Matthew 22 [:32]: "Abraham lives." Also in John 11 [:25]: "He who believes in me, though he die, yet shall he live." Thus David's house and throne are firmly established. There is a Son occupying it eternally, who never dies, nor does he ever let die those who are of his kingdom or who accept him in true faith as King. That marks the true fulfillment of this verse which declares that David's throne shall be eternal. Now let all the devils and Jews, Turks and whoever wants to concern himself with it also name one or more sons of David to whom this verse regarding the house of David applies so precisely and beautifully, since the time of Herod, and we shall be ready to praise them.

To such kingdom and throne of David we Gentiles belong, along with all who have accepted this Messiah and Son of David as King with the same faith, and who continue to accept him to the end of the world and in eternity. Jacob's saying in Genesis 49 [:10] states: "To him shall be the obedience of the peoples." This means not only one nation, such as the children of Israel, but also whatever others are called nations. And later[201] we read in Genesis 22 [:18]: "In thy seed shall all the nations of the earth bless themselves." In this verse we find the term "Goyim," which in the Bible commonly means the Gentiles, except where the prophets also call the Jews this in a strong tone of contempt. To summarize, the blessing of God through the seed of Abraham shall not be confined to his physical descendants, but shall be disseminated among all the Gentiles. That is why God himself calls Abraham "father of a multitude of nations" [Gen. 17:5]. There are many more such sayings in Scripture.

The reason that Scripture calls this kingdom "David's throne" and that it calls the King Messiah "David's Seed" is found in the

---

[201] This should of course read "earlier."

fact that this kingdom of David and the King Messiah did not come from us Gentiles to the children of Abraham and Israel, but came from the children of Abraham and Israel, as the Lord himself says in John 4 [:22]: "Salvation is from the Jews." Even if we are all descended from Adam and partake of the same birth and blood, nevertheless all other nations were shunted aside and solely Abraham's seed was selected as the nation from which the Messiah would come. After Abraham only Isaac, after Isaac only Jacob, after Jacob only Judah, after Judah only David were chosen, and the other brothers, each in his turn, were pushed aside and not chosen as the lineage from which the Messiah was to come. But everything, all things, happened for the sake of the Messiah. Therefore the whole seed of Abraham, especially those who believed in this Messiah, were highly honored by God, as St. Paul says in Acts 13 [:17]: "God made the people great." For it surely is a great honor and distinction to be able to boast of being the Messiah's relative and kin. The closer the relationship, the greater the honor.

However, this boasting must not stem from the idea that Abraham's and his descendants' lineage is worthy of such honor; for that would nullify everything. It must be based rather on the fact that God chose Abraham's flesh and blood for this purpose out of sheer grace and mercy, although it surely deserved a far different lot. We Gentiles, too, have been honored very highly by being made partakers of the Messiah and the kingdom and by enjoying the blessing promised to Abraham's seed. But if we should boast as though we were deserving of this, and not acknowledge that we owe it to sheer, pure mercy, giving God alone the glory, all would also be spoiled and lost. It is as said in I Corinthians 4 [:7]: "What have you that you did not receive? If then you received it, why do you boast as if it were not a gift?"

Thus the dear Son of David, Jesus Christ, is also our King and Messiah, and we glory in being his kingdom and people, just as much as David himself and all children of Israel and Abraham. For we know that he has been instated as Lord, King, and Judge over the living and the dead. "If we live, we live to the Lord, and if we die, we die to the Lord"; that is, we will also live after death, as we just heard, and as St. Paul preaches in Romans 14 [:8]. We look for no bloodthirsty Kokhba in him, but the true Messiah who can give life and salvation. That is what is meant by a son of David sitting on his throne eternally. The blind Jews and Turks know nothing at all of this. May God have mercy on them as he has had and will have on us. Amen.

Neither can one produce a Messiah to whom the statement in Daniel 9 applies other than this Jesus of Nazareth, even if this drives the devil with all his angels and Jews to madness. For we heard before[202] how lame the lies of the Jews regarding King Cyrus and King Agrippa are. However, things did come to pass in accord with the words of the angel Gabriel, and we see the fulfillment before our eyes. "Seventy weeks of years," he says, "are decreed concerning your people and your holy city." He does not mention the city by name, Jerusalem, but he simply says "your holy city"; nor does he say, "God's people," but simply "your people." For this people's and this city's holiness are to terminate after the expiration of the seventy weeks. In its place a new people, a new Jerusalem, and a different holiness would arise in which one would no longer have to propitiate sin annually by sacrifice, worship, and holiness in the temple and yet never become righteous and perfectly holy, because the atonement had to be repeated and sought anew by sacrifice every year.

Rather the Messiah would bring eternal righteousness, make misdeeds of no effect, check transgressions, atone for sin, fulfill prophecies and visions, etc. Where sin has been forever removed and eternal righteousness is found, there sacrifice for sin or for righteousness is no longer required. Why should one sacrifice for sin if it no longer exists? Why should one seek righteousness by service to God if this righteousness is already at hand? But if sacrifice and worship are no longer necessary, of what use are priests and temple? If priests and temple are no longer necessary, why a people and a city who are served by them? It must develop into a new people and city which no longer needs such priests, temple, sacrifice, and worship, or it must be laid low and destroyed together with the useless temple and worship, priests and sacrifice. For the seventy weeks pronounce the final judgment and put an end to them together with city and temple, priests, sacrifice, and worship.

---

[202] Cf. above, p. 243.

The Christian church, composed of Jews and Gentiles, is such a new people and a new Jerusalem. This people knows that sin has been removed entirely by Jesus Christ, that all prophecy has been fulfilled, and eternal righteousness established. For he who believes in him is eternally righteous, and all his sins are forever made of no effect, they are atoned for and forgiven, as the New Testament, especially St. Peter and St. Paul, strongly emphasizes. We no longer hear it said: Whoever offers guilt-offerings or sin-offerings or other offerings in Jerusalem becomes righteous or has atoned for his sin; but now we hear: "He who believes and is baptized will be saved; but he who does not believe will be condemned" [Mark 16:16], no matter where in the wide world he may be. He need not travel to Jerusalem; no, Jerusalem has to come to him.

David, too, proclaimed this in Psalm 40 [:6 ff.]: "Sacrifice and offering thou dost not desire; but thou hast given me an open ear" (that is, the ears of the world, that they might hear and believe and thus be saved without sacrifice, temple, and priests). "Burnt offering and sin offering thou hast not required. Then I said, 'Lo, I come; in the roll of the book it is written of me; I delight to do thy will, O God.'" Indeed, this is the Messiah who brought righteousness through his will and obedience. This is the message of the books of Moses and of all the prophets. Thus also Gabriel says that the sacrifice will not be adequate; he declares that the Messiah "shall be cut off and have nothing" [Dan. 9:26]. Of what will he have nothing? Find out about what he is talking. He is speaking to Daniel about his people and his holy city. He will have none of these, so that their holiness will no longer be with him and in him. Thus Psalm 16 [:4] says: "I do not want their libations of blood, nor will I take their names upon my lips."[203]

So also we read in Isaiah 33 [cf. v. 24]: "The people who will dwell in the new Jerusalem will be called *Nesu awon, levatus peccato*: a people forgiven of all sin." And Jeremiah 32 also promises another, a new, covenant in which not Moses with his covenant shall reign, but rather, as he says: "I will forgive their iniquity, and I will remember their sin no more" [Jer. 31:34]. This is, indeed, a covenant of grace, of forgiveness, of remission of all sins eternally.

---

[203] As rendered in Luther's German version.

That cannot, of course, be effected by the sword, as the blood-thirsty Kokhbaites aspire to do. No, this was brought into the unworthy world by pure grace through the crucified Messiah, for eternal righteousness and salvation, as Gabriel here declares.

As was said before, this saying is too rich; the whole New Testament is summed up in it. Consequently, more time and space would be needed to expound it fully. At present it will suffice if we are convinced that it is impossible to understand this statement as referring to any other Messiah or King than our Lord Jesus of Nazareth. This is true also for the reason that at that time, in the last week, no other Messiah than this was killed; for as Daniel's words clearly indicate, there must be a Messiah who was killed at that time.

And, finally, also Haggai's saying fits no one else. For from Haggai's time on there was no one who might with the slightest plausibility be called "the *chemdath* of all the Gentiles," their delight and consolation, except this Jesus Christ alone. For fifteen hundred years the Gentiles have found their comfort, joy, and delight in him, as we perceive clearly and as the Jews themselves confirm with their cursing to the present day. For why do they curse us? Solely because we confess, praise, and laud this Jesus, the true Messiah, as our consolation, joy, and delight, from whom we will not be parted or separated by weal or woe, in whom and for whom we will confidently and willingly live and die. And the more the Jews, Turks, and all other foes revile and defame him, the more firmly will we cling to him and the dearer we will be to him, as he says [Matt. 5:11 f.]: "Blessed are you when men revile you and persecute you on my account. Rejoice and be glad, for your reward is great in heaven." All praise and thanks, glory and honor be to him, together with the Father and the Holy Spirit, the one true and veritable God. Amen.

So long an essay, dear sir and good friend, you have elicited from me with your booklet in which a Jew demonstrates his skill in a debate with an absent Christian.[204] He would not, thank God, do this in my presence! My essay, I hope, will furnish a Christian

---

[204] Cf. above, p. 137.

(who in any case has no desire to become a Jew) with enough material not only to defend himself against the blind, venomous Jews, but also to become the foe of the Jews' malice, lying, and cursing, and to understand not only that their belief is false but that they are surely possessed by all devils. May Christ, our dear Lord, convert them mercifully and preserve us steadfastly and immovably in the knowledge of him, which is eternal life. Amen.

INDEXES

INDEX OF NAMES AND SUBJECTS

Tartars, 22, 35
Temple, 73-74, 83, 173-174, 176, 187, 210-213, 221-229, 303-304
of Haggai, 210-229, 234, 237, 298
Jews bereft of, in exile, 66, 79-80, 84, 97, 138, 233, 239
of Solomon, 198, 213, 223, 225, 228-229
Ten Commandments, x, 52-53, 88-95, 101-102, 107-109, 160, 169-170, 226-227
Eighth, 258
Fifth, 264
First, 90-91, 93-94, 167
Fourth, 94-95
Ninth, 95
Second, 226, 286
Tenth, 95
Third, 91-93
Tentatio, 208
Terence, 228
Tetragrammaton, 242, 256
Theodoret, 117 n. 20
Thersites, 249
Thiele, Ernst, 28 n. 31, 30 n. 34, 37 n. 40
Thummin (*see* Urim)
Thuringia, 15 n. 7
Tiberius, 298
Titus, 138
Toleration, 279 n. 185
Trachtenberg, Joshua, 131 n. 21, 212 n. 92, 214 n. 97, 217 n. 102, 226 n. 116
Trajan, 234, 236
Trier, Holy Coat of, 50
Trinity, 290 n. 197
Triplex usus legis, 103 n. 8
Turkey, 36, 293-294
Turks, 22, 34-36, 49, 51, 80 n. 18, 129, 164, 175, 177, 266 n. 170, 274, 277, 301, 303, 305
Tyre, 86

Uprising, 14 (*see also* Authority, resistance to; Insurrection; Rebellion; Sedition)

Urim and Thummin, 224
Usury, 125, 167, 169, 217-218, 227-228, 242, 255, 271-276, 284, 288
Luther's view of, 169 n. 31, 242
prohibition of, 270, 275, 285 n. 193

Veil (over the Scriptures), 155 n. 18, 171
Venusberg, 27
Vespasian, 138, 237
Victor of Carben, 130, 176 n. 37
Vienna, Archbishop of (*see* Faber, John)
Violence, 14
Virgil, 244 n. 149

Walter, Johannes von, 5 n. 2
War (*see also* Peasants' Revolt)
against the Protestant states, unjustifiability of, 17-18, 29, 32, 34-54
just, doctrine of, 7
possible outbreak of, feared by Luther, 6, 13-16, 18-19, 33-35
Smalcald, 9
Thirty Years', 9
Wilderness, 75-77, 153, 185, 292
Williams, George H., 116 n. 19, 235 n. 136
Wittenberg, 106, 108, 115, 116 nn. 16 & 19, 165 n. 27, 191, 212 n. 92, 245
University of, 101-102, 105
Witzel, 102
Woman, Seed of, 219-221
Women, Jewish view of, 141-142
Worms, Edict of, 6
Wrath, 114, 192, 241 (*see also* God, wrath of)

Zebulun, 203
Zechariah, 298
Zedekiah, 250, 258
Zerubbabel, 225
Zurich, 123
Zwickau prophets, 116 n. 17
Zwingli, Ulrich, 104
Zwinglians, 59

INDEX TO SCRIPTURE PASSAGES

323

Micah
4:1 f. — 215

Haggai
2 — 134, 188, 237
2:6 f. — 219
2:6-9 — 176 n. 36, 201 n.
  71, 209-229, 234 n. 131
2:7 f. — 223
2:9 — 213 n. 94, 214 n.
  97
2:9b — 229

Zechariah
5 — 227 n. 117
5:2 — 226
5:6 — 226
9:9 f. — 282
11:12 — 226
12:10 — 226
14 — 251

Malachi
2:14-16 — 95

Matthew
3:7 — 141
3:9 — 141
5 — 227
5:10 — 16
5:11 f. — 305
5:22 — 40
10:13 — 12, 12 n. 3
10:14 — 276
10:34 — 219
10:40 — 278
11:18 — 141, 254
12:34 — 277
15:4 ff. — 227
16:18 — 117, 269
21:13 — 227
22:21 — 19
22:32 — 301
23 — 227
24:15 — 51
26:24 — 294
27:22 — 271
27:42 — 282
28:20 — 117

Mark
16:16 — 304

Luke
1:48 — 222
1:50-53 — 111
3:17 — 263
6:39 — 172
10:6 — 12
10:16 — 278
11:15 — 256
11:22 — 219
13:34 — 133 n. 12
19:46 — 227
21:20 — 139
21:22 f. — 139

John
3:6 — 144
3:20-21 — 25
4:22 — 140, 302
5:23 — 278
7:22 — 85
7:31 — 281
7:41 — 281
8:20 — 254
8:39 — 141
8:44 — 141
8:51 — 295
8:56 — 301
11:25 — 295, 301
11:47 — 282
15:23 — 284
16:14 — 54
19:15 — 271

Acts
2:5 ff. — 204
3 — 298
4 — 298
5:29 — 54
13:17 — 302
25:16 — 21

Romans
1:18 — 114
2:4 — 112
2:13 ff. — 170 n. 32
2:14-15 — 111
3 — 159
3:1 ff. — 159
3:27 — 144
3:29 — 94
4:15 — 114

5:13 — 110
7:23 — 119
9:2 — 291
9:5 — 140
10:2 — 175
10:10 — 54
11 — 253, 267
12 — 29
13 — 34
13:1 — 91 n. 29
14:8 — 302

I Corinthians
2:14 — 175
4:7 — 302
15 — 244

II Corinthians
3:13 ff. — 171
12:9 — 112

Galatians
2:11-14 — 112

Hebrews
13:8 — 118

I Peter
5:8 — 118

II Peter
2:22 — 162
3:18 — 112

I John
5:16 — 12

Jude
13 — 37

Revelation
1:8 — 118
14:13 — 42 n. 48

APOCRYPHA
I Maccabees
1 — 225
1:10 ff. — 207 n. 82

325